Modern Job Search

By

Kurt Schmidt

Modern Job Search

Published by Converging Point, Inc.
© Copyright Kurt Schmidt 2014
Cover Design: Chris Shomo / Renaissance Interactive

© Copyright Kurt Schmidt 2014
ISBN: 978-0-9960768-1-4

Table of Contents:

Introduction

I'm a corporate headhunter and I'm good at my job. I'm good at finding the right candidates for my clients, helping everyone prepare and get through interviews, and negotiating offers. Even so, there are still offers that get turned down, commissions that go unearned or long running projects that fall apart at the last minute. Outsiders consider dealing with these things the most difficult part of my job. It's not.

The weight I carry around comes from conversations with people I know need jobs but don't fall within my focus disciplines or industries. Good people; friends, colleagues, and candidates, some of whom have jobs now but want something different, others who are unemployed and really need to get back to work, and recent graduates who are just starting out.

The nature of my work is that I will only ever have jobs for a very small percentage of people. Being a good headhunter means learning as much as possible about a few types of positions in a couple of specific industries and focusing. By definition, a lot of other industries and jobs are excluded. Here's some perspective: I would be wildly successful if I placed one out of every hundred people that contact me. This isn't the kind of thing most people think about but it's true.

However, after 15 years, I do know what it takes to get a job, even when there are none to be found. I've invested a lot of time developing the techniques and strategies in this book and I know they work. My paychecks and, in fact, my survival, are proof.

Parts of what follows have already been told to friends, colleagues and candidates during phone calls, in meetings, or in whatever time could be found. This book represents the first time I've put it all together. The journey beyond the introduction will take you through every part of the job search process from figuring out your value proposition to negotiating offers. The approach is holistic because success comes from mastering the entire process, not just one part.

The people and experiences included in the narrative are real and so are the results. I've read a lot of resumes and have matched a lot of candidates and companies. I've setup countless interviews and negotiated more offers than I can remember. Each success allowed me to continue. Each failure put me one step closer to being thrown out of the game. In order to persist, and in fact, thrive, good headhunters learn what works and adjust very quickly. The volume of resumes, candidate submissions, interviews, offers and placements is such that there's data to analyze and methods to compare. This is significantly different than what a typical job seeker might experience. As a result of all of this work and enough success to earn the privilege to continue, I have accrued a body of knowledge that has been repeatedly tested. I wrote this book because I wanted to share what I know in order to help more people.

There is a common foundation to all jobs – Every job is an expression of someone's need for help. Using that idea as the base, the job search process in this book focuses on defining value, identifying people who recognize that value, learning their language and how to approach them, and demonstrating the desire and the ability to help. The applicability is universal: If someone needs help, show them you can help. Everything else is here too, including: resume writing, interviewing, getting offers, negotiating, resigning and starting a new job. However, understanding and accepting the first part is what's really important.

Is this book going to help you find a job?

Yes. Plain and simple. If you follow the process described and do it with integrity and enthusiasm, you will find a job, and not just any job, a good one. Perhaps just as important, using the strategy in this book will also give you a much greater sense of control over your job search. Instead of sending resumes out into space, getting few if any replies and little to no usable feedback, following this process will allow you to create conversations, develop relationships and find open doors instead of dead ends.

Control inspires confidence. Imagine the confidence that comes from really knowing that you have the tools you need to start from nothing and find a good job. Believe me, as a headhunter working on commission, having a proven process for marketing candidates and knowing for sure that it works goes a long way to helping me keep my cool. As is stated repeatedly throughout the book, there's little that differentiates my candidate marketing campaigns from your personal job search. My ability to sleep peacefully at night no matter what the job market looks like isn't any different than what any empowered job seeker should feel if they too know what to do when the time comes. If you're not sure, you will be after reading this book and trying the process for yourself. Even if you're not looking for a job right now, being prepared provides the kind of confidence that will help you perform better in your current job.

I really believe that everyone needs to work. Everyone needs a job. The world is a better place when people are gainfully occupied and employed. It's better for all of us, myself included. That's why I've worked hard to make this book as accessible as possible in language, structure and price. Everyone who reads this will find something they can use.

*****

About Me: I'm currently the President and owner of an executive search firm focused on filling supply chain management and strategic sourcing positions in Fortune 500 manufacturing and energy companies.

Past and present clients include: BP (British Petroleum), Halliburton, Emerson, Trane, Flextronics, AGCO, Danaher, American Standard, Exterran, Cameron, Dell, Iomega, Ingersoll Rand, Whirlpool, Motorola, Compaq, Hitachi, Hewlett Packard, Thyssen-Krupp, Tyco Electronics, John Deere, Black and Decker and many others.

Chapter 1: Understanding Your Value in the Marketplace

Karen wants a new job and she's come to me for help and advice. Advice is probably the best I can do since I have no chance of placing her with one of my clients. Karen is a good friend and I know she's frustrated so I'll help her if I can.

I am a headhunter. To my friends it seems like my job is to get people jobs but it's not really. My job is to help my client companies find people with surgically specific experience for jobs that are very difficult to fill. In a great year I will help six or seven hiring managers hire candidates with the expertise they need. It's not a high volume business and it is not meant to be. However, after almost fifteen years in the staffing industry I know what Karen needs to do to get a new job and I can tell her, as I've told countless friends and colleagues over the years.

The conversation usually goes like this:

"I want a new job. I'm frustrated and I feel like I am in a rut. I want to work in another industry, maybe in another type of role. I want to grow."

"What do you do?"

Karen is in marketing and business development for a major wireless network provider. I know what she does but I need to hear her explain it to me so I can see if she knows what she does. Fairly often, particularly in larger corporations, people can't really explain the impact of what they do beyond the names of their roles, so this is a good exercise.

"I'm the Head of Customer Marketing for my region."

"Yes of course, I know that but what do you do?"

"What do you mean?"

"What do you actually do? What are you going to do tomorrow morning when you get to work? What will you accomplish this year? Why do you do it?"

It's usually the last question "why," that is the toughest because I'm not looking for a self-interested answer like "because it is fun." I'm looking for an outward impact type of answer. If Karen is going to find a new position, particularly outside her industry, it is important that she understands the value she brings to her organization, how to explain it, and how her experience and knowledge will benefit other organizations. Simple right?

"Well, it's all on my resume. I'll send it to you so you can have a look."

"Okay, great, send it. I'll read it and then we'll talk again."

Karen has a good resume. Her experience is nicely laid out in chronological order starting with her most recent position and ending with her education. All of the dates are there so I know where she's been. For each position she has the names, titles, a brief summary of her role and bullet points that cite specific accomplishments and give some sense of scale. I can use this to help her find the answer to the "why" question we talked about earlier.

Why anyone does what they do at work, strategically, is their value within their organization. It's more than a mission statement or a goal in that value is a precise term and has context. Extracting and understanding value is the true first step to identifying the right kinds of organizations and positions to pursue. Karen looks hesitant when I say this to her at our next meeting. All of a sudden it appears that what we're going to talk about is different than what she expected. What did she expect?

10

Probably like most people, she figured that we'd polish up her resume, talk about cover letters and review interview strategies. In my way of thinking though, all of those things are several steps out, so if she wants my advice we're going to have to start at the beginning.

Value is the beginning. It's objective, measurable, communicable and transferable. Our society and economy operate on the exchange of value. I'm not an economist but, after making a career out of self-employment in one form or another, I think about value every day in a variety of contexts.

The first time I really thought about value was during a job interview at an executive search firm. I was 25 years old, a couple years out of college with a degree in English Literature and floundering in a job market and economy that I largely didn't understand. I was making a living selling insurance to small businesses but I was unhappy. I felt that there were other things out there for me and that I could do more. The interview was for a position as an executive recruiter, a type of business that I had never even heard of at the time. I had just been told that the average fee collected by this firm for getting someone hired with one of their client companies was almost $20,000.00. I was shocked! How in the world could they get away with charging so much just to get someone a job?

Clark, the interviewer, co-owner and founder of the firm, had my attention. These people were making good money in a slow economy. They looked relaxed and sounded smart. The office was nice, well appointed, organized, and professional. I could see myself there.

Clark had a vision and I had fortunate timing. I never applied for this job and it was never advertised. Instead, I wanted to test my English degree in the world of finance and was looking for a job selling securities. The opportunity to meet with Clark came as a result of an earlier interview with a partner in a small brokerage firm. The original interview was more of a favor to my parents than something I earned. The partner at the brokerage firm, Steve, was a nice guy and I must have done well enough in our conversation to spark some interest. I can't recall what we talked about. He said he would like to be able to give me a chance but he couldn't just then. Instead he told me he would give my name to a friend of his who was considering bringing in some help. I had no idea what business Steve's friend was in and he didn't say.

Clark called me a week later and after a long telephone conversation, he invited me to come in to speak with him in person and meet some of the other people at the firm. It was an interview. Even after talking with Clark on the phone I was still unclear about what his firm actually did to produce revenue. I understood his idea though. Clark wanted to see if he could take one or two people right out of college with no measurable experience and develop them as corporate headhunters. For him, this was something new, an experiment. The other people on the staff at his firm were industry veterans from companies like General Electric, Coca-Cola and International Paper. Clark came from GE. In his last position he was a Vice President of Materials Management for GE Medical in Milwaukee. A few years before our meeting, Clark and his wife, Carol, a psychologist, decided to leave GE to move to Savannah and open an executive search business. They were doing very well and it was time to grow.

"You charge $20,000.00 for getting someone a job?"

That was my level of understanding when he first said it. He showed me the white board where each recruiter listed their work-in-progress. At the top were the placements for that month with the fees charged written beside the names of the companies and candidates placed. Below the placements were lists of interviews and potential placements that might close this month. The total production for the month was summed up at the bottom. This very small group of people was producing over $100,000.00 a month, every month.

Why were companies paying so much for this? Or rather, the question that I would not be able to answer correctly for some time yet: What was the value these headhunters exchanged for that $20,000.00 fee?

It took a couple more interviews for me to finally work up the nerve to ask Clark for the job. I got it. It would take me another year and more to figure out how to make a living at it.

The answer to the question about the value a recruiting firm brings goes something like this: In a typical hiring scenario, particularly in cases where the position requires very specific expertise, the normal hiring process might consist of placing advertisements in a variety of media, having the human resources staff review resumes, schedule interviews, both telephone and in-person, and ultimately, hopefully, identify a well-qualified candidate then blindly make them an offer.

In terms of time and resources, the interviews alone can be very expensive. Conducting a lot of interviews to find just the right candidate can be prohibitive. For example, on-site interviews for most of my projects require flying candidates and sometimes even managers into a central location to meet. From a total cost standpoint, it is easy to see how simply interviewing; including candidate selection, staff setup time, short notice plane tickets, hotel rooms for both candidates and managers imported from other divisions, and everyone's time, can be pricey. Therefore, reducing the number of interviews required to fill a position is one way to create value.

In many cases, the fee paid by a company to a corporate headhunter is really a cost savings when compared to the amount of time and money that might otherwise be spent on advertising, logistics, travel and other expenses, including on-site interviews. Even fees far exceeding $20,000.00 can become efficient for large companies that need special people.

Instead of creating, placing and paying for advertisements, reviewing hundreds of resumes, scheduling series of telephone screens, inviting multiple candidates in for on-site interviews, and finally taking chances on offers; my clients save money by only having to look at two or three resumes, schedule two or three telephone interviews and maybe only fly one candidate in for an on-site interview. Since I help negotiate their offers, we are also able to greatly reduce the risk of turn-downs and failure. Add to that the potential for getting the whole thing done a lot faster and there's a pretty good case for going to an outside expert.

This is the value I deliver as a headhunter. I save my clients money by reducing the time and effort required to fill critical positions. My compensation, the fee I charge, is derived from both the value the market places on the service provided and as a reflection of the costs avoided. This is how I want Karen to define her role. One way of doing this is to get Karen to take a step back and look at the big picture.

"Why does your job exist?"

"I don't know. I'm not sure I understand what you're asking."

"Okay, let's put the question another way. Why does any job exist? What are jobs?"

Over the years I have developed a method of preparing candidates for interviews that speaks to this question as a way of getting them to see the needs behind the job. I always start by saying:

"Nobody ever wants to hire anybody. It's a pain in the ass."

Jobs come as a result of a goal or problem, a need, that an organization wants to address. Whether they know it or not, in creating a job, organizations are conducting a make versus buy analysis. Sometimes the solution is found internally and just requires a reallocation of resources. Other times the organization concludes that it has to seek outside help by contracting with another organization or creating a job. Jobs are one way that an organization addresses its needs. Every job has its root in someone somewhere saying: "How are we going to do this?"

Value is what you contribute in order to fulfill the organization's needs. Your goal as a potential employee is to create value and be compensated for it in order to satisfy your own needs. The concept of creating value in exchange for compensation is universal and applies to all jobs.

Value is commonly expressed as money. A simplified way of looking at how you create value is to ask:

"How do you make or save your employer money?"

In today's economy there are literally millions of different types of jobs, some much more specific than others. In each case there is an explicit need to fulfill. In order to get that job, you have to be able to identify and speak to that need. You also have to understand your value, whether or not it applies, and how to communicate it to an organization in a way that they will recognize.

This is what I explain to Karen as we review her resume together.

"What need do you fulfill right now in your job as Head of Customer Marketing? How do you make or save your company money?"

Karen explained to me that she travels all over her region and gives presentations to both her company's customers and their customers. She acts ahead of the sales teams to let their customers know about upcoming technologies that may improve their performance as wireless service providers, increase sales or reduce costs. She speaks with large end users of her customer's services in order to inform them about new services and products available through her customers so that they might increase their orders benefitting both her customers and her company. In this way her function paves the way for corporate sales teams to save time closing deals or make bigger deals with existing customers. Karen also manages customer relationships after the sales process by maintaining dialogues, helping to solve problems, strengthening relationships and building credibility.

I told Karen, based on how she explained her job, the function she performs has been proven to add value to the sales process, resulting in sales increases that are greater than the costs associated with employing someone to do the job. That is why her job exists.

Businesses are in the business of making money. Jobs at companies exist only if they are profitable for the company. Good companies are constantly reviewing who and how they hire in order to try to create the most value and profitability for the least cost. Conversely, they are also always looking at how to eliminate positions in order to save money and, again, increase value. This is not a moral issue; jobs at any organization only exist as long as they contribute to the goals of the organization. To get and keep a good job it is important to understand the value the job creates as it pertains to these goals. Or, put another way, if you can't clearly discern the value that your job creates for the organization that employs you then you better start looking for a new one!

In Karen's case, after talking about it we can summarize the need she addresses and the value she creates in one sentence: Karen reduces the time and effort necessary for sales people to sell her company's services while also creating opportunities for larger sales.

Now Karen needs to understand how she specifically performs within this function. Is she good at her job and why? How do we measure her results? Does Karen's work really increase sales? If so, how much?

Karen's company creates goals for each department and in many cases each position. They review their goals at monthly meetings to see if they are on target. Each person has their own subset of goals within the department's set of goals and further within the company's goals. Inside her own company Karen knows if she is on target and performing well. However in order to communicate her performance to people outside her company Karen needs to break out her accomplishments in ways that demonstrate value in a language that other organizations with similar needs will understand and appreciate. She can do this by going back to the question above: "How do you make or save your company money?" Karen needs to be able to cite specific instances where her work resulted in increased sales or reduced costs. On her resume, her accomplishment list might include examples like this:

- Organized and managed "New Services in Wireless" Symposium for Southern Region Enterprise Customers enabling the sales team to schedule appointments with 8 existing customers and 2 new potential customers resulting in new contracts valued at $4.2 Million per year.

- Developed and implemented Customer Relationship Management Program for Southern Region Enterprise Customers allowing for 24 hour monitoring, instant support and issue escalation, resulting in a 10% decrease in customer attrition, saving $3.5 Million per year.

These types of accomplishments provide tangible numbers that demonstrate the impact of her effort. Other companies that function similarly will be able to recognize the value that Karen creates.

For Karen, extracting and communicating the value she brings to her company is not that difficult. This is her third position in the wireless telecommunications industry and she has over 12 years of experience. There are expectations for her role and her company tracks performance. If she is seeking a position similar to the one she has or in the same industry then the needs and value requirements will be similar and the recipients of her inquiries will be able to understand where she might fit in and contribute. If Karen is seeking a position outside her industry then she'll need to do research to find potential employers that have similar needs and will understand her value proposition.

What if you don't have any experience in the industry in which you want to work? Either you want to change industries or you are just starting out. How do you identify and communicate the value you can bring? Can you fulfill a specific need that will make or save an employer money and if so, can you prove it?

First off, are you qualified for the job you want? If so, how? Prior experience? Education? The job market is an extremely competitive place. Most of the time it is a buyer's market meaning that companies and organizations, the owners of the jobs, have the advantage. They can be very particular about who they hire and will only hire people who can demonstrate that they can add the most value, make the largest contribution and have the biggest impact towards meeting their goals. In short, companies cannot be counted on to be particularly creative or opportunistic when it comes to hiring. They want what they want and rarely compromise. In order to be successful in your search it is critical to be realistic about the kinds of positions you should spend your time pursuing. In today's market it is difficult to impossible to talk someone into giving you a chance. In fact, the idea that anyone is going to give you anything is not a productive way to think. Nobody is entitled to anything regardless of education, skills or experience. It is up to you to identify the value you can bring to the party and communicate it to the people who need it most.

So what do you do? You do what I do: Research and ask questions!

Karen told me that she thinks she would like to change industries. She is considering trying to work for a handset manufacturer instead of a wireless services network provider. She is interested in companies like Apple or Samsung. In order to change industries, Karen needs to figure out what similarities there are and whether or not the experience she has in increasing sales opportunities for wireless network providers has value for handset manufacturers. She needs to understand their businesses and learn the answers to questions like: How do handset manufacturers sell handsets and who do they sell them to? Do handset manufacturers have people called "Head of Customer Marketing?" If so, what do they do? Is it similar to what she does now?

There are a lot of ways to get the answers to these questions. First, Karen should try to find job descriptions for marketing positions at all of the handset manufacturers that she can identify. She doesn't need to apply to any of these positions. For now, it's good to just read the descriptions, study the language and get a sense for what these people do. To get a feel for the industry she should also read everything she can on company websites, in press releases and in industry news publications. She needs to start to think like a handset manufacturer to understand their needs.

For example, it is likely that handset manufacturers sell a lot of their products to wireless service providers who then sell them to end users. Wireless service providers are Karen's current customers so there could be a synergy. A handset manufacturer may see value in the fact that Karen already has relationships with many of the same customers.

Another way to look at it is to consider the potential sales process. Do marketing people who work for handset manufacturers also give presentations and symposiums to introduce their new products to customers and large end users? For example, Karen has experience giving presentations to school systems and government agencies who use wireless services provided by her customers, the wireless service providers. She describes new technologies that will become available from her company to generate interest and create larger orders for her customer, resulting in larger sales of network services for her company. Do handset manufacturers sell handsets in bulk through their customers to end users?

The answers to these types of questions will help Karen understand whether or not she has a realistic chance of being seriously considered for a regional marketing position at a handset manufacturer. If there are few similarities in the requirements or process, her chances will be slim. She needs to recognize this in order to make the best use of her job search time and increase the quality of her results.

In most cases, the further she gets from her industry or discipline, the less likely it will be for Karen to get a position that increases her responsibility or compensation. The value of her experience decreases as she moves further away from her core. That is not to say change is impossible or even ill advised, rather that it might require other compromises.

At one point, walking past a shoe store after having coffee together, Karen says: "I'd really love to work for Nike or Puma. I love their products and feel like I could help them in marketing."

"What sacrifices are you willing to make in order to go to work for either of those companies?"

"What do you mean?"

"Well, would you hire a car mechanic to fix the roof of your house? Or, if you did, would you consider paying him or her as much as someone who specializes in roof repairs?"

"No…"

"Exactly. You would not perceive that you would get the same level of value from a car mechanic working on your roof as you would from a roof specialist. Therefore, you value it less. Now, if you're Nike, in most cases, would you expect to get more or less value from someone outside your industry? If the answer is less, then the value you would receive in the form of compensation for working there may also be less. The sacrifice you may have to make to get a job at Nike could be that you initially have to take a lower level position with less responsibility and less pay. The challenge for you is to identify how your experience can add commensurate value to Nike's processes, then to communicate that value to them in a way that they recognize."

Karen doesn't really like to hear this but in most circumstances I've encountered, particularly in working with larger organizations, this perception is true. Karen might be a marketing genius, whose ideas are universal, transcending all industries and going right to the heart of human buying behavior but to get on board with Nike after coming from the wireless network industry she's going to have to earn some credibility and maybe make sacrifices. The vast majority of employers are conservative and don't like to take chances. If Karen is competing with candidates from inside the athletic shoe or sporting goods manufacturing industry then she may have to make a very compelling case to get an interview.

What if you're just starting out? Identifying value and communicating it in terms that apply to specific positions and demonstrate money earned or money saved is a lot easier if you have experience but what if you don't?

Anthony earned a degree in Human Resources Management from a well-regarded university last year. A few months after graduating he applied, interviewed, received an offer and accepted a position with a regional executive search firm opening a new office in his city. Before accepting the job he did the best he could to develop an understanding the firm's position in the market. Even so, after six months the regional manager, his direct supervisor, left for a job at a large consulting company. The new regional office was left floundering for several months without a manager as the head office tried to figure out what to do. During this time clients left and business dropped off. When the head office finally acted, part of what they did was reduce staff. Anthony's position was eliminated. He left with a total of nine months experience and a bachelor's degree.

There's no way one of my clients would ever use me to hire someone with as little experience as Anthony but he was referred by a friend who promised I could help. The first time we met I could tell by the look on Anthony's face that what I was suggesting to him was a little scary. Again, he thought we would talk about his resume and cover letters. When I didn't mention either in our first conversation it was clear that he was struggling to connect-the-dots between what I was telling him and getting a job. He was expecting tips and tricks for mastering the "copy and paste your resume into everything you can online" strategy. Instead, the approach I explained starts the same way for him as it does for Karen or anyone else: Identify and prepare to communicate value!

If your body of experience is smaller, you have to be creative and find other ways to show value. Nobody expects that recent college graduates will show up with years of relevant and applicable specific experience. The value that companies look for in recent college graduates has more to do with attitude, work ethic, potential and interest. How do you demonstrate these things without citing specific relevant work accomplishments or putting empty phrases like "hard worker" or "team player" on your resume?

As a Junior Personnel Consultant, Anthony did get some experience and was familiar with some of the major companies in his area. He even had a few contacts. More importantly, he had a general sense of what job function he wanted to perform. He didn't know the specifics though. In order to be able to identify the value that he might add to a company or organization, Anthony's first task, like Karen's, is research. I told Anthony:

"Go find companies that interest you and look for entry level or minimum experience level jobs that you like and realistically have a chance to get based on your education and interests. Find as many as you can and develop a list. Don't apply, just read the descriptions and consider the language from a needs standpoint. Read about the companies; get a feel for their businesses, structures, goals and cultures. We'll talk about your value proposition and how to approach them when you have a list of 100 companies that you like and can show me 20 job descriptions for positions you think you are qualified to do. "

Anthony's jaw dropped when I said 100. However, unlike Karen who has twelve years of industry specific experience and might be able to identify twenty or so companies that would immediately recognize and value her skillset, Anthony is a blank slate in many ways, not tied to any specific industry by experience. Additionally, the area in which he wants to work is Human Resources which performs a similar function across almost all industries. He needs to offset the lack of specificity in his value proposition with increased numbers. Finding 100 companies that have Human Resources Departments is a lot easier than finding the same number of companies who value people with expertise marketing wireless network technology to wireless service operators and enterprise end users.

"Let's see that work ethic Anthony!"

I told Anthony to use the next few days and take the same amount of time that he would spend looking at online job boards and mindlessly pasting cover letters and resumes into applications and instead identify and really read about companies and jobs that interest him and make a list. I bet him that if he trusted me a little bit, he would ultimately get a lot more out of this list than he would by firing off one application after another. Unfortunately I can't bet too much without feeling guilty since Anthony is unemployed.

So far I have told both Karen and Anthony that in order to learn about their value and how to communicate it they need to do research and to be realistic. What do I mean by "research?" Research into what?

What I'm telling them to do is what I do every day.

For a large part of my time as a headhunter I have preferred marketing candidates over recruiting for specific companies. "Marketing" candidates means taking my best candidates and contacting companies on their behalf with the hope of being able to find a suitable position and place them regardless of posted job openings. Since I am paid by the companies, the "marketing" approach is exactly backwards. Usually headhunters accept a position under contract from a company either for a commission or on retainer and go recruit qualified candidates. The value for them is on the job because by filling it, they get paid. For me though, marketing candidates has always been more satisfying. It's a risky approach. The only thing I have is time, if I spend it poorly, marketing a candidate that I cannot place, then I lose. Starting out, I don't know where or even if I'll place the candidate I'm marketing.

To effectively market and place a candidate requires an understanding of both a candidate's value proposition and a company's or industry's need. Over the years I've specialized in Supply Chain Management positions for large companies in the manufacturing and energy industries. As a result I have learned about the kinds of issues these companies face and the goals they set for themselves. I have learned about their needs. I have also spoken with thousands of Supply Chain Management professionals and have learned how they address their employer's needs – their value to their organizations. This is research. When I find a company that has a need that matches the value proposition of a candidate that I am marketing good things happen. The only magic is the quality of the research and the quantity of the effort.

I get calls and emails from prospective candidates all the time. Since I've advertised myself as a Supply Chain Management headhunter the bulk of the inquiries come from people seeking Supply Chain positions. Even so, I can't help most of them because I am specialized within my discipline. However every once in a while I get a call out of the blue from someone I can help.

I can't remember exactly how Tom got my name but he did and he called early on a Monday morning. Our first conversation was typically brief.

"Hi Kurt, my name is Tom Brown. I heard that you might be a good person to speak with about finding a new position."

"Hi Tom, tell me a little about your background and what kind of job you're seeking."

"Well, currently I'm a Materials Manager with a large electrical infrastructure manufacturer in Memphis. I'm responsible for all of the Supply Chain functions for two large manufacturing facilities with a staff of about fifty. I'd like to find a similar position but in Houston, and hopefully, a step up in responsibility and compensation."

By the end of that first call I've heard enough to know that Tom might be a marketable candidate. He's in Supply Chain, in manufacturing, and at a recognizable, good quality company. However before I can determine his value, both to another company and as a candidate I should work with, I need to learn a lot more.

"Okay Tom, I may have some ideas for us. Can you send me a copy of your resume?"

Tom's resume arrives a few minutes after we hang up. We have some more phone calls to complete and questions to answer before I'll know for sure if Tom is a marketable candidate but we're off to a good start. Tom has a solid education background including a bachelor's degree in engineering and an MBA. He's been with two companies in sixteen years and was promoted several times in each. In his current role as Materials Manager he's been able to save his employer money by improving inventory management procedures, resulting in less on-site inventory; he's identified and negotiated contracts with lower cost offshore suppliers; and he's improved supplier quality by implementing a supplier certification program. In addition, he managed to do everything while the company was going through a rapid growth phase. His accomplishments show specific savings of millions of dollars for his employer over a several year period. He has clearly demonstrated value.

To complete the picture of Tom's value to his company and within the industry I have to understand his compensation, both his current compensation and his expectations or requirements. We tackle that in our next phone call. From my perspective, it's important that Tom's current compensation is not too high for his desired type of position and that his expectations are realistic. Tom is good in both cases. His salary and bonus are low enough to make him appealing to other companies but not too low, and his expectations are reasonable, within 10% to 15% above his current level.

The result of our conversations is that, based on everything we've shared and my knowledge of Supply Chain Management in the manufacturing and energy industries, Tom and I were able to discern and quantify his value proposition. The approach is the same for Tom as it was for Karen and Anthony except they are figuring out their own value propositions and setting their own expectations.

The next step for Tom, again as it was for Karen and Anthony, is research. Obviously in Tom's case, I'm doing the research. Since Tom has very specific experience, like Karen, my goal is to identify a minimum of twenty companies that might need someone like him. I know that his company buys a lot of steel and fabricates it into large utility towers. I know the manufacturing facilities that Tom supports are large, each over

300,000 square feet and the type of manufacturing they do is slower, producing larger end products that are often customized for specific applications. It's a complex environment with a lot of different parts in inventory. It's a global operation, sourcing supplies and shipping products around the world. Facts like this will help me identify companies that may have similar needs or challenges.

Since Tom wants to move to Houston, my target area is already established. The next question is whether or not there are at least twenty manufacturing or energy companies large enough with similar global supply chain operations in Houston. It turns out that there are. Houston is the capital of the energy industry in the USA, including all of the supporting manufacturing. Houston is a great target location for Tom.

Now it's time to dig a little deeper and find twenty specific companies. I start by looking up the names of the largest manufacturing and energy companies in Houston. Since there are so many and Tom is currently with a manufacturer, I focus on manufacturers. It's not hard to find lists of the largest employers in any city or state. Going through the list I look at company websites to learn about their products and services. I read their press releases to see if they are growing or shrinking, good health or bad, and where they rank in their industries. Since Tom's current company is heavy into steel fabrication I look for companies that use and fabricate products from steel. Using the information I got from Tom about the types of products, type of manufacturing, size and geographic range of his current company, I look for companies that are similar. Some may be direct competitors, some may be suppliers or customers of his current company or related product manufacturers. Others may have little to do with the exact industry of Tom's current employer but still use lots of steel or other raw materials. All of them will have Supply Chain Management organizations that manage complex, large scale global manufacturing operations.

The last thing I do is check the careers page for each company. It's a long shot that any of these companies will have an open position that might make sense for Tom right now but it's worth checking. More importantly, I'm hoping to find any openings in their Supply Chain Management department that might give me hints as to their priorities and structure.

At the end of this I will have a list of at least twenty companies that will recognize the value that Tom can bring. It is not important that any of these companies have the perfect job for Tom right now. The purpose of this research is to understand whether or not it is possible for Tom's value proposition to match a need at one of these companies at any time. This is both a qualitative and quantitative approach. The list should include as many of the highest probability companies as possible. To be effective it also has to be a large enough list so that over a period of time there will be a very high likelihood that one or more of the companies will need someone like Tom. This list will be what I use as the foundational research piece for marketing Tom in Houston. Over time, it will grow, a lot.

This is a business for me. It is a defined process that I've honed over the years in order to place people and earn a living. For you, this is a good exercise to help determine your value proposition and which types of organizations need it most. We'll use the same strategy in the next chapters to identify specific potential contacts within the companies or organizations on our lists and learn even more about their needs ahead of packaging ourselves (or in my case, Tom) and approaching them.

The other important part of this chapter is establishing a new point of view or frame of reference. The idea behind exploring value and needs is to change your thinking from asking questions like: "Is this the right job for me?" to "Can I really help these people achieve their goals?" The idea that your job search is not about you is repeated a lot in all of the chapters of this book except the last one, which is about you.

In a buyer's market, your job search should be about finding the company or organization that will best benefit from your experience and expertise and then clearly showing them how you can help. Remember all jobs have to create value and address a specific need. If there's no value or need, there's no job.

Chapter 2: Value Comparison, Network and Contact Development

Anthony spent the last two weeks since our meeting applying for jobs online and not getting replies. He didn't do what I suggested and now he's frustrated.

"I didn't do what you suggested because I couldn't see how doing this kind of research would directly lead to getting a job."

"How is completing applications online working out for you?"

"Not so good. Or, well, I don't really know."

"Why don't you know?"

"I probably applied for forty jobs in the last couple of weeks but I haven't received a single reply."

"Isn't this what you were doing before you and I spoke a couple of weeks ago?"

"Yes."

"So, you're telling me that you're still doing the same thing and getting the same results. Are you surprised by this? Why didn't you take a couple of days and try what I suggested?"

"I know you said we were going to work from the list I was supposed to do but I didn't feel productive just reading stuff and not doing anything."

I'm tempted to be unhappy with Anthony for not listening to me since my time is valuable but I understand what he's saying. I have been there. Instead I ask him to trust me a little bit and explain that the list was only the first step in a process that does have a definite beginning and end.

He says okay and promises to come back with a list of 100 companies and 20 jobs that he has NOT applied to. I promise that if he does this I'll take the time to explain the next step.

The list, whether it is Anthony's broad-stroke, 100 company list or a highly targeted list of 20 companies for either Karen or Tom, is important. By doing the work to create the list, you, me, Anthony and Karen are learning a lot about the landscape in which we want to succeed. We're learning about the industry or sector, we're learning about the top organizations within it, and we're learning about some of the challenges these organizations face. Secondarily by actually looking at open jobs (and not applying for them) we're learning the language and structure of the organizations that interest us. All of these things will make us better prepared to speak to their needs and communicate value when it is time to go after a position.

Karen is by nature an over-achiever and showed up to our next meeting prepared. Despite the fact that she's on the road four days a week conducting presentations and organizing new technology seminars, she somehow found the time to research and list not 20 companies but 40. She's also included several job openings that she thinks might have potential. She didn't apply to any of them.

Instead of only including wireless handset manufacturers, her main area of interest, she also thought about other kinds of companies that might be somehow related to her current company, including internet service providers, desktop and laptop computer manufacturers and online media companies. Out of curiosity and a desire to explore, she researched and added a few energy companies as well.

Karen's list includes mostly larger companies like her current employer. She read about each one as best she could using sources like the companies' websites, financial websites, customer product or service reviews and employer rankings done by business magazines. When possible, she even went shopping to see the products or services these companies provided and how they marketed them to their customers.

The last thing Karen did was rank the companies on her list in several ways, including how closely they were related to her current employer by type of business or industry, similarities in company cultures, their geographic locations and by how much they interested her. She surprised herself during the ranking part because after doing all the work and thinking about it, she found that her top five companies included three energy companies, one wireless services provider and one computer-electronics manufacturer. There are handset manufacturers on the list as well but not as many and not ranked as highly as she expected they would be when she started. Karen has a good starter list to use as a foundation for the next step.

Tom's list came out a bit differently than Karen's. It's more specific and industry related. I came up with 20 companies in Houston that are all large manufacturers using significant amounts of steel to make heavy, industrial or energy industry related machinery. They all have similar manufacturing styles in terms of production volumes and complexity. Inevitably, all of these companies will have developed Supply Chain Management organizations staffed with people who have similar backgrounds and experience to Tom. I didn't find any open positions that are an exact fit right now but that doesn't matter. For my purposes in candidate marketing, and the level of specialization in Tom's background, I didn't expect and don't need to find any posted job openings immediately. Tom and I reviewed my list over the phone. He was familiar with some of the companies on the list and approved of them and the rest as prospects. I explained to him that we may or may not find an open position at one of these companies right now, and that it was not important at this stage. The list is a first step in developing a network of contacts that will recognize Tom's value proposition and provide information and guidance.

Now it's time to build something from these lists. Let's learn about the kinds of people that work for some of the companies we've included.

One of the top companies on Karen's list is Samsung Electronics. She thinks their products are really cool. They are much more diversified than her current company and that is also of interest to her. She likes the way they are positioning themselves and their business lines seem to be doing well. She found a handful of job descriptions online and some of the language is similar to her own job description and some of what she has on her current resume.

The next step for Karen is filling in the blanks. So far she's looked up a variety of companies, read about them and listed the ones she likes. Then she searched for jobs in those companies and found a few that were interesting. Now she needs to learn more about the kinds of people who do these types of jobs, what their backgrounds look like, who they report to, and how they operate within their departments and companies.

This part of the process is important since it will help Karen calibrate and get specific. By taking the titles of the jobs she found and using them to search for information about the people who have them now, Karen will discover if her experience is similar to theirs. If it is, then she is on-target. If it isn't, she needs to go back and look for more and different job listings. The goal is for her to figure out what people who have similar experience are doing now and how they got there. Hopefully she will be able to identify people who are her peers. Additionally, Karen might be able to see which other companies these people have worked for, potentially allowing her to expand her original list.

As she is learning more about the types of people who have the jobs she wants, she needs to continue and figure out to whom these people report. The hiring managers for these positions are the owners of the jobs and the people that she most wants to be in contact with.

Since Karen has some corporate experience and corporate structures tend to be similar, she can guess a little about the titles of the managers. She is a Manager now who reports to a Director. She is realistic so she doesn't think she is ready to be a Director in a company that is the same size as her own or larger just yet, however she does want to be a more senior Manager. Karen is considering Director level jobs at smaller companies though. The first set of job listings she liked were all Manager level jobs so it is probable that some report to Directors, or, depending on the organization, Vice Presidents.

For example, one of the jobs she found was called "Product Marketing Manager." The job description included items like strategic marketing, communication development and customer relationship management supporting new product launches for enterprise level customers. It sounds very similar to what Karen is doing now except this job is responsible for a larger geographic region and has more staff. The company is also larger. This position would represent an increase in responsibility and probably also compensation for Karen. Based on the title, there is a high likelihood that job reports to a Director of Marketing of some kind. The hiring manager's title could be "Global Marketing Director" or "Americas Marketing Director," including North, Central and South America. Or, depending on the organizational structure, the title may have more to do with function instead of region and could be something like "Director of Product Marketing."

It is the same for Anthony and Tom.

In Anthony's case he is looking for positions like "Internal Recruiter," "Talent Acquisition Specialist," and "Human Resources Recruiter." He wants to work on the internal recruiting staff of a large company. The hiring managers for these positions will have titles like "Recruiting Manager," "Talent Acquisition Manager," and "Human Resources Manager." These are Anthony's targets.

Tom is currently a "Materials Manager." He's looking for a "Senior Materials Manager" or Director level position. We will contact senior Directors and Vice Presidents of Supply Chain, Procurement and Materials Management.

Figuring out the titles of the owners of the jobs you want is not rocket surgery.

How does this apply to your own job search? If you want to be a "Sales Associate" or any other member of a sales team, it is likely that the hiring manager will be called a "Sales Manager," "Director of Sales," "Business Development Manager," or something similar. If you want to be "Manufacturing Engineer," then look for a "Manufacturing Engineering Manager." If you want to be a "Customer Service Manager" then start by looking for a "Director of Customer Service."

Sometimes the title for the hiring manager is on the job description itself. If you get a hiring manager's title from one description it might be similar to the hiring manager's title for another position. Experiment as you're doing research. Be creative!

As we're talking about all of this I can tell that even Karen is now a little concerned. She's following the logic but she's wary about the work and the payoff. Fair enough, we're not yet attacking the jobs themselves, we're still gathering information.

"How in the world am I going to find all of this information?"

"You know, we're so fortunate now."

"What do you mean?"

"I'm going to show you a whole world of information, how to get it and how to use it."

"What's that have to do with being fortunate?"

"Well…"

Karen and I are friends so she'll put up with one of my stories about how it was in the old days because she knows it makes me happy to tell stories.

When I started out as a headhunter, I didn't have a computer on my desk and the firm didn't have an internet connection. I was young, from outside of any industry and didn't know anyone. The staff at the firm shared big giant company directories, essentially huge phone books with the names of companies broken down by state and industry. The books cost $500.00 each and we got new ones every year. We had file cabinets filled with handwritten candidate information forms. We all kept notebooks, real paper ones, filled with notes about people we spoke with, specific company data, phone numbers, fax numbers and all sorts of other information. This is how we formed mental pictures of the organizations we worked with before we had the internet. Gathering information was much more difficult than it is today. Every shred of data I got came from calling people, often cold, and writing down everything they told me. Sometimes people were great and willing to talk, other times not so much. Either way, getting even the most generic information often took a long time. As a result I learned to keep good notes, value the information I got, and to be efficient, persistent and fearless. The same discipline and work ethic that allowed me to survive and thrive in pre-internet times continues to serve me well today in an environment of effortless information overload.

Karen, like the rest of us today, is fortunate because it is now easy to get all the information anyone could ever possibly want and more, much more. Everything she needs is available if she's willing to ask the right questions and go looking around. However in an environment with too much available information it is easy to ask the wrong questions, get distracted and spend a lot of time gathering useless information. To counter that, we're going to focus on using a few good resources and trying to gather the most useful information possible.

The tools and methodology I am showing Karen are exactly the same as what I use to market candidates and make placements.

Internet geography changes over time. Websites that are very useful today may be gone tomorrow. It's easy to become overwhelmed with the options. In the last few years I have found two that I use much more than any others: Indeed.com for fast and easy job listings research and LinkedIn.com for deeper research, contact identification and relationship development. Both will probably last and continue to improve over time.

Indeed.com is a simple job listing aggregation website. It scours the internet looking for job listings that come directly from company websites, search firm websites, job boards and online publications. It is easy to use, only requiring the most general information for basic searches (keywords, title, company name, city, state or zip code). Advanced searches allow you to be more specific and add filters.

You can setup a free account that will allow you to save searches and receive daily or weekly updates via email. It is like Google for jobs, even in appearance. Like any website, it's good to experiment. I use Indeed.com to quickly see if there are any listed openings within the disciplines and locations that interest me. Typically I search by job title(s) and location.

I have no doubt that there are millions of job seekers and other headhunters searching Indeed.com for jobs too. Since I am working with candidates trying to find positions with existing or potentially new clients,

I never apply to any of the jobs I find. My goal is to see who is doing what and where.

I am not recommending that Karen or Anthony apply to jobs they find there either at this time. Applying online can end up being a black-hole kind of process resulting in a lot of effort and little return. Everyone is applying online and most are using a shotgun approach to blast out resumes by the hundreds. It can be a lot of work and, more importantly, it creates a lot of work. Have you ever considered where all of the resumes and online applications go? While you may be doing your homework and only applying for jobs that you are qualified to do, many people are not, they are just applying to everything. The end result is that your resume and everyone else's go through a system, some more complex than others.

Large companies have very sophisticated databases and software that actually reads resumes for keywords before either forwarding them to an internal recruiter in human resources or not. In smaller organizations the link you click to apply online may generate an email to a human resources person who receives all of the resumes, applications and cover letters directly. Other job postings will literally have an email address at the bottom which will attract not only resumes but also all sorts of spam and other junk mail. At the end of this, maybe, your resume will find itself in front a live human resources person who probably has hundreds of other resumes to review and measure against a likely generic job description. Ideally this is not where you want to be but it is often the best result of the process. Certainly this is not where I would want any of my candidates to end up. While people do get jobs this way, the odds of getting noticed are long, regardless of qualifications and experience, and getting applicable feedback is next to impossible. Chances are you won't even get a reply. No feedback equals no opportunity to calibrate your search or improve your efforts either!

For now, we're just going to use Indeed.com to find jobs, read the listings and learn about the titles, responsibilities, language and requirements. When paired with what we're also learning by reading company websites and other resources, understanding the job postings helps complete the basic picture of our target jobs. Even if you're a professional and have a great understanding of what you do, how you do it and for whom, this exercise can help you figure out if other people see and express things the way you do. We're going to use the information we get in job postings from Indeed.com in the next steps to clarify our understanding of the jobs we're after, refine our lists and develop specific contacts.

The second website, LinkedIn.com, is a much more complicated and highly developed resource. You may be using it already. A Google search called "How to use LinkedIn" will produce hundreds of articles and even a few books. LinkedIn.com is constantly adding more features and functionality. Starting out, it can be a little intimidating so it is important to have both a sense of how it works and some idea of what you are trying to accomplish.

What is LinkedIn.com exactly? It is a networking website that allows users to create a profile, search for other users and connect with them, join professional groups and associations, research companies and look for job postings. As of right now, LinkedIn.com has well over 250 million members in 200 countries.

Different than basic search website like Indeed.com, LinkedIn.com requires some development and customization. You have to find contacts and build your own network. The network you end up with is qualitative and quantitative. The quality and quantity of your search results will be directly based on the amount of effort you put into creating your network. It is important to have a specific goal or set of goals for using LinkedIn.com.

My goal for LinkedIn.com is simple: I want to know as many of the most qualified Supply Chain Management professionals at a variety of levels in manufacturing and energy production as possible. I want to be able to contact potential candidates about job opportunities or potential hiring managers about marketable candidates like Tom. My search results need to support my goal, period. I don't invite anyone who is not related to my goal to join my network. For me, LinkedIn.com is not a social network, it's for business. Karen's goal should be to know about and have the ability to contact as many professional peers and potential hiring managers possible within the discipline that she wants to work - Marketing. The same is true for Anthony and everyone else.

All that is required to get started on LinkedIn.com is to sign up for a free account and build a profile. The website will walk you through the process. LinkedIn.com has very useful tips about profile building on its "Help" page. Initially, your profile should end up looking like a looser, more summarized or highlighted version of your current resume with some additional information. You can include a summary of your skills, experience or qualifications, a list of your current and previous employers, your education background and some personal interest information. Remember to also list some accomplishments; how you saved or made your organization or company money, or created value. People will see your profile and the information needs to be relevant to your goal. Your profile doesn't have to be perfect right now. You will find ways to improve your profile as you develop your network on LinkedIn.com and review peer profiles.

The next time I saw Karen she had created a profile and spent a little time exploring the website. She still wasn't sure how to use it though.

"Okay, so I've got a profile now. What's next?"

"Well, to communicate with people and make connections, you've got to find them. Remember I told that your results on LinkedIn.com will be both qualitative and quantitative. That means that we should be specific in what we look for and how we do it. Going back to your company list, let's see if there are any employees from those companies on LinkedIn.com. Let's start with Samsung Electronics for example."

Using the search box on the home page and selecting "Companies," Karen and I type in "Samsung Electronics." The top result is the right company: "Samsung Electronics, Korea, 263,000 employees." Clicking the link for the company leads to a summary page that describes what they do and shows how many employees are on LinkedIn.com. Clicking the "number of employees" link on the right side of summary page opens a new page that lists employee profiles sorted by relevance, meaning their relationship to you.

Your network on LinkedIn.com is based on 1st, 2nd and 3rd degree relationships. First degree relationships are people that are directly connected to you. If you've just started you won't have any 1st degree connections. Second degree relationships are people who are directly connected to your 1st degree connections. Third degree relationships are people who are connected to your 2nd degree connections.

My own network includes well over 1000 1st degree connections and has taken a couple of years to build. My connections are all Supply Chain professionals that I have contacted via invitation, email or telephone call. My +1000 1st degree connections have well over 100,000 of their own connections. Their connections are my 2nd degree connections. My 2nd degree connections are connected to an additional 15,000,000 connections who are my 3rd degree connections. As a result, my searchable network of Supply Chain professionals, based on the total of my 3 degrees of connections is approximately 15,000,000 people. This number increases every time anyone in my network adds a new connection. Even so, my network is very specific. Had I invited additional connections who were not as specifically related to Supply Chain Management in manufacturing or energy then it is likely that my searchable network would far exceed 15,000,000, however my specific search results would not be as accurate as they are now. Larger isn't always better. I don't want so many results that sorting through them is impossible. I want the best results for my purpose, not more, not less.

Another way to expand your searchable network on LinkedIn.com is to join groups. LinkedIn.com has groups for employees of the same corporations, college alumni, non-profit organizations, trade groups and industry-specific groups. There is a link for "Groups" on LinkedIn.com's main page. You can search the Group Directory for appropriate groups and request to become a member.

Again, my goal is to develop a network of Supply Chain professionals that I can contact about opportunities or outstanding candidates. I am a member of groups like "ISM – Purchasing and Supply Chain Professionals" and "Supply Chain Management Practitioners & Experts." Members of these groups fit the profile of the kinds of people I want in my network. I am not a member of any groups that don't include members that fit the profile of the kind of people I want to find in search results.

It is always important to remember that your search results will be based on the quality of your network. Your goal for developing your network on LinkedIn.com should be specific and purposeful.

Somehow, after my brief explanation about relationships on LinkedIn.com, Karen still thinks it is complicated and is a little intimidated.

"Wow, this sounds complicated! I'm a little intimidated."

"It's easier if you have a goal. What's your goal?"

After a moment of thought:

"I want to find marketing people at a variety of levels who work for the kinds of companies in consumer electronics, telecommunications and energy that I want to explore. I want to be able to learn about their backgrounds, figure out where I fit in and maybe contact them."

"Brilliant!"

Going back, Karen and I are looking at the list of employees we found for Samsung Electronics. We've refined the list a little bit by typing the word "marketing" in the "Keywords" section to include only people who have the word "marketing" on their profile somewhere. We've also selected "United States" in the location section. There are a lot of Samsung Electronics employees with "marketing" on their profiles in the United States, however, Karen can't see many names yet, only titles. She can read the profiles though and start to learn a little bit about who she might want to connect with, including both peers and potential hiring managers, but so far, that's all.

"How do I find out their names in order to contact them or add them to my network?"

The reason that Karen can't see the names on the profiles is because she doesn't have a relationship with any of these people. Since she has no 1st degree connections, she doesn't have any 2nd or 3rd degree connections either. She also hasn't joined any groups yet.

"The search for Samsung Electronics was just an example. I wanted to show you that it was likely that there were some Samsung Electronics employees in marketing on LinkedIn.com. Now, let's back-track a little bit and try a different approach and another search. Let's search for groups that are related to the type of marketing and communications work that you do."

The fastest way for Karen to be able to see the some of the names on the profiles that came up in the search results for Samsung Electronics is to join some groups and become related to the other group members. When you join a group you will be able to see the other members' names. You can post and review discussions in the group, you can view group job listings, and importantly, you can contact other group members by sending them invitations to connect.*

*LinkedIn.com users who want to invite a new person to join their network by connecting have to select one of several options describing how they know the person in order to complete the invitation. When this book was originally published, those options included: "Colleague, Classmate, We've done business together, Group, Other," and "I don't know (insert name)." Recently, LinkedIn.com deleted the "Group" option and replaced it with "Friend." Before this change, users could only invite other people to join their network if they could cite some relation, as a colleague, classmate, or group member. With the addition of the "Friend" option, users can now invite anyone without having to cite any previous relation or provide the person's email address as validation ("Other" option). Groups are still a valuable tool for identifying potential contacts with common experience but the new "Friend" invitation option negates the need for a "Group" invitation option. While there is a 300 character limit on invitations, using them is a good way to break the ice and request permission to email someone directly. Note: I personalize every invitation and when I use the "Friend" button to validate an invitation, I always acknowledge that my new hopeful contact are not (yet) friends and apologize for using the term to send the invitation.

Karen and I go to the main page of the "Groups Directory." The first Group that came up in the default search result is called "White House." The summary on the White House group page says that it is the official White House group page on LinkedIn.com. Karen finds this very interesting and wants to join.

"Should I join this group?"

"How does joining this group help you satisfy your goal for LinkedIn.com? It looks interesting and there may be some marketing and communications people who are members but you might get better results by looking for more specific groups."

Instead of joining the White House group, Karen and I type "marketing" in the keywords section of the search box for groups. Our first search includes over 13,000 groups. Obviously we need to be more specific. Adding the word "telecommunications" to "marketing" in the keywords section reduces the number of results to 57. The first result is a group called "Telecommunications Professionals Network." It's a professional group for people in the mobile wireless communications industry and has over 25,000 members. The next group is called "CTAM" which stands for the Cable and Telecommunications Association for Marketing and has over 5000 members. Some of the others on the list look promising as well.

Joining a group is as simple as pressing the "Join Group" button on the group page. Some groups allow new members without approval, others have administrators who look at the join requests and approve or disapprove. Karen reads the summaries of the first two groups and opts to join them. Since both groups require approval for membership they will show up in the "My Groups" section of LinkedIn.com's group page as "membership pending." Typically it only takes a day or two to get group approval. If it takes longer, there is an option to send a message to the group administrator.

Karen and I modified subsequent group searches by removing the word "telecommunications" and adding new words like "wireless," "electronics" and "energy." The results of all of these searches included groups that might be beneficial for Karen to join, like "Mobile Insiders" which has information about networking, discussions and jobs in the mobile, wireless and telecommunications industries. After a few searches with varying terms, Karen identified and applied to join 20 groups that supported her goal. She also applied to join the "White House" group too because she liked it.

Because she selected groups that matched her experience and interests as described in her profile, Karen was approved to become a member for all of the groups she selected. Now when she performs company searches like the one we did previously for "Samsung Electronics" she will be able to see the contact names on the profiles of Samsung Electronics employees who are also members of any of the groups that she belongs to. It's a good start.

"Great, I can see the names of some of the people when I do searches for companies! Now what do I do?"

"Wash, rinse and repeat."

One of my favorite life quotes. It comes from shampoo and in the context of washing your hair, is totally unnecessary, particularly if like me, your hair is short and unruly no matter what you do. However in many other aspects of life, this simple mantra, which to me extols the virtue of practice, is good.

What Karen should do now is continue to learn more about who she should be contacting, the peers and targets who will recognize her value and work for companies that might need her expertise. She also needs to start thinking about how she should present herself, using her understanding of the language of her industry and discipline. Lastly she should begin considering what she will say when she does make contact and how she will speak to value and needs. All of this means repeating these first few steps.

- Using her original list of 40 companies to look for jobs on Indeed.com

- Trying to find out more about each of the companies on a variety of sites like Yahoo Finance and the companies' own websites

- Using LinkedIn.com to identify actual people who do or own the jobs she likes

It sounds like a lot to do but it's not really if you have the right tools. The goal for now is to develop specific knowledge about which companies or organizations you want to work with and who works for them in a similar function to your own. This knowledge will be applied in the next steps of the process and the results will be much, much more efficient than if you would have used the same amount of time to simply apply to jobs on online.

This is what I do when I work with candidates. Remember the list of large Houston based manufacturing companies I made for Tom? The next step for me is to use my LinkedIn.com network of +1000 direct contacts and 50 groups to search for specific contacts that are at the Manager, Director and Vice President levels in each of the companies on the list. I suspect I'll be able to expand my list both vertically and horizontally by using the information I find on my contact's profiles.

Expanding the list vertically means generating more contacts within a specific company. For example, a Director of Materials may be connected to a Director of Procurement in the same company and they both might be useful contacts. While I can only see another person's contacts if we are connected, I can see if anyone commented on that person's profile or left a reference. More importantly, I can see profiles that came up in similar searches done by other people.

Expanding the list horizontally means finding other companies to add to the original list. It is likely that I overlooked some good companies in my first attempt at making Tom's marketing list. However, I can get ideas for more companies by reviewing the profiles of the people who come up in my LinkedIn.com searches and seeing who they have listed as previous employers. This is an easy way to expand the original company list and increase our odds.

The next step is to develop lists of specific contacts based on our company lists and continued research. The lists should include both peers and targets. It is important to make an actual list before just contacting people one by one for several reasons. The first reason is efficiency. Right now, we are in research mode. We're reading, making notes and developing contact lists. We're not finding one contact, dropping research and switching to an entirely different task. We're doing research and getting names. Also, and perhaps most important, having a list is an accomplishment in itself. Your list will change, names will be erased, new names will be added, but having a list of people to contact is tangible, foundational, provides direction and is a great step.

At this stage for Karen, with her list of 40 companies, I suggest developing a list of both peers and targets of 120 initial contacts, or three per company. This is similar to what I'm doing with Tom's list. My goal is to identify 3-4 contacts for each of the 20 companies on his list.

In Anthony's case it's a bit different, recall that he and I discussed coming up with a list of 100 companies. Because Anthony is at the beginning of his career and his interest in Human Resources is not industry specific he should be able to find 100 companies pretty easily. Again, since he has little real experience he has to offset his lack of specificity with numbers. He has to approach more people and develop more contacts. However, it's not necessarily more work. The contacts he's seeking are at the Manager level and there are more Managers than Directors or Vice Presidents, so he will find more of them more easily. For starters, I'm suggesting that Anthony try to find 2 contacts for each of the companies on his list for a total of 200.

Why don't I suggest Karen and Anthony start making contact as soon as they have a list?

The short answer is that they are not ready. In fact, I'm not ready to make contact with anyone on Tom's behalf either. Why not? Part of what is happening during all of this research and list making is that you, me, Karen and Anthony are all learning more about the language of the specific types of jobs, companies and people that interest us. In each of our cases it makes sense to use this language to package ourselves in order to communicate value and speak to needs before making contact and potentially saying the wrong thing. The names on our lists are valuable and it is important to use them wisely.

This strategy is the same, whether you are looking for a job at a large company or a small one. The tools may differ, LinkedIn.com for example is geared towards larger companies and organizations, but the process is the same. The goals are to figure out which companies or organizations will value your expertise and experience the most, who in those organizations specifically to eventually contact, and what language, buzz-words and experience highlights to communicate in order to make the greatest impact. It doesn't matter what resources you use to accomplish these goals, whether it's online, via telephone or in person. There are thousands of websites for conducting this kind of research. LinkedIn.com and Indeed.com are just the best tools for me right now and even they are subject to change. Depending on the type of positions you're looking at or the type of organization, there may be other websites that are more beneficial. The important thing is to get specific: specific organization and company information and specific contacts. We may not hit a home run using this first company and contact list but without getting specific in our approach it will be difficult to recognize what isn't working and make adjustments. In addition, our lists of companies and contacts form a good foundation that will allow us to monitor and track our progress in a task oriented way.

The next thing we'll do is use the information we've gotten about the companies or organizations that interest us and the people who work for them to create resumes that incorporate their language and speak to their needs. We've got our lists of companies, targets and peers, now, before contacting them, let's work on our presentation.

Chapter 3: Packaging Yourself and Preparing to Start

Resumes are important but they are not the most important part of your job search. A resume on its own will not get you a job. However, ensuring that your resume keeps the process moving is critical.

Typically people spend a lot of time creating resumes that they think will stand out. From my perspective, as someone who sees a lot of resumes, most of this time is wasted. Getting just the right spacing, fitting the most information possible on only two pages, using multiple distinctive fonts, clever indentations, underlines, bold, italics and more won't help that much if the right information isn't there or you don't get your resume to the right person.

Think about it. There is a good chance that you've just spent hours and hours doing battle with Microsoft Word in order to align the dates for every position or make sure all of your bullet points match just so that you can copy and paste the resume into an online application that strips out all of your formatting anyways. That is not time well spent. No matter how you send your resume if the information on the first few lines isn't applicable or relevant most hiring managers and recruiters won't finish reading it. We don't have time.

The useful lifespan of even the best resumes is less than 30 seconds. That's how long it takes me or any other hiring manager or recruiter to scan your resume to see if you're a fit for the position we're trying to fill. If you're a fit the resume gets tagged for further review and possible contact, if not it gets filed. That's the reality. To have a successful resume you've got to present the most relevant information in a clear and ordered format, nothing more and nothing less. And again, relevant information is only relevant if the person reading it thinks so. The mission of your resume is to answer some questions but not all of them and provoke a desire for further contact.

Again, this is not about you. As much as you'd like to think your resume is your life story, your portfolio of brilliant accomplishments, your moment to shine, it's not. Your resume's defining characteristics should be that it contains the facts and is easy to read very quickly. In the hands of the right person that's all it takes.

A lot of what we covered in the first two chapters will help you produce a good resume. If you skipped ahead to get to this chapter thinking you didn't need the first two chapters now would be a good time to go back. It doesn't take long and (hopefully) you paid for them along with the rest of the book so you might as well read them!

In the first chapter we did research to develop an understanding of value and needs in the context of the value that you can bring to an organization and the needs that you can help fulfill. We looked up positions that interest us and developed lists of companies that we believe will recognize our value and need our help.

In the second chapter we took that thinking to the next level and did research to learn about the people who do the jobs we want and how they fit into the organizations or companies that employ them. We even got specific and generated lists of people we'd like to contact. Along the way we learned more about the language these companies use to describe themselves and their goals. We also learned how their employees describe their specific responsibilities and accomplishments.

We've figured out who we want to approach in terms of companies or organizations, who we want to be in terms of job titles and responsibilities and some of the names and titles of the owners of our target jobs. We've also learned about what these companies value.

We have done a fair amount of work so far. Karen did this for her job search and I did it in order to begin to find a position for Tom. Anthony was running behind a little bit but he is up to speed now too.

After all of this we should be able to create good resumes. What is a "good resume?" Remember the part in the first chapter where Karen and I were discussing what she does in her position? Karen sent me her resume and this is what I had to say about it:

"Karen has a good resume. Her experience is nicely laid out in chronological order starting with her most recent position and ending with her education. All the dates are there so I know where she's been. For each position she has the names, titles, and a brief summary of her role and bullet points that cite specific accomplishments and give some sense of scale."

That's it. It's very simple. Taking a closer look, we can see that Karen's resume has five modules that are clear, concise, and logically ordered:

1. Contact Details: Name, Address, Telephone Number and Email Address

2. Summary: A very short one to two line summary of her value proposition that can be modified per specific job opportunity.

3. Experience: The names of her employers, position titles and accomplishments.

4. Education and Certifications: Karen's education, listed with the most recent or most advanced formal degree on

top, followed by lower degrees and professional certifications.

5. Interests and Activities (optional): Depending on the company or organization, some may value civic or volunteer activities, some may value sports participation, for specific positions there may even be value in other kinds of hobbies.

The information contained in each of Karen's resume modules is interchangeable allowing her to update it easily and speak to specific needs.

There is no module for references on Karen's resume and there shouldn't be. My advice regarding references is simple: Make them ask. Why? Because anyone you give as a reference should be alerted that they may be contacted on your behalf by a specific organization about a specific job. Your references should not be generic or available on your resume so that anyone can call them at any time. They should be selected based on the opportunity and their ability to provide helpful and appropriate information. It is up to you to control who is contacted, in regard to which opportunities and when.

When getting ready to use your resume, the key question to ask is whether or not the information you are considering including adds value to the position to which you're applying. If the information adds value, directly and not in some roundabout way that you made up, then add it; if it doesn't, don't add it.

As a headhunter, I am only interested in finding facts or figures that tell me if you can do the job I'm working on. In fact, perhaps like many headhunters and human resources people, I do this in reverse. The fastest way for me to process a candidate is to look for reasons why they don't fulfill a particular need. It is not a judgment process. Someone may be a fantastic Manufacturing Engineer, but if I'm looking for a Commodity Manager, then the Manufacturing Engineer is most likely out. Per project or search, the process is binary, in or out.

Creating a resume that is easy to process and contains only the most relevant information means that people like me can find, harvest and apply what we need more quickly and efficiently. We like that. Conversely, a cluttered resume that includes too much or irrelevant information, omits dates or other facts ultimately makes the reader work harder and requires too much time to process. A resume that is too long or difficult to read transfers work from the job seeker to the potential employer and often ends up going unread.

Let's get specific and go through each module of Karen's resume part by part starting with the fonts and font sizes.

Karen's entire resume is in a basic generic font. In her case Arial. Arial is good, so are the other most basic fonts. Her name, employer's names and section titles (Summary, Experience and Education) are in bold, font size 12. Everything else is regularly weighted (normal), font size 10. Her position titles are underlined. The only other formatting tool that she uses are standard round bullet points for her list of accomplishments. There are no italics, no additional font sizes and no more underlining. There is nothing fancy and it is easy to look at and read quickly. It is more important for a resume to be easy to look at than it is for it to fit on a certain number of pages. Having too many font sizes, too many things in bold or italics, too much underlining or any other highlighting effects makes it more difficult to read.

On the top of the first page she has her full name, address and contact details, all centered or left justified.

Karen Smith*

123 Maple Street

Anytown, USA 10010
Tel: (212) 555-1212
Email: Karen@gmail.com

Below her contact details, Karen has a short Summary that describes her value proposition or speaks to the most basic needs in the job description for the position to which she is applying.

Summary:

Highly experienced business-to-business marketing professional adept at creating long term strategic marketing plans, managing enterprise customer relationships, facilitating new customer development and increasing sales

Karen's Summary is short and general. Its purpose is to provide the reader with enough information to want to continue reading. A really good summary will mirror the first sentence or two of an applicable job description. If you're a hiring manager who has just started looking for someone who can help develop "long term strategic marketing plans" or "manage enterprise customer relationships," then Karen's Summary will entice you to keep reading. Mission accomplished.

If a Summary goes on for more than just a few lines it can become redundant since the specific accomplishments below should provide the same information in greater detail. As a module of her resume, Karen can change or edit her Summary as necessary for any position of interest.

I'm not a huge fan of starting a resume with an Objective Statement because they are usually very self-focused. Everyone wants to "grow in their career, develop more skills" or "attain a leadership position." If I'm looking at your resume, then it's not really necessary to tell me why I'm looking at it: You want something! Otherwise, you wouldn't have sent it, right?

Karen's Experience module starts right below her Summary. Her experience is listed in chronological order beginning with information about her current or most recent position on top. The first line has her employer's name, division or department if relevant, location and total dates employed. Below that is a short summary explaining what her company or organization does or who they are. The next line includes her title and, because she has had multiple positions in the same company, the dates she has been in her current position. Immediately below is a one or two line explanation of her responsibilities. After that are her most important accomplishments, the ones that made or saved her employer money and are most applicable and relevant to other potential employers who need help with similar challenges.

Experience:

ABC Wireless Networks, Anytown, Maryland, June 2007 - Present
ABC Networks is one of the largest telecommunications hardware, software and services companies in the world offering a complete portfolio of mobile, fixed and converged network technologies, consulting and systems integration, network implementation, maintenance and care and managed services.

Customer Marketing Manager, Southeast Region, August 2010 - Present
Responsible for managing long-term and strategic relationship marketing for enterprise customers and new customer development in ten states in the southeastern United States

- Organized and managed "New Services in Wireless" Symposium for Southern Region

Enterprise Customers enabling the sales team to schedule appointments with 8 existing customers and 2 new potential customers resulting in new contracts valued at $4.2 Million per year.

- Developed and implemented Customer Relationship Management Program for Southern Region Enterprise Customers allowing for 24 hour monitoring, instant support and issue escalation, resulting in a 10% decrease in customer attrition, saving $3.5 Million per year.
- Continued…

Karen's accomplishments are specific both in content and language. Anyone can see how she either made or saved her employer money. Her accomplishments are designed to speak to hiring managers who need help doing the things she's done. Because she has included actual numbers, dollars and percentages, we can see the scope and scale of her work.

Accomplishments are tangible. In any situation, the things you did that are accomplishments are the things that had real, measurable positive results. Simply stated, what did you think of, create or implement that either made or saved your employer money? Did you help conserve a resource or time? Did your work contribute to adding customers either internally or externally? Did your management of existing customers allow your employer to keep them or continue to develop them? Did you create a process that improved efficiency? Did you sell or create a product or service or work on a team that did?

Karen has 12 years of experience and is in her third position and second company. There are three jobs on her resume with several accomplishments listed below each one. How did she determine which accomplishments to list? And how many did she include for each position?

Karen and I met for coffee again recently to discuss her resume. Or, in her words, "finally discuss her resume."

"I sent you my resume a while ago, before doing all of this research finding companies, jobs and contacts. Now I'm not sure my resume is still good enough. What do you think?"

"The formatting is good, your summary and experience probably apply to some of the positions you want to pursue, and it's setup so that you can update and edit things easily. That's good. You'll probably want to review some of the jobs you looked at and some of the profiles of potential peers you found on LinkedIn.com to see how your accomplishments compare to theirs."

"How do I know if I'm including the right accomplishments? And how many should I have?"

"Tell you what. Let's go through them to make sure and update your resume a little bit while we're at it."

"Okay, what should I do first?"

"How do you feel about another list? It's easy, I promise."

"Oh no, not another list!"

"A really good exercise for this resume and future resumes is to write down as many accomplishments as you can think of for each job you've had. Put each job on a separate page, put the title at the top and just start writing them down. For your current job, this becomes a living list of accomplishments that will grow over time. We'll review, compare them to some of the jobs you're interested in and rank them for each position when you're done. Don't make this hard, just start writing and go with it."

Again, because Karen's resume is modular, we can go back and take out or add an accomplishment for any position at any time as it suits whatever opportunity Karen wants to pursue. Having a list of accomplishments for each position makes updating and editing easy.

I've suggested that Karen make a separate list for each position because it's easier to cut than to create. I've also encouraged her to just start writing with no concern about ranking her accomplishments or fitting a certain number into a certain space just yet. This part of the process is only about getting things down on paper. Hopefully this will enable her to think creatively. When she's done, she should have a varied and detailed list.

Once we have a list for each position we'll review her accomplishments and rank them in best results order. The best results are the ones that made the biggest impact. Results are tangible, dollars saved or made, or percentages that show improvements. Measurable accomplishments are things like increased sales, enlisted more customers, avoided costs, improved performance, increased quality, reduced delivery time, reduced return rate, and increased satisfaction. Think creatively, every position has areas in which things can be improved. How have you improved things?

Ultimately we are going to fit Karen's entire resume on two pages. It's not a rule but for her level of experience, two pages is a good size. We'll select and include enough accomplishments from each of her positions to fill the space. The most important and relevant accomplishments are the ones in her current position. We'll include more of those. We'll include fewer accomplishments from her previous positions not only because they are less applicable to the positions she's seeking now but also because they are no longer as current.

In order to fit her resume on two pages, Karen has space for five accomplishments for her first position and three or four each for her second and third positions depending on the length of each accomplishment. When she's done there will be enough room on the second page for her Education module and a little extra if she needs to include an Interests and Activities module. The specific accomplishments she includes on any version of her resume will vary depending on the needs of the positions she's interested in. Because Karen created individual lists of accomplishments she can simply copy and paste them to update her resume.

Karen's Education module is near the bottom of the second page of her resume. It is okay to put the Education module in one of two places on your resume, either just below the Summary ahead of Experience, or after Experience at the end of the resume or ahead of the optional Interests and Activities module. Often, depending on the client, a candidate's education is the first thing I look for, before reading through their experience. However, it only takes a second to scroll past the Experience module and get to the Education module on a well-constructed resume. Depending on the length of a career, education may have more or less importance than experience. In Karen's case, because she has 12 years' experience, her experience is more important, even though her education is excellent. The opposite is true in Anthony's case because he has far less experience. When we work on Anthony's resume, we'll put his Education module at the top.

Formatting the Education module is simple. Put the most recent college degree or formal education at the top. Include the type of the degree earned and graduation year on the top line and the name and location of the school on the second line. Repeat for lesser degrees and professional certifications.

Education and Certifications:

Masters of Business Administration, 2000

University of Maryland, College Park, MD
Bachelor of Science Degree: Marketing Management,
1998
University of Maryland, College Park, MD

Why is it important to include the year that you received your degree? A lot of people who have had long careers skip putting their graduation years on their resumes because they don't want to reveal their age. They may also skip some of their earlier positions for the same reason. This is a mistake.

One of the key things that human resources people and recruiters look for are gaps in career history or chronology. Having a gap raises unnecessary questions. There may be age discrimination in some cases but in my experience finding the right mix of skills and education is hard enough without also having to filter by some set of discriminatory standards. Discrimination is inefficient. Regardless, you are who you are, and trying to hide it or mislead in the hopes of getting an interview only moves back the inevitable. Surprises are never good in the hiring process. Don't surprise potential employers.

From a time management standpoint, you should want to know sooner rather than later if a company is or isn't interested for any reason. If they don't think you're a fit for the position or their culture, you should move on. You are also evaluating them. It is important not to spend time trying to get in or fit in situations that have too much resistance. There are plenty of potential employers. Making sure all of the information is on your resume eliminates unnecessary questions and saves time. Complete your chronology. The right employer will value your experience.

In the beginning of this chapter in the list of resume modules I wrote that the Interests and Activities module was optional. Typically I don't really care about a candidate's interests or activities outside of his or her career. I'm not apologetic about it, I'm efficient. If my purpose is to find someone who can help my client source a specific kind of processed steel from Eastern European suppliers, then the fact that he or she enjoys needlepoint on weekends doesn't add value. That said, if one of my client's hiring managers is an avid golfer and I know about it, I might encourage a candidate who is also a golf enthusiast to mention it in passing in an interview if the opportunity arises. I still don't need to see it on their resume and it's not the kind of thing I would consider while recruiting for the position.

However there are organizations that value community involvement, civic activities and volunteerism. If you're involved in any of these kinds of things then it is probably not a bad idea to have an Interests and Activities module prepared. You can always add it.

Karen added an Interests and Activities module because her employers tend to be very large corporations that sponsor various types of events and have community outreach programs. Similar potential employers will probably see value in the fact that Karen, a marketing professional, is well connected in her community. Karen's Interest and Activities module follows the format of her other modules.

Interests and Activities
Active Member/Volunteer, Junior League
International, 2003-present
Volunteer, Adopt-a-Classroom, 2004-2005
Volunteer-Company Lead, United Way 2003-2004

That's it. Karen's resume is complete. There are no addendums or other additional documents. She doesn't have a long and a short version. She has five modules: Contact Details, Summary, Experience, Education, and Interests and Activities.

Because of the number of accomplishments she selected from her lists, Karen's resume fits neatly on two pages. Because she created separate lists of accomplishments for each position she can add or delete any of them at any time very easily in order to customize her resume for any specific position. Karen, being an overachiever also created a list of template summaries so she could update the Summary of her resume easily too.

Resumes really should only be one or two pages. In most cases, going longer than two pages provides more detail than is necessary to accomplish the mission. Remember, the goal of a resume is to answer enough questions to provoke a desire for further contact, nothing more.

Providing too much information or answering too many unasked questions can have the exact opposite of the desired effect. A lot of us are looking for reasons not to tag you for further contact. It's simply more efficient. If I have to sort through a hundred items to try to find one that fits a certain set of specifications, the easiest thing to do is to develop ways to eliminate the ninety-nine that don't fit.

I have seen very good resumes from people with as much as twenty-five years' experience on a single well-spaced page. Conversely I've seen resumes from people with much less experience stretched out to three or four pages.

The longest resume I received recently was eight pages! Imagine, I had a candidate who thought his career was so special that he spent eight pages telling me about it. He probably didn't think of it this way, but having an eight page resume means he is asking every person who receives it to spend a significant amount of time reading it. Most people don't have a lot of time.

His resume would be a lot better if it got to the point more quickly. At eight pages he's trying to cover too many options. He's not thinking about a specific employer's particular needs. He's going for everything. A resume that long is unfocused. It says: "I didn't spend time trying to understand exactly what you're looking for but I'm sure I did it at some point and I can probably do it again. You can find it in here somewhere if you really look."

A long resume represents a transfer of effort that does not respect the relationships involved in the job search process. He's making the reader do the work he should have done. People who receive his resume feel that and it creates resistance. He should have reviewed the potential opportunities and spoken to the needs specifically, instead of making someone like me try to find value buried between the non-applicable. Most importantly, having a resume that is too long is counter to its purpose. You don't want to provide so much information that there are no more questions.

For candidates with little experience, like Anthony, the problem isn't that the resume is too long, rather that it might be too short. Earlier I told Karen to create a list of accomplishments for each of her positions with the idea that it's easier to cut than it is to create. I wasn't kidding. It is much easier to deal with having too much information as opposed to too little. If your resume is running long the solution is simple: Go back to the job descriptions that interest you and find the most important things. Take out the parts of your resume that don't speak to the most important things and your resume will be shorter. The problem is different when you feel like you don't have enough experience to fill out your resume. You can't create experience so, what do you do?

Anthony was really excited that we were finally going to talk about his resume.

"I'm really excited that we are FINALLY going to talk about my resume!"

"Finally! What do you mean finally? Don't you think that you are better prepared to write your resume now that you've done all the research that I suggested?"

"Well, yes, actually. I am much more prepared than I was before."

"Okay, great. We've already talked about the modules you need for your resume so I imagine you're struggling with content. Is that right?"

"Yes. I only had that one job after I graduated and that was only for nine months. I got some things done but only as much as I could do in such a short period. I feel bad about that, like I am not competitive or people won't see me as a good candidate."

"First, you shouldn't feel bad about anything. What happened to your job was not something you could control or influence. It happens. Businesses arbitrarily reduce employment all the time. It is part of the risk you assume when you seek employment and accept a position. Hopefully next time you'll be more prepared for it so it won't be so traumatic."

"Do you think there will be a next time?"

"Probably. If you work for a large corporation and are many levels removed from the top decision makers it is difficult to view things strategically. As a result, a case may develop in which it makes sense for them to reduce staff. You can get caught up in a layoff and never see it coming. It's good to be prepared."

"Oh, that's kind of scary."

"It's true though and it's smart to think about these kinds of things ahead of time. Accept the risks. Now let's get back to your resume. Consider this, your level of experience is similar to anyone else who has nine months of experience."

"What do you mean?"

"Expectations. Your potential employers won't expect you to have landed on the moon already with only nine months of experience. If they are hiring people to fill positions where they only need or want a small amount of experience then you're just right. Companies and organizations hire people with limited experience for entry level positions all the time. The challenge is not portraying your experience as more than it is, rather doing the homework to target opportunities that are made for people who have your level of experience. You've done that. All we have to do now is take what you've got, extract the most valuable components and present them in a compelling fashion."

"You really make that sound good, and easy."

"Thanks. It is good and, since you did the homework, it won't be too difficult either."

I reminded Anthony that we discussed some of this earlier, from Chapter One:

"The value that companies look for in recent college graduates has more to do with attitude, work ethic, potential and interest."

Now it is time to apply that thinking and create a resume for Anthony that speaks to the idea that he is someone with a good attitude, strong work ethic and potential, albeit with little experience. Because Anthony wants to pursue entry level or one-year experience level positions in Human Resources and Internal Recruiting the potential employers he is going to contact will expect to see his level of experience. In writing his resume, Anthony is going to select material for his modules that best demonstrates his interest, good attitude, work ethic and potential.

The highlight of Anthony's budding career is not his experience but his education. In terms of time, Anthony spent four years getting his education but only has nine months of career experience. Instead of putting his Education module after his Experience, we'll put Anthony's Education module right after his Summary.

For the type of position he is seeking, Anthony has a very good education. Since Anthony has a Bachelor of Science degree focused on Human Resources Management and is seeking an entry level Human Resources position his education is highly applicable.

Because Anthony has limited career experience but a good education it can be helpful for him to expand his Education module to include any special courses or projects he completed that further demonstrate his value, interest and potential in Human Resources Management. These can be listed like accomplishments like in the Experience module. Anthony's Education module is just below his Summary and looks like this:

Education:

Bachelor of Science: Human Resources Management, June 2011
Rochester Institute of Technology, Rochester, New York

Specific Subjects Studied in Human Resources Management:
- Advanced Human Resources Administration
- International Human Resources
- Training Design and Delivery
- Interviewing Techniques
- Compensation and Benefits Administration

Related Projects:

- Presentation: Training Design, Implementation and Results Tracking in a Manufacturing Environment
- Presentation: Benefits of Outsourcing in Human Resources
- Term Paper: Recruiting in the Digital Age

Memberships:
- Student Member, Society of Human Resources Management (SHRM)

If Anthony has done good research and identified positions that are realistic for him to pursue, some of his course work will match some of the knowledge that potential employers are seeking in candidates for entry level positions. In addition to listing the degree and some areas of study, Anthony also included some projects and presentation titles in order to demonstrate specific and applicable knowledge. A potential employer who is looking for help in tracking the benefits of training might find value in the fact that Anthony has done research and completed a presentation in that area.

In the nine months that Anthony was employed after he graduated from college, he did get some good experience and does have a few accomplishments. Anthony's Experience module is setup the same way as Karen's but placed just after his Education module.

Experience:

ABC Executive Search, Anytown, New York, September 2011 – May 2012
An international executive search and human resources administration company

Junior Personnel Consultant

Team member for recruiting projects supporting manufacturing, construction, IT and financial industries; including client communications, advertising, candidate sourcing, interviews and evaluation, negotiations and placements

- Recruited and placed District Retail Manager for XYZ, Inc. in 6 weeks, ahead of schedule, beating competing personnel staffing company and earning new positions for the firm
- Recruited and placed Program Manager and Brand Manager and for ACME, Inc., doubling project scope by identifying two high-value candidates instead of one, resulting in two placements
- Manage logistics and coordination of client and candidate meetings and interviews
- Manage client communications including project status updates, candidate evaluations and negotiations

When Anthony and I put all of this together we discovered that his Contact Details, Summary, Education and Experience modules filled about three quarters of one page. So, we added an Interests and Activities module and included the fact that Anthony has done some traveling internationally and goes kayaking and scuba diving recreationally. These interests and activities speak to Anthony's energy level and enthusiasm and help fill the small remaining space on the only page of his resume without making it appear crowded. There's nothing there that can hurt. Anthony's resume is now complete.

During the time that I spent with Karen and Anthony I was also doing my job, working with Tom to get him prepared to market. We've had several more phone conversations and Tom has shared a lot more detail about his current position. We discussed the scope and scale of his responsibility and the improvements he's made in the time he's been with his current employer. Tom's resume was already pretty good. All of his modules were there, his chronology was complete and he had specific accomplishments for each of his positions. We added a couple of new accomplishments for his current job and wrote out several more separately so we could adjust his resume for particular positions or organizations. From a structural standpoint, Tom's resume looks a lot like Karen's and fits on two pages even though he has a few years more experience.

With the initial research done and everyone's resumes completed, all three of my test subjects are ready for experimenting! In a sense, that's what we're about to do. We're going to experiment by contacting people to see how they respond, and then we're going to use the results to calibrate our approach and get better.

If you have followed along so far, like Karen and Anthony, you should have developed a sense of your value proposition and have identified a few jobs you want to pursue. In addition, you should have an initial list of companies you like and believe you can help. You should also have a good starter list of contacts that are peers or potential hiring managers. Lastly, you'll have a good resume in a format that you can update or modify depending on specific needs.

In the next chapters we're going to take all of this material and knowledge and put it to work. We're going to contact people! Because we took the time to do the research first, instead of just throwing together a resume and blasting it out, our approach will be more specific, better targeted, and ultimately more successful. Because we learned the language and understand more about our own value and the needs of the organizations or companies we will approach, we can be more confident. The things we have done so far make us more competitive and better prepared.

Karen and Anthony are ready. They both feel better and more confident about why they are seeking the jobs they want. They understand where they can contribute and how, and they are empowered as a result. I feel very good about marketing Tom as well. I spent enough time with him to really understand what he's doing and how he adds value. I've identified the kinds of contacts who will know what I'm talking about when I call or email and we've put together a solid resume. We're all ready for the next steps. Let's get started!

Chapter 4: Making Contact

Every time you speak with someone during your job search the conversation you're having is an interview. Every email you send is an interview. Every phone call, every introduction and every handshake, these are all interviews. This is important.

I can't say how many introductory emails I've received that are written so poorly or are so full of errors that I can't help but form an impression of the sender. The impression is not a good one. Considering that spell check is built into to almost every email program or browser, typographical and spelling errors are tough to reconcile. It's simply attention to detail, which is a very important attribute for any of the jobs on my desk. Someone who hasn't taken the seconds required to make sure that they have spelled my name correctly (it's in my email address!), correct basic grammatical errors or at least include punctuation is someone who is not taking this very seriously.

This is not a complaint. From a pure efficiency standpoint, a poorly written email means that I don't have to continue reading. It saves time to find out so early. It sounds harsh but the question I have to ask is: Will this candidate's emails to my hiring manager clients be this bad? If they are, it will hurt an already competitive, statistically difficult process and the chances to earn a commission will decrease. As a rule, it isn't good for me to do anything that will worsen the odds of making a placement. I have to do my best to strive for perfection every time. I don't show my clients candidates they might hire, I show my clients candidates they will pay to hire. Notice the distinction; it sets the bar pretty high. The fees are not cheap and the value proposition has to be clear. I am not only competing with every other headhunter out there, but also all of the walk-ins, referrals, internals and other "no-fee" candidates. If I want to earn a living I have to be better than all of them. Keep in mind, you might be competing with me, or, if not me, certainly everyone else. Are you ready?

The same is true for resumes. We spent the entire last chapter discussing the formatting and content of a good resume. The fact that there should not be any misspelled words or typographical errors in your resume is implied. It's not good to spend a lot of time creating a resume only to put it out there with errors.

I value my contact lists similarly. I don't want to waste valuable time doing research to find good potential contacts only to send them poorly written email. Do you think they are going to give any more leeway than I would when it comes to errors?

How do I avoid this? I write, read, re-write, edit, review and then send. I make notes for calls ahead of time. I make an effort to get to the point quickly, to write crisp and concise emails. I respect the time of the people I'm contacting and I do my best not to make mistakes. The effort required to make sure is smaller than the effort required to do all the preparation work in the first place, and definitely less than what is required to go back and fix an error after the fact.

That's it, lecture over.

We've spent a fair amount of time getting ready for the things we'll do in this chapter. If you've done everything that Karen and Anthony did for themselves, and I did for Tom, then you should have a clear understanding of your value proposition, a good list of potential contacts and employers, and a good working resume. You're ready for the next step.

In this chapter I am going to show Karen and Anthony exactly how I will market Tom using steps that they can repeat for themselves. We're going to write and send a lot of email. Anthony and Karen are going to do things that normal job hunters don't do and I'm going to do what I always do to get my job done. We're also going to spend some time talking about our goals for the conversations we're hoping to have and how to frame our communications to support of our goals.

Marketing candidates, and marketing yourself, is an art. It took a lot of practice and experience to learn the methods that were the most effective and comfortable for me. There are obvious steps and more subtle steps. There's timing and an understanding of the process to consider.

Most people will only have to do an actual job search a few times in their lives. For example, it is likely that you got a job through a contact once, or stayed with the same company and were promoted, or any number of other variables that resulted in you getting a job without having to conduct a full-blown cold-start job search. In contrast, as a headhunter, when I'm not recruiting on specific positions for established clients, I'm marketing. I am probably marketing half of the time. I market candidates for a number of productive reasons, placing the candidate I'm marketing is only one of those reasons. A lot of marketing activity results in new client development and future placement opportunities.

Recently I marketed a very strong materials and logistics management candidate to a company I'd been reading about and wanted to engage. I did a little research and found an appropriate contact. There was no way to know if the contact I found needed someone like my candidate but marketing her in was a good conversation starter. That particular call didn't result in an opportunity for the candidate I was marketing, however I did get a referral to another manager who needed a different type of candidate. So, instead a job for my candidate, I found an opportunity to recruit a different type of candidate for another job.

How does that relate to you and your job search? If that happens, you've had a good conversation with a new contact who gave you a referral to someone else who could be a potential hiring manager. No matter what else happens or doesn't happen, that in itself is a good result.

How exactly do I market a candidate like Tom, or the woman in the previous example?

We covered how Tom and I first started talking in the first chapter. He called me after getting my name from another one of his contacts. We spent some time on the phone reviewing his qualifications and goals. Then we discussed potential companies and I did some research to create a list of companies and identify contacts. Lastly we updated and edited his resume. This all happened in a period of about two weeks. The next step is applying all of this development work to start dialogues, build relationships and ultimately identify opportunities that we can turn into jobs.

Remember in the second chapter when we made our lists of companies and contacts? Karen and I talked a little bit about ranking them from high potential / high interest to low potential / low interest. I did the same for Tom and have two lists. The first is our original list of twenty companies. The second is the break-out list of four or five contacts in each of the twenty companies. Both lists are ranked based on Tom's industry, qualifications and interests. I'm going to start in the middle of the contacts list. I don't want to start with the highest potential / highest interest contacts because it would be good to get some replies and feedback so I can hone my message first. Every contact is valuable and every communication, whether it's an email or phone call, has to be the best I can do. It is smart to practice a little bit before getting to the best of the contacts. I'll probably only get one chance with each of them.

How do I get all these email addresses? And what about using LinkedIn.com invitations to get them?

For people that I've already connected with on LinkedIn.com, there are two ways of making direct contact. LinkedIn.com has a message feature that allows users to send each other mail within the system and most 1st level contacts will have a direct email address listed and available under the "Contact Info" tab below their picture (or name if there's no picture) on their profile pages.

If the person I want to contact is on LinkedIn.com but is not yet a connection or if I don't have their email address, LinkedIn.com's invitation function can serve as a quick way to introduce myself. I can ask someone to connect, for permission to send them a personal message via email, or even for their advice. LinkedIn.com recommends not sending invitations to people you don't know but I'm pretty sure that common interests and a desire to connect make it okay to try to meet new people. Everyone I know has been doing it for years. Even so, the headline on their invitation page asks: "How do you know (contact name)?" and lists several options: "Colleague, Classmate, We've done business together, Group, Other, I don't know (insert name)," and most recently "Friend." As I wrote in Chapter 2:

"While there is a 300 character limit on invitations, using them is a good way to break the ice and request permission to email someone directly. Note: I personalize every invitation and when I use the "Friend" button to validate an invitation, I always acknowledge that we are not (yet) friends and apologize for using the term to send the invitation."

The 300 character limit really does impact how much you can get across in the text of an invitation but I've found that it is usually enough for me to craft a personal message that gets to the point and inspires a response. Like the email messages we'll discuss below or resume writing from the previous chapter, everything you send to a prospective contact, hiring manager, peer, or anyone else during the course of your job search has to be well written and error free. And, like everything else, it takes practice.

I always start my invitations with a greeting, "Hi (first name)" then add a quick line about myself: "I'm an executive recruiter specializing in supply chain jobs in energy and manufacturing." Usually there's just enough room after that to ask a question or request contact information. Sometimes I write that I have an opportunity and ask them to contact me if they are interested. Other times, like any job seeker might, I tell the recipient that I found their background interesting and wanted to connect to network or seek advice. The vast majority of the invitations I send prompt the recipients to at least look at my profile. Most get a response too; either the invitation is accepted and I can send a longer direct message, or the recipient contacts me directly. Of course, I'm regularly doing the work to make sure my profile is ready for views – again, like my resume or anything else that I might present to a prospective contact, client, or employer.

LinkedIn.com is truly a great resource and even though there are over 300 million members, there are still people who don't use it. If I need to reach someone that is not on LinkedIn.com and I want to send them an email instead of calling, there are a couple of well-known options I can try. The first is easy: Guessing! Most large companies use similar structures for creating email addresses. The most common include examples like:

- firstname.lastname@companyname.com

- firstinitial.lastname@companyname.com

Try these with the (.) between the first and last name or without and your email might get through. Smaller companies like mine might just use the first name and the domain. If you don't want to guess, call the switchboard operator and ask for an administrative assistant in the department where your prospective contact works and ask for their email address. The structure will most likely be the same as the person you want to reach or you can ask the administrative person to forward your message.

There are a lot of ways to get contact information for the people you want to reach. Other obvious methods include Google or Facebook searches. Lesser known methods include using the resume search tool on the job aggregation site Indeed.com. In fact, doing a "Title" search using Indeed.com's resume search tool is a great way to identify contacts in the first place!

No matter how we get the email addresses we need the next step is composing a well written and effective message. That's where Tom and I are right now. We need to put together the text of our first email. The goal of this email is not to get Tom a job. That's too much and it's self-interested, both for me and for Tom. Sending a single email that asks for a job, or for someone to hire Tom, doesn't speak to value or frame the conversation in a way that is useful. In fact it doesn't set up a conversation at all. If I ask a potential hiring manager if they want to hire Tom all they can say is yes or no. The vast majority of the time the answer will be no and then we're done. It is almost like blindly applying to positions online. I don't want a yes or no response. I want an open response. I don't want to corner my contact; I want to speak with them. This is just the beginning of the communication process.

The goal of the first email is to make contact and attempt to establish a rapport that results in a continued conversation, and an exchange of information and ideas. I don't want to ask for something without offering anything. I am going to ask for something though, advice. And I'm going to offer myself as a worthwhile contact. Remember if you're in the right place, communicating with the right people, you too, like Anthony or Karen, are also a potentially valuable contact. The right people want to know about viable candidates in their fields even if they are not thinking about hiring someone right now. In addition, I am going to use empathy and demonstrate value in terms of how I work and who

I work with. I want to be a headhunter who is seen as someone who markets candidates so that the contact I'm reaching out to perceives that I might help them too if they need it.

Asking for advice from the person I'm contacting puts them in a position of authority and knowledge, which is complimentary. I am seeking and would value their expertise and opinion. Since I've chosen my contacts very carefully and have done my homework, they will recognize the language I use to describe Tom and that will establish credibility. The contacts I've identified and selected to send marketing inquiries to on behalf of Tom are all potential hiring managers or peers. Good hiring managers want to know about strong candidates in their fields regardless of their current hiring needs. Additionally, they have peers in similar hiring capacity positions who they can refer who may need someone like Tom right now. Lastly, these potential hiring managers and peers usually don't mind knowing another headhunter who works in their discipline just in case they too are receptive to hearing about opportunities.

How does this relate to you marketing yourself? Advice is easy. It is a low resistance request. If you've done a good job on your lists, everyone you contact will be in a position to offer some type of advice, both peers who have the type of job you're after and potential hiring managers who might need help. What are you offering as a candidate? Again, if you're contacting potential hiring managers in your field, they should perceive value in knowing someone who is qualified to contribute to their needs, whether or not they want to hire right now. If you're contacting peers, keep in mind that they are also future hiring managers and creating relationships with them can have benefits later if they are promoted. You're also going to make them feel good by reinforcing the value of their own career decisions and seeking their advice. How do you feel when someone tells you that they value your opinion and would like your advice? You feel good. The emails we're sending should cause the same feelings.

All of the contacts on all of our lists have jobs and every one of them has very likely engaged in a job search at some point in their career. The cutthroat, heartless, brutal world of business is populated by people just like you. Everyone who is employed and everyone on all of your contact lists owes someone a favor for helping them become employed. The debt may be as small as "they took my call, spent two minutes with me when I was looking and gave me the name of the person who hired me." One result of that experience is that they remember. If you can indirectly trigger that memory you have a good chance of getting them to think about what you are going through now. Reminding someone about their own job search can result in a situation where they can make a payment on their debt. They may not be able to repay the person or people who helped them but they can help someone else a little and that feels good. All you're asking for is advice and again, advice is easy.

They, the buttoned down, suited, overworked, nondescript masses of corporate America, are, underneath it all, real individuals with feelings. They definitely remember searching for jobs and how stressful it was. And, when asked for something easy like the name of a contact, some details about how they got their jobs, or a lead to a company that might be hiring they help more often than you might think.

Who are you asking for advice? You are contacting people who have or have had the job you want, people who hire for the job you want and people who are related to the job you want. So what do you say?

For me, this is fairly direct because I can immediately state that I am a headhunter working in the same discipline as the people I'm contacting. From there, the message that I'll send is very similar to the message that you, Anthony and Karen will send. It's short, to the point, includes some important highlight content and asks an open question or two. The long explanation above about empathy and targeting is really important but the actual emails are fairly short. Remember this has to be easy for people to respond to. Think: low resistance.

After many drafts and edits, the first email message I will use to market Tom to contacts on LinkedIn.com looks like this:

> "Hi (First Name only),
>
> I'm an executive recruiter specializing in supply chain management positions within the energy and manufacturing industries. I found your profile while doing research for a candidate I am helping and I'd like to ask your advice.
>
> The candidate I'm working with is a Materials Manager for a well-known utilities infrastructure manufacturer in the southeast. He's purchases about $250 million per year in steel commodities, is responsible for inventory management at two facilities and has been promoted repeatedly. He has an MBA and a BS in Engineering. I am trying to help him find a new position in Houston so he can be closer to family.
>
> What is your opinion of the market in Houston for people with his skills and experience?
>
> Who do you know that hired someone like this recently or may still be looking?
>
> Thanks for your help. I really appreciate your insights.
>
> Best Regards, Kurt Schmidt"

In the first short paragraph I introduced myself, explained how I found them and why I'm sending an email. Then I put them in a position of authority by letting them know that I value their advice. It's concise and logical.

I included some key highlights about what Tom is doing in the second paragraph. It is important to provide relevance so that the person receiving the email doesn't have to work too hard to see value. It is also helpful to give a sense of scale and scope. Tom's title explains what he does. The short description of his current employer shows the relation to my contact's employer (manufacturing, steel). The dollar amount that Tom manages shows the scale of his responsibilities. The fact that he's been promoted repeatedly with his current employer demonstrates that Tom is valuable. The last sentence, describing Tom's desire to move to Houston in order to be closer to family, is empathetic.

If the first two paragraphs work, the recipient of my message will feel good because I sought his or her advice. They will recognize Tom's value because I did the homework ahead of time to make sure that they were an appropriate contact, a potential hiring manager or peer, and included relevant highlights in my description. And, they will understand and relate to Tom's motivation.

Secondarily, they will see that I'm a headhunter who takes the time to contact companies on behalf of candidates. Sure, if any of these contacts hires my candidate I am going to send them a giant bill, but that's beside the point. I'm still taking time to help someone. In my business, cold marketing like this is not the norm. Most recruiters spend all of their time recruiting. Or, if they market candidates at all it's only to established clients. I'm going one step further. And, hopefully, on a subconscious level, they will think that I might do the same for them and I might.

Lastly, I only asked two simple questions. Again, asking someone's opinion is good. I asked this person for their opinion of something fairly large, assuming them into an elevated vantage point. I didn't ask for too much, just some thoughts. The answers to either question won't commit them to anything and are free and easy. I didn't ask if he or she had a position now. Maybe they do, maybe they don't. Maybe they will give me a name or perhaps they are reluctant to do so. We'll see.

Hopefully the sum of all of the things I tried to do will be enough to generate a response. Any response is fine. Going into this, I know that I won't get a response 100% of the time. In fact, I'll be thrilled if I get a response 15 or 20% of the time. No matter what the percentage is, the vast majority of the replies will be closed, like: "I really don't know of anyone who is looking for someone like that right now." I always reply, and I'm always polite, I thank the person for taking a moment to read my email and send an answer. Then I keep their information. They may not be interested in offering anything more at this time but at least they replied. If I have something relevant I will contact them again. I'll be consistent and I'll always offer value. Over time, perhaps a relationship may develop. If not, the truth is, email only takes a moment and there are so many possible positive results that it is almost always a good investment of time for me to reply, be professional and polite.

This is a numbers game. I'm going to send a lot of emails. I have my list as a base to work from and I know that I will be able to add plenty of names to it during the campaign.

There are six possible responses to a first marketing email:

1. No Response - Self Explanatory: This will be what happens most of the time. For some people it will happen more often than for others. It happens to me constantly. To maintain my positive attitude I think of my emails like self-guided missiles: Fire and forget. I fire them off and move on. If I fire enough of them, I will eventually hit the right target.

2. Nothing Open, No Guidance: "I don't have an open position for someone like that right now and I don't know of anyone else who is looking."

3.   General Guidance: "I heard that 'Company X' wants to hire someone like your candidate right now. You might check them out." Or "did you check our careers web page?"

4.   Good Referrals – Specific Contacts: "I don't have anything open right now but I know someone else who does. Here is their contact information."

5.   The Potential Position: "We don't have anything open right now but that might change in a few months. Check back with me later or send a resume for me to keep on file."

6.   The Miracle – an Open Position: "Your timing is great because I am indeed looking for help right now. Please send the resume and I'll get back to you if we're interested."

In recruiting there is a seventh possible response as well: "The Candidate," in which the person I've contacted for guidance about a candidate is also looking for a new job and wants to become a candidate too. They will send me their resume, I'll review it, we'll schedule a call and the process starts over again. If I like them, I'll market them.

Of the six potential responses (or non-responses), four have actionable items. Five of the responses provide an opportunity to reply. The number is five because even the number two response "Nothing Open, No Guidance" should still elicit a nice "Thank You" email.

1.   No Reply: Nothing to do. Forget about it. Keep the contact for future reference though.

2.   Nothing Open, No Guidance: As mentioned previously, when I get this response I always reply, thank the person

I've contacted and at least encourage them to contact me if there's ever anything I can do for them. Sometimes they do.

3. General Guidance: This is good. First, I can add another company to my list if I don't have it already. Then I can do research to identify appropriate contacts. My reply to this response is short and simple. I thank them for getting back to me and offering a lead, then I ask if they know someone specific at the company for me to contact. Lastly, I offer to return the favor and keep in touch like before.

4. Good Referrals – Specific Contacts: This is even better. Now I have both a company and a contact to add to my list. I'll do some research before emailing the referred contact to make sure he or she is the right person and to see if I can find any better contacts at the company. When I reply to the original contact, I'll ask if I can use their name in my introductory email to the person they referred. It's helpful to be able to cite someone in an introductory email in order to establish credibility, but it's always best to get permission first. Again, I'll thank the person for replying to my original email and tell them to contact me anytime if they need something.

5. The Potential Position: This is a very open response and I can reply in a number of ways. If I just send a resume without asking any further questions it closes the conversation so it's good if I can come up with a question or two. Before doing anything, I'll get Tom's permission to send his resume because most likely I am going to send it, along with my background notes. I'll keep the questions simple but helpful, for example: "Where do

you need the most help right now?" "When would be the best time for you to have someone join the team?" Of course I'll ask for feedback about Tom's background and applicability. Even though I know this is a low probability lead, I will still put it on my calendar and I will be sure to follow up.

6. The Miracle – an Open Position: I call this one "The Miracle" because it is difficult to find someone who is actually looking for exactly the kind of person I'm marketing right now. Of course, I've practiced and done a lot of homework so it does happen.

How do I reply to "The Miracle" response? The easiest thing is to just send Tom's resume and my background notes. However, that may not be the best thing. What if Tom is not the right person? If I just send his resume without asking any questions my potential responses are only yes or no and that's risky. I'll send Tom's resume, with his permission, because I want to give my contact what he wants. I'll also ask a few questions because it would be good to know more about the job. Maybe I have another candidate who is a better fit than Tom. All of a sudden, marketing has turned into recruiting.

Some of the questions I'll ask are qualifying questions like: "What is the most important thing that this person will need to be able to do for you?" The answer to this question will help me determine whether or not Tom is the best person to suggest or if I know someone better. I will also ask about the title of the job and if there is a job description available somewhere. Ideally I'll be able to find it online and make sure Tom's resume speaks to the needs before I send it. However sometimes jobs are not posted and I'll have to take my chances. At a minimum, I want to know the title of the position, highlights about the needs, and the desired compensation level. I'll ask these questions in a reply before sending Tom's resume or even in a call. We'll talk about calls a bit later.

When I receive a reply about a relevant open position during a marketing campaign sometimes I'll change my goal from potentially placing the candidate I'm working with to creating a new client relationship. I won't stop marketing Tom but there could be other opportunities that are worth exploring. Obviously this is different for me than it is for you. Your ultimate goal is to get yourself a job. My ultimate goal is to get everyone a job. In order to achieve my goal it is necessary to demonstrate that I am not a one trick pony who only has one good candidate. The questions I'm asking should imply that I want to evaluate the position against my other candidates in order to determine who would be the best fit. It goes without saying that I will thank my new contact for getting back to me.

My original email and the replies I get are different than what yours will be but they are not that different. It is easy to see how to convert my marketing email into your job search email and how the replies you might receive can fall into the same categories.

In the first paragraph of my marketing email for Tom I introduce myself as an executive recruiter. You're not going to do that but you are going to introduce yourself, honestly and concisely. For example, here's what Karen might say:

"Hi (First Name Only),

I'm a Customer Marketing Manager for ABC Networks. I found your profile while doing research to learn more about marketing management in handset manufacturing and I'd like to ask your advice."

Karen's first paragraph is polite, short and to the point. While it is different than mine because she's not a headhunter, she can still put her contact in a position of authority by seeking his or her advice.

If Karen has done her homework and developed a good list the person she is contacting will be in marketing as either a peer or a potential hiring manager, in the same industry or another industry. As a result, Karen will establish credibility in her first sentence with her job title and company name.

The second paragraph of Karen's email should read a lot like mine for Tom. It needs to provide scope and scale information. It's important to keep it short and only hit the high points. Depending on the responses, there will be an opportunity to send a resume later. For now, Karen's goals are to frame the conversation and to create enough interest, empathy and understanding to generate a response.

"Right now I organize and manage technology presentations to enterprise customers and end users for the Southeastern Region. My team has helped deliver over $5 million in new sales this year as well as improving customer retention by 10%. So we're doing pretty well."

Again, if Karen is communicating with the right people, her accomplishments will resonate and make sense. Karen's second paragraph also sets up her questions. Recall, Karen would like to get out of wireless networking and possibly into handset manufacturing or another industry. Karen needs to learn whether or not her experience in wireless networking is applicable in other industries. Now, with context, she can ask:

> "Is what I'm doing similar to how you're marketing to your customers? Do you think the skillset is transferrable?"

Or if Karen can see that her recipient changed industries before getting into marketing in handset manufacturing, Karen might ask a questions like this:

> "What challenges did you face when you first moved into the handset manufacturing industry? Was it an easy or difficult transition?"

These questions imply that Karen is interested in making a move into the handset manufacturing industry without saying so directly or asking for anything other than advice. Either or both of these questions are probably enough for this first email. If Karen gets a response the conversation will continue and she can ask other questions. Karen closes with a short line thanking her new contact.

> "I really appreciate your insights. Thank you.

> Best Regards, Karen Smith"

That's all. It's very important to keep it short. Notice, Karen didn't offer anything else or overdo it. She did not attach her resume or even mention that she could send it. She didn't ask about any open positions or for any other contacts. She only asked a question or two. Depending on whom Karen is contacting, peers or potential hiring managers, in her industry or not, she can always change the questions. The emails are modular, just like her resume. For example, she might ask more direct questions of a potential hiring manager in a closely related industry, like:

"How could someone from outside your industry help you the most?"

"What skills and experience would you like to have on your team but don't now?"

All of these questions demonstrate interest and imply the Karen is potentially looking to make a change. At the same time, they are not self-interested questions. Karen is showing a desire to learn and add real value where she can.

Like in my example for Tom, Karen has up to six possible responses with up to five opportunities to reply and four actionable items. Her responses will be different than mine. Some might cut to the chase in regard to understanding that Karen is seeking a job and simply say, "We aren't looking right now." Others will actually give her contacts or advice and answer her questions creating opportunities for continued conversations. Most of the time, like me, Karen won't get a reply.

However, if she sends this email to the people on her original list, and continues to add contacts and email them as well, she should end up with enough responses to generate a second round of conversations, either with contacts from the original list or with new referrals.

Counter intuitively, this first introductory, advice request email is even easier to write if your level of experience is more like Anthony's than Karen's or Tom's. People expect that Anthony, with only nine months experience and a degree, needs advice. He's new and just venturing out into the job market. It's no secret. His first email might read like this:

"Hi (First Name Only),

I'm a recent graduate with a degree in Human Resources Management and almost a year of experience in executive recruiting. I found your profile while doing research into the different types of roles in Human Resources. I'm trying to learn more about some of the challenges HR professionals face and I'd really like to ask your advice.

What is the most important thing you do to help your company?

How can someone with my level of experience add value to an organization like yours?

I really appreciate your advice. Thank you.

Best Regards, Anthony Johnson"

Again, Anthony's email follows the same simple structure as mine and Karen's. It is a little shorter since we combined the introductory and background paragraphs but it accomplishes the same thing. Another example of a good question for someone with limited experience, like Anthony, to ask is:

> "What are some of the challenges you faced when you
> first started out in Human Resources?"

My email is different from Anthony's and Karen's in that I am more directly asking about possible job opportunities. However, again, it's not that different. While Anthony and Karen didn't ask about specific positions, the fact that they are both seeking guidance about needs within their respective disciplines implies that they are looking for an opportunity.

The introductory emails we've written are not set in stone. As we get replies or if we don't, we'll review and edit.

So what is it we're doing by sending out all of these emails and asking people we don't know for advice? Do they know that we are really looking for a job?

We are looking for jobs, and yes, they know. However, more important than just looking for a job, we are looking to learn about and identify ways in which we can help. This is the same as looking for a job with one small exception: helping is something you do for others or within a team, a job is something you get for yourself. This small exception should set the tone for all of your communications. Your recipients will feel the difference. It was fun explaining this to Anthony.

"I have no idea what you mean by this. Of course I'm looking for a job. I want everyone to know: I want a job. I want to make money."

"I, I, I, is the only person in all of your sentences. What about them? Is that what you want them to think, what I just thought, that all you want is for someone to give you a job?"

"What do you mean?"

"You should not want someone to give you a job."

"Yes I do. I really do."

"Wouldn't it be better if they wanted your help because you showed them that you had something to offer and were interested? Do you see the difference?"

"Okay, sure, I think so."

"If this is all about you wanting a job, then they have to give you something. If, however you can make this about them wanting your help, then they are asking you for something."

"Now I understand. But don't they need to know that I am looking for a job specifically? This help thing sounds very vague."

"Believe me, they know you're looking for a job. The difference is in how you present yourself when asking about it. Remember when we talked about value and where jobs come from? Help is the received value that balances the equation. Help is a job.

If you can regularly focus the conversation on their needs, their goals, how they accomplish things, their biggest problems and challenges, then they will perceive you differently than if you only focus on your goals and your needs. They will perceive your self-confidence instead of your self-interest. This is part of what keeps the conversational door open.

One of the questions we talked about for your first email was: 'How can someone with (your) level of experience add value to an organization like (your contact's company)?' Consider the difference between that question and a more typical question that someone might ask like: 'Do you have any openings for someone with my level of experience?' See the difference? Which of those two questions sounds more confident and less self-interested? How do you think that tone might affect the answer? Which of those questions has the potential to go further?"

"This seems like such a small detail. Is it really important?"

"It's not just this one question. It's an approach and an attitude."

What I am describing to Anthony is important. The idea is that if you can demonstrate value you can generate interest. In this sense, value is more than a specific and tangible list of accomplishments it is also an attitude. Showing a desire to contribute and help without first focusing on "what's in it for me?" is not only confident and modest, but also demonstrates a very mature understanding of what a job is. A job is not something you are owed or entitled to. A job is something you earn.

The approach we take is reflected in what we do or don't do and what we say or don't say, and when. Our approach is the frame of reference that we create through our communications and how we present ourselves. What does this mean specifically? What exactly should we do to create the proper frame of reference? And, importantly, what shouldn't we do?

First, we've done some of the work required in the research leading up to our introductory emails, we know generally how we can help and who might value our contributions. Now we're making contact to seek guidance and demonstrate that we are interested in learning and contributing. The obvious implication is that we are seeking jobs, Karen and Anthony for themselves and me on behalf of Tom, however we are not asking for jobs. Instead, we are asking for advice and information and we are thankful and appreciative of anything offered. We want to engage and learn.

We are not just blasting out resumes and immediately asking people to read our histories and decide if we fit, forcing them to do the thinking for us. Instead, we're asking for a small thing, a little advice and guidance, maybe a contact or two. We are doing our own thinking.

We are not sending long emails that list out every job we've ever had and selling, selling, selling ourselves to everyone. We are including a little bit of background information to establish credibility and demonstrate that we understand who we're contacting and why.

We are not specifically asking for a job, applying for a job or doing anything that sets up a yes or no response. We are asking open questions and hoping for a reply, any reply. There are no wrong answers to our questions and in almost every reply situation there are opportunities for us to continue the conversations. We are doing our best to encourage a response and avoid closed conversations.

We are not answering every possible question about ourselves or explaining every little detail as to why we're looking for a job. We are not asking our hopeful email readers to work on our behalf. Our emails are short, logically written and to the point. We are giving them enough information so that if they are interested, they might ask a question or offer some advice. We are trying to focus on their needs without telling them our life stories.

We are not saying anything negative about our current situations or complaining. Believe it or not, I get introductory emails all the time from potential candidates who, when describing their interest in seeking a new position, provide a laundry list of negative issues with either their current job or their previous position. Everyone has an impulse to explain things, however it is important to consider how the emails you write will make people feel. Over-explaining and complaining is extremely self-interested. Don't say anything negative about your current company, your current boss, or that it is no fun to be unemployed. Negative communications create negative feelings. There are correct and positive answers to questions about your motivation but it is best to wait until asked.

Don't talk about money! First, as mentioned earlier, it is implied that you are looking for a job. Jobs pay. If you bring it up now you setup a binary situation: too much or too little. There's no conversation in that. Also, what is your salary or desired compensation? It's yours – you're talking about yourself again. This process, at this stage, as repeated throughout this book, is not about you. Your compensation goals are best discussed only when asked, and then there is a very specific, correct way of answering.

Don't express a sense of entitlement. It sounds cynical but nobody deserves a job.

Lastly, don't say anything that doesn't add value to the conversation. The components of the first email we developed all add value for the recipient. Our request for advice elevates them into a position of authority. Our highly specific and targeted accomplishments resonate with our well researched recipients, establish credibility and show that we've done our homework. Our questions show that we value their opinions and are interested.

The purpose of our first email is to get a reply and start a conversation. It is short and to the point. Don't make your recipients work too hard to discover why you contacted them. Encourage them to respond and potentially ask you a question. When this is successful and conversations start, information begins to flow, new contacts are developed, your lists grow, you learn more about what's important and make progress. This first email is probably not going to get you a job but it will add to the body of activities that will result in employment.

Now, let's send this email out a few times and see what happens. I don't suggest to Karen and Anthony that they send an email to every one of the contacts on their lists immediately. Rather, like I'll do for Tom, I tell them to try sending 10-15 the first day while continuing to do research to expand their original lists of companies and contacts. Do the same the second day, third day, and so on. By not sending out all 100 emails at once, we are reserving the opportunity to make changes, either on our own as an afterthought or based on a reply, or lack of replies.

Sending emails like this is as easy as copying, pasting and pressing send. Admittedly I re-read almost every one of mine before hitting send just to make sure there are no errors, but otherwise, it is a simple process. There is nothing to fear in reaching out to the people on our lists. Remember, "Fire and forget." We are ready for this. We know how we can contribute, we've identified people who will recognize our capabilities and we've created resumes that speak to what we can do.

Marketing Tom, I go into this knowing that I won't get replies most of the time. Of the replies I do get, some will lead nowhere, others maybe somewhere. I'll get leads that don't play out, referrals to contacts I can't find, jobs that are too low, too high, already filled, not open to recruiters or otherwise off limits. My list will expand and contract. I'll keep finding new contacts and sending out first round emails. It will take time. There will be days when I feel like I got nothing done and days when I feel like I got a break. Ultimately though, I will place Tom with a company and I will earn my commission. If it doesn't happen easily, it will happen as a result of persistence and absolute unwavering daily work. Regardless though, it will happen. Out of all of these emails and all of these contacts, all the leads, referrals and everything, the fact is, I'm only looking for one job for Tom. The same is true for you, Anthony and Karen.

In the next chapter we'll spend some more time talking about something I call "understanding the numbers" which deals specifically with how to manage the ongoing campaign that is your job search and how to derive satisfaction from completing all of the small things involved.

This is real progress. We are reaching out and we will get a reaction.

Chapter 5: Understanding the Numbers

It's been a couple weeks since Anthony and I have had a chance to speak. Actually it's been a couple of weeks since I've left the office to do anything. I wanted to catch up with Anthony so I invited him for coffee to both get an update and break up my routine a little bit.

"Hi Anthony, how have you been doing? Staying busy?"

Anthony has had a chance to mix up his time little bit too since he was able to get some temporary work helping manage logistics and planning for a series of presentations at a friend's company. It's a good thing and will last another week or two. So far, he has met a few new people, learned some new things and is making a little money. He's also been continuing to send out emails and make contacts for his job search. It's always helpful to have a variety of tasks so that no one task becomes too monotonous.

Anthony tells me that he likes this type of project planning and coordinating. It makes him feel like he is really helping to get something done.

"For the first time in a while I feel like I'm part of something and it's nice to go home with a bit of a sense of accomplishment."

"Yes, never underestimate the satisfaction you can get from getting even small things done!"

"It makes me think about my job search though, and also how you do your job."

"What do you mean?"

"Well, you told me before that it takes weeks or months for you to place one person and even then, nothing is ever certain until that person shows up for work and you get paid. You have to project way out there and really focus and yet I know most of your projects fall apart. It's got to be really, really frustrating; like me sending out emails and applications and getting nothing back most of the time. Sometimes I feel like I'm never going to find what I'm looking for. How do you deal with it?"

"That's a great question and very insightful, both in regard to what I do, and for what you or anyone else is going through during a job search. It can be frustrating and it is very important to learn how to manage that frustration and find ways to be satisfied as you're doing the work."

"So what do you do specifically? I know you're working on marketing that guy Tom and I haven't heard from you in a couple of weeks so I know you've been busy. How is it going?"

"In regard to Tom, I don't know. I don't have any real results yet but I'm sure it's fine."

Anthony looks a little puzzled because I said "I don't know" with a look of total confidence despite the fact that there are no tangible results yet. Logically, after two weeks' work it should seem underwhelming at best if not disappointing to have made so little progress.

"Wait, so you've spent two weeks working on marketing Tom, don't have anything to show for it and yet you can still sit back and say everything is fine and really mean it. How do you know everything is fine? How can you be so confident?"

"First I didn't say that I have nothing to show for my first two weeks of marketing Tom, I said I have no real results. A real result for me would be something very tangible, a workable job, a telephone interview, or an on-site interview. Just because I don't have any of those yet doesn't mean that the two weeks have been wasted. I did get replies to some of my initial emails and have added some new contacts to my lists, both for Tom and for future searches. Even intangibles count. Because of the large amounts of information I deal with there are unintended consequences or unexpected opportunities that can completely change the game. However, none of that is important in regard to Tom specifically, just to time in general."

"Now I'm lost! Usually I can follow what you're talking about but this doesn't make any sense. You're telling that you only got a few new contacts after two weeks' worth of work; I don't know how many hours we're talking about but probably a lot, and that you are okay with that because of something, something and 'time in general?' I totally don't understand. I would be at least a little frustrated by now but you're not. Why?"

"You're right, I'm not frustrated. I'm okay. One of the reasons why is that I know what I'm getting into and what to expect. Your mood, or mine, is based in part on understanding the process and managing your expectations. There are a few things that help me with this and maybe they can help you too.

The first thing goes back to when we talked about value and needs earlier. If you, like me, have done the research and know you're right about the value you're bringing; and you've correctly identified people who will recognize and may need that value, then you should feel confident. You have two parts of a three part equation solved. You know that you are in the right place with the right message. The third part is timing and timing takes time sometimes. This is why the research in the beginning is so important. Not only does it provide confidence but it also significantly increases the odds of success and reduces the amount of time required to complete the process. The rest of what allows me avoid frustration has to do with what I call *understanding the numbers* which is about taking satisfaction from achieving tactical goals and meeting daily targets."

"Right, I remember talking about value and needs, and based on the research I did, I do feel confident about how I can bring value and address a company's needs; how I can help. I also understand about increasing the odds. I'm not sure I get what you're saying about understanding the numbers though."

"You know how I'm always talking about process, process, well like any process, there is a beginning and an end. There are also markers along the way, targets that have to be hit to achieve the ultimate goal. I call knowing about these targets and incorporating them into my project expectations understanding the numbers. The idea is based on an If / Then formula and it goes like this: If I make a certain number of calls, or send a certain number of emails every day for a certain period of time, then I will find jobs. If I get a certain number of jobs to work on, I will be able to schedule interviews. If I schedule a specific number of interviews, I will get offers. If I get enough offers, I will make a placement.

When I fill in the blanks of the formula and replace the word 'certain' with real numbers I can forecast what I have to do to earn a commission. When I take that forecast and break it up into monthly, weekly and daily tasks, I can predict how long it will take and what I need to do each day. With that information laid out in kind of a project map or plan, I can derive satisfaction from completing daily and weekly tasks. I can scratch them off my list as I do them and that makes me happy!"

"I think I'm following. You have an ultimate goal, placing Tom, or, in my case getting a job, right? You also have a process, which we're talking about and I'm learning. The process has targets or smaller goals that allow you to measure progress along the way, and by doing that you feel satisfaction?"

"That's it sort of but I think you'll get a better idea how this works if we put it into practice so you can see exactly what I mean."

Here's what I tell Anthony: This is my formula for marketing Tom, starting from the final vision of a completed placement in the future and working back to today:

- For me, completing one placement means scheduling at least three or four first interviews with Tom or any other candidate

- Scheduling three or four first interviews means getting access to work on four or five jobs

- Getting access to work on four or five jobs means finding at least ten

- Finding ten jobs means communicating with (via phone or email) 200 to 300 target contacts

- Reaching out to that many target contacts means sending at least fifteen emails and calling another ten people per day for each of the three or four candidates I'm marketing at any one time, on top of any other recruiting work

- Having new people to contact regularly requires a couple of hours of research per day

- All of this combined, including managing the process once the candidate and the company are engaged and ultimately completing a placement will take from eight to twelve weeks

- Effectively managing risk means working on at least three or four marketing campaigns and two or three recruiting efforts at once, minimum

The detailed version of this formula tells me what I have to do every day for every step of the process. I literally type or write out my daily tasks every morning and I make sure they support my ultimate goal. Then I mark them off the list as I do them. If I do what I am supposed to do on any given day, I can go home satisfied that I did my work regardless of the immediate result (or lack of). Paired with the confidence I have derived from my value and needs research this is a powerful combination. I feel good and I know that if I keep working, sooner or later the timing will be right too.

"Where did you get all of those numbers and how do you know that they are true?"

"The numbers for marketing Tom come from my own experience in recruiting over the years. I keep track. I know that typically, if I put together three or four good quality first interviews, then usually I make a placement. The numbers help me create tactical goals, setting up three or four interviews for example. There are no guarantees that the numbers will play out this way every time and the words typically and usually bear that out. However, over the years, three to four interviews for one placement has been my average.

Your numbers will be different but the process is the same and there will be a set of numbers that can be identified. The key for you, or anyone else working on a job search, is understanding this way of looking at things at the beginning. Anyone can look back at their own job search when it's done and see what their numbers were. Being able to forecast it, break it down and identify tasks that can be completed in a day or a week is different. It is important because it is within these numbers that we can derive satisfaction even during what seems like the least productive of days. It is empowering.

For example, today I will send out 10-15 emails on Tom's behalf. I will also make 10 or so phone calls and do research. Regardless of the results, I will leave the office satisfied with the work I did marketing Tom because I did it, and just as critical, I did it well. I will have accomplished my mission for the day and I'll go home and get ready to do it again tomorrow."

"What happens if you do that every day for months on end and never get any replies? What if you send out hundreds or thousands of emails and make phone calls until your fingers lock up, your tongue wears out and your ears fall off and still don't find something for Tom? What happens then?"

"Part of what I'm confident about is the integrity of this process. I know that what I am doing works and has worked for me for a long time. Sure there are risks involved, it's a risky business, but the process I'm using and teaching you is designed to minimize those risks. If you listened carefully, you noticed that when I said I'm going to send out my daily emails and make my daily calls I also said that I am going to do it well. That's no joke. Quality is critical to both general success and daily satisfaction. I don't just send out emails or make calls to fulfill a quota. I do it to achieve an ultimate goal and I treat each one as if it is foundational to that goal."

"Even though I am confident today as a result of the research I did earlier, how do I maintain confidence during my job search? Especially on days when I work really hard and nothing seems to happen? How do you do it?"

"First off, there will be days like that. In fact, to be honest about it, most of the days you spend working on your job search will be like that.

Remember though, you are only looking for one job. It is really important to keep things in perspective."

"What do you mean?"

"The goal matches the effort. For me, right now, a typical placement results in a commission of around $25,000.00. Regardless of what other people might think, for me, $25,000.00 is a lot of money. My most basic absolute minimum goal is to make one placement every three months. So there is little reason to be frustrated at the end of the first two weeks. Frankly, I am usually surprised when it takes anything less than three months to get a placement, but sometimes it does. I figure everything averages out over time anyways. Sometimes I make more than one placement at the same time or several in a month. Other times nothing works for months on end."

"Okay, I understand how it works for you but how does that apply to my situation?"

"Like I said, you're only looking for one job. You're looking for a good job, hopefully a job that will develop into a career that will last for many years. That's a pretty big goal isn't it? How much work is something like that worth? A lot right? How many times are you willing to face rejection in order to achieve that goal? How many emails are you willing to send in order to get one back that leads to the long term good job you're seeking? How long should it take?"

"Okay, I see, a big reward or goal can require a lot of work."

"Yes, excluding luck, which I don't believe in anyways, a quality result requires a quality effort. Knowing that going in creates an expectation for you that this may take a while. So you pace yourself. You should setup regular achievable goals, like me, 10 to 15 emails a day, a few phone calls, a couple of hours of research, etc. Keep the overall goal in mind but focus on the completing the tasks and achieving the small goals with the highest level of quality that you can and take satisfaction from that every day."

"Sorry, I have to ask, why don't you believe in luck?"

"Because one of these days, maybe in a week, maybe in a month or more, you're going to bounce into my office and tell me that this has been your lucky day because you just got an interview with a great company, or you just met an excellent contact, or even better, that you just got a fantastic job offer. When you do I'm going to knock you on the head and remind you that you worked really hard to get it. There was no luck involved. You increased the odds of success by proactively sending out a high quality message to as many relevant contacts as you could. By now, you should have the idea that if you send out at least a thousand relevant and specifically targeted emails over a several month period, some of them will arrive at the right place at the right time. There's a good chance one of them will be a part of what gets you a job. Saying it was luck discounts your effort. If it happens, it will be because you did it."

"Right, no luck involved. I got it. So what do I do now?"

"Well, sorry but I'm going to take off now because I have to work. Before I go, tell me, did you get anything from this conversation?"

"Several things actually, first that if I do good enough research early, in order to understand value and needs, it will give me confidence. Secondly, that I need to break up the work into parts and set a pace for myself that includes tasks that I can complete and measure in order to keep track of my progress and not get frustrated."

"Don't forget one last thing, the idea that the size of the goal or reward is relative to the amount of effort put forth. If you want to shoot for the moon, be mentally prepared for the journey."

I really enjoy these conversations with Anthony, aside from my hope that these ideas prove helpful for him, his energy level and interest kind of recharge my batteries. It's also a good way for me to revisit my own practices so I can stay on track.

During a job search, all of us can expect to contact several hundred people, if not thousands, over a period of potentially months. We will have to spend a lot of time doing additional research to identify new companies and contacts to add to our lists. Most of the time we won't get replies to our first contact emails. Of the replies we do get, most will offer no real opportunity to continue the dialogue other than to courteously respond. Many of the emails that do turn into conversations will not go much further than a referral or two or some general advice. However, if we work hard enough, we can turn all of this activity into a few interviews and of those, maybe more than one will result in an offer and ultimately a job.

The course your job search takes may not end up being a straight line. It might include a lot of starts, stops, direction changes and adjustments. Often when I'm marketing a candidate I think in terms of generating a buzz, creating a critical mass of activity, or just using my energy to push outwards and exert force into space. I'm sending out lots of email and making lots of calls. I know the vast majority of won't hit anything or produce any useful results but it doesn't matter. They are all necessary in order to create enough momentum to achieve my goal. Sure it would be nice if I could cut through all of the waste and identify the one target hiring manager that needs to hire someone like Tom right now and sometimes that does happen. However, most of the time it doesn't. In the long run, it is easier to just do the work.

In my mind candidate marketing is like the lifecycle of a rainstorm. It all begins with heat and the transfer of moisture upward forming patchy white clouds. At some point, clouds that started out as disparate wispy floating bits of white begin to turn gray and thicken with water, becoming opaque. Then they turn blue and dark and solid. The weight of the water becomes palpable. When the weight is too much, when the clouds reach critical mass, it rains.

My job is to seed the clouds, to build them up, bring them closer together and increase the density of the water, weight and unreleased energy until the rain comes. When the mass of my outbound communications gains momentum and I start receiving replies that I can build upon, my marketing campaign will begin to have a life of its own. The opportunity for results will increase and I know eventually it will rain. I just have to keep pushing until it does.

We're sending out emails, like we were in Chapter 4. We're taking satisfaction from both hitting our daily targets and doing quality work. We've got our ultimate goal in mind but are focused on daily tasks. Pretty soon we'll start getting replies, maybe not a lot at first but they will come. In Chapter 6 we'll take this to the next level, we'll discuss how to deal with the replies we receive from our first round of introductory emails and what to do if we don't get replies.

Chapter 6: An Open or Closed Conversation

The purpose of this chapter is to explore how conversations happen and how to create the transition from sending out emails to speaking with actual people and getting interviews. Even though every conversation is unique in how it originates, develops and concludes, there are very specific types of responses that we can discuss. The best way to demonstrate this is to provide more details about how I'm marketing Tom, then show how your situation, or Karen's, Anthony's or any other job seeker's is not that different. The situations I describe below are not only real but also representative of typical results for both the types and number of replies I receive and how those replies can be categorized and acted upon.

In the context of sending out our first round of introductory, or in my case, marketing emails for Tom, what defines a conversation? Almost all of the replies I've been getting from the initial marketing emails sent out on Tom's behalf fall within one of the six main categories described in Chapter 4:

1.   No Response

2.   Nothing Open, No Guidance

3.   General Guidance

4.   Good Referrals – Specific Contacts

5.   The Potential Position

6. The Miracle – an Open Position

However, every reply has to be evaluated on its own merit. Simply said, some replies are better than others even if they are in the same category. Some replies invite responses from me that include more questions and are *open conversations*, other replies may provide information but don't elicit a response and are *closed conversations*. Some open conversations are more open than others. And, it is okay that most people don't reply.

I received 36 replies out of the first 100 emails sent for Tom based on my original contacts list. This is a very good result. Of the 36 replies, 20 could be classified as "Nothing Open, No Guidance." All 20 basically said: "I don't have anything for someone like that right now and I haven't heard of anyone else who is looking." Even though these might be closed conversations, I responded to every one of them, as described in Chapter 4. They all got a courteous and short note saying at least, "Thanks for getting back to me about this. Please don't hesitate to contact me if I can do anything for you in the future. Best Regards…" In a few cases where they said more or gave any indication that there might be future opportunities, I added a question like "If you could hire someone right now, where do you need the most help?" I don't really expect responses but if they come, I will evaluate them individually again. In terms of marketing Tom, none of these replies are directly useful right now, however each of these contacts were carefully chosen and did take a moment to reply so developing any kind of rapport with them might be helpful in the future.

The most important thing about email conversations is to actually read the email. Note, I left out a potential opportunity in the responses above. They were all worded a little differently but each response was classified as a Category 2, "Nothing Open, No Guidance." However, any of them could have just as easily been in category number 5, "The Potential Position." How so? Without meaning to intentionally mislead, people tend to be very conservative with information in the beginning of a conversation. That is why it is so important to read and listen very carefully.

For example, the exact wording used above is: "We don't have anything for someone like that right now." It's thin, but that could mean they might be looking for someone, just not someone like Tom. If I don't ask about it, I'll never know. So in my reply, to potentially open up the conversation, I might add: "You indicated that you are not looking for someone like my candidate right now, however I got the impression that you might still need help. What kind of person are you looking for today?"

It's a gambit but a cheap one and sometimes a good way to continue a conversation. It costs just a moment to add another question to an email. If I get a reply saying: "Yes we are looking for someone…" I will have created a potential job order and might be able to do some recruiting and develop a new client. Again, this particular situation might not be immediately applicable for direct job seekers but the point, not to overlook any detail and consider every option, is universal.

The other 16 replies I received out of the 36 total replies broke down like this:

Five of them fit the headhunter only category, number 7, "The Candidate." Reading that I do executive search work focused on supply chain management and strategic sourcing in energy and manufacturing, these contacts asked if they could be included as candidates for future openings. Remember "wash, rinse and repeat?" I'll go through the same exercises with each of these five as I did with Tom. First I'll request that they send their resumes, then I'll schedule calls to review their backgrounds and interests in order to discern their value propositions, and lastly, I'll evaluate whether or not I want to market them or simply keep them on file in case a need arises. I'll also explore why these people want to leave companies I thought of marketing to. What does it say about their current companies? Do others want to leave? Why? Is it worth tracking jobs there? Would it be better to take people out?

Nobody is going to ask to be your candidate, or Anthony's or Karen's. However you may contact people who tell you that they would like to change jobs themselves. For you, like it is for me, this can be a helpful bit of information. The questions I listed above, the ones I'd ask anyone who wants to be a candidate, are useful for you as well. Again, either something is wrong with this company (if others want to leave) or there could be opportunities there. It's worth exploring and even trying to contact others to see if they would reply similarly.

That leaves eleven replies from my first 100 emails. Of those, two offered general guidance (Category 3) consisting of things like "I heard so-and-so is hiring" or "Have you tried contacting this company?" I follow up on every piece of information I receive. Even though replies like this typically don't ask for a response other than "Thanks I appreciate the information, let me know if I can return the favor sometime," I still sometimes add another question. For example, asking if the contact knows someone at the company they referred is easy enough. Most of these replies end up as closed conversations, consisting only of the contact's fist reply, still though, it's something, and they did reply so perhaps I will email them again sometime.

I also received some specific contact referrals to add to my list. These are very valuable. Considering that we all did our best to identify relevant contacts in the first place, the people they refer are often also good contacts. It sounds over-simplified but quality knows quality. Think of it from your own point of view. Would you attach your name to something that wasn't good, even if it was just a very small thing like a referral? Probably not. The other valuable thing about specific contact referrals is that you can usually cite the referrer's name in your introductory email to the new contact. This is another way of establishing credibility and will help get your email read. Often the referrer will specify that it is okay to use their name. If they don't it is very important to ask first. When I reply to ask permission to use the referrer's name I usually add a question about why they suggested that contact, for example: "Do you know if he/she has a specific need now?" Any additional information is useful and will contribute to making the next email even better.

We will all get specific contact referrals. This is one of the best possible results so be thankful, be professional and don't forget the original referrer. Remembering and getting back to them later with any results, positive or negative, is a great way to continue a conversation.

At this point there are only a few replies left. Cutting to the chase, I did not get any "miracles." Finding a viable, open and appropriate job for Tom as a result of an email sent to a single contact in the first round of 100 emails is called a miracle for a good reason.

Four of the last eleven replies were the specific contact referrals I described above. I got eight new contacts to add to my list. Because they are specific referrals I expect my reply rate to be much higher and potentially much more useful. Out of eight new introductory emails, I am hoping for at least five new replies and maybe something tangible like a specific job lead.

That leaves five replies from the original 100 emails. Two of those went into a sub-category that I call "The Heartbreaker." We'll all get a few of these. Simply put, they say, "Sorry, we just hired someone like that." With every reply there are positives and negatives. The good news about this one is that we're probably in the right place, just at the wrong time. A reply like this affirms that we are on the correct path and, depending on the context, there may still be a few questions to ask.

First, if they just hired someone perhaps their new hire is leaving a job at another company. It would be good to know a bit more because there might be a replacement opening available. Discovering that the person you contacted just hired someone is not a dead end; it can still be a potential job lead. It's okay to ask something like: "Out of curiosity, what company was your new hire with previously? Is their background similar to mine (or Tom's)?" Again, any information is helpful. When this happens to me, I try to confirm that I am on the right track in terms of job type and qualifications or, at least, try to figure out if I wasn't. If I learn that the person they were seeking and hired is completely different than Tom I'll ask some more questions and possibly change my research for marketing Tom.

It's also good to ask if they anticipate needing more help soon. Companies that hire one person are often hiring others. They might be building a whole new team. This could still turn into a resume sending opportunity. It may not be the most immediately valuable resume sending opportunity depending on what's happening, but there is still a chance to develop more of a relationship with the new contact. There is also always the possibility that their new hire won't work out and they will have to open up the job search again. Developing a rapport with someone new, creating opportunities to maintain contact and making sure they have a resume on file could be very beneficial if something happens.

These are all small percentage opportunities but anything is possible and enough small percentage opportunities can result in a high percentage of coverage. We always want to address as many options as we can.

I'm down to the last three replies out of my original 100 marketing emails for Tom. The good news is that all three of these are Category 5 replies meaning that there is a potential position and maybe an opportunity to send Tom's resume.

The first reply was from a Director at a medium sized power plant capital equipment manufacturer. He said that he thought his company would be seeking someone like Tom in the next six months. They are growing and may move someone internally to create a position. He does not have an open requisition or an approved job but he would be interested in learning more and having Tom's resume on file.

There is a lot going on in a reply like this. It can setup a variety of opportunities and I need to proceed carefully. The easiest thing to do would be to simply send Tom's resume with my notes, mark the date in my calendar and make a note to follow up with this contact in a few months. Many people will do just that, including many recruiters. However, this closes the conversation for a while. Or worse, just sending the resume creates a situation where I have to wait on him for the next communication. It is always better to be in control of communications when possible and create the opportunities for outbound messages without overdoing it. There are situations that require waiting, however each situation deserves analysis to see if there is a way to avoid it. In this case it would be better to keep the conversation open, get more information and see if I can strengthen the new relationship. How can I do that? And, more importantly, how can you do it too?

My first move is to call Tom to see if he is interested in the company, vagueness of the role notwithstanding. I do this to get Tom's permission to send his resume to my contact at the company. I describe sending his resume as "exploratory" and don't promise anything other than feedback. It is always important to get permission to send a resume. I may have said it earlier but it bears repeating: There are no good surprises in this business. I need to be sure that Tom is interested, knows where his resume is going and will follow my lead through the process. Even after I have Tom's permission I am still not 100% sure I'm going to send his resume just yet. There is another opportunity to explore first.

I would really like to learn a bit more about what's happening at this company in terms of business health and growth potential. It would also be good to know what this Director has in mind for his team and where he needs help or has challenges. Getting more information will not only help me determine if Tom is my best candidate for the pending job but also extend my conversation with the Director. In fact, what I would really like is to have a real conversation.

One minute later I have the main telephone number to his company at his location. It is not hard to find company phone numbers though the posted numbers on their websites may not be that useful. We are not looking for the "800" number that customers use. To reach a specific employee, by name, it is usually better to call into the main corporate switchboard number. The easiest way to get a main switchboard number is to either enter the company's street address in Google or, if they are a publicly traded company, look them up on Yahoo Finance and check their profile page. Larger companies will have automated attendants that will allow you to enter an employee's name in order to get their extension. Smaller companies will have live operators you can simply ask.

It's time for me to make a phone call. At this point, you are probably thinking that calling someone is okay for a headhunter but as someone seeking a job of their own, this is way too bold and subverts the normal practice of sending in a resume and cover letter. At least, that's what Karen thought when we talked about whether or not she could do something like this in her own job search.

"You think I should just pick up the phone and call someone like that? That's crazy! I'd be so nervous. I wouldn't even know what to say. It seems really pushy too. Won't he think I'm too aggressive?"

"Well, this is what I do, and, there's no rule saying you can't do it too. If this was your situation it would be worth noting that you have very little time invested in this contact so far and probably more to gain than to lose. The two things you need to make this call are a basic plan and an approach to the conversation, something that opens the door. You just have to think it through. Start with this: What would you like to accomplish? Consider both an ultimate goal and a tactical step or two for this specific call."

"So if someone says that they don't have a job right now but believes there will be one in the future, I guess ultimately I would like them to think of me when the job becomes open. I'm not sure what you mean by 'tactical steps' though."

"Your ultimate goal is exactly right but it would be tough to accomplish on this one, likely very short call. You can forward your goal though. For me good tactical steps would mean getting the opportunity to ask a few insightful questions about the situation and the director himself, reinforcing my credibility, furthering our dialogue and setting up opportunities for continuing the conversation. Think of it this way: What if you are able to remain in touch and develop regular communications so that if a new job becomes available, you are the first person he calls?"

"Yes, that would be incredible."

"So, do you see how calling right now could be a pretty good first step?"

"I guess you're right but your position in this process is different than mine. If I'm sending the introductory emails we talked about, how would someone like this Director even know that I'm looking for a job?"

"Why else would you be contacting someone like this and asking questions about the types of challenges he or she faced when changing industries? It's implied. The questions you asked were good and not self-interested. You demonstrated a desire to learn and a willingness to add value. Even though you are looking for a job, you are not blindly selling yourself. Maybe it will happen differently for you but there is a very good chance that you will run into potential positions the same way I do and you can call people. It's okay. Sometimes it's fun."

"So what are you going to say when you call this guy? And what should I say if I want to call someone like this?"

"For me this call is about many of the same things that it is for you. For both of us, it is a very short, unscheduled first telephone interview and should be treated that way."

"This is an interview? What do you mean? Why is this call an interview for you?"

"I need to establish and reinforce my credibility in order for my firm to get access to the job, to the client, and to future jobs; in effect for my company to ultimately *get the job*. You also need to establish and reinforce your credibility to get access to the job. So we are both trying to get a job, right? This is the first little call so, again, we won't get all of that now but we can hope to take a step towards it."

"Okay, that makes sense. So what are you going to say first? And what should I say?"

"Before I pick up the phone and start dialing, I am going to make a handful of notes about what I'd like to cover if I get him. I'm not going to write down every specific question exactly, instead I'm just going to note some key words. I don't want to sound scripted and I don't want to do most of the talking. The approach will be something like this:

> 'Hi (contact name), this is Kurt Schmidt. Thanks for
> getting back to me about the candidate I mentioned
> in the email. Before I send his resume I wanted to
> take a moment to learn a little more about your goals.
> As your team is expanding, where do you think you
> will need the most help?'

Ideally, if I stop talking right here, my new contact will share more details about the potential position and I'll be able to ask a few more short questions. The most important things to learn are where he needs help, what's happening in the company, how it impacts his department, where he thinks there will be needs in the future, and when he believes he will be able to hire someone. It is worth noting that none of the things I hope we'll talk about have to do with Tom specifically, unless he asks. In fact, I might purposely make sure I don't even have Tom's resume in front of me."

"Wait, aren't you trying to market Tom to this potential hiring manager for a future position in the first place? Why don't you want to have Tom's information there and ready?"

"While I am trying to market Tom to this contact, having his resume in front of me may cause me to make one of the classic errors that people make on calls or during conversations like this. I do not want to go into this call and sell Tom. I want to listen. I want to ask questions. I want to stop talking and learn. If I have Tom's resume in front of me I might accidentally continue my question and turn it into a statement. Instead of stopping after asking: 'Where do you think you will need the most help?' there is a huge temptation to continue and say something like: 'Because my candidate has done X, Y and Z.' If I do that, this call will fail. I will be selling instead of listening. Yet, many people, including me, do that all the time. There will be a natural pause when my contact figures out who I am and what I asked. It's okay. I'll pause too and I'll wait for him to talk. Then I'll write down everything he says. This is important for both of us, however in my case, part of my value proposition is that I have access to lots of candidates, not just Tom. If I sell instead of listening, I may not hear a detail that suggests that maybe Tom isn't the best candidate and I should send someone else. In your case, listening now will not only help you better understand what's happening and enable you to improve your resume, it will also show some real maturity and self-confidence which will differentiate you from other candidates. It goes almost without saying that if you let the person you're speaking with do most of the talking there is a better chance that he or she will leave the conversation feeling good."

"Okay, I understand how it works for you and how this can be valuable in terms of your business but it still seems like something most job seekers won't do or maybe it's just not a normal strategy. I am not sure how this would work out if I did it."

"Let's go back and look at exactly what I said on that call and see if it would work for you. All I said was:

> 'Hi (contact name), this is Kurt Schmidt. Thanks for getting back to me about the candidate I mentioned in the email. Before I send his resume I wanted to take a moment to learn a little more about your goals. As your team is expanding, where do you think you will need the most help?'

What would happen if you said the same thing, except referring to your own resume instead of someone else's? What's so different? You still want the same information and that information will only help you do a better job, which benefits both parties."

"I guess I could ask the same question. However, this still seems really aggressive and forward to me and I'm worried that the call won't go well. What if I make a bad impression or the director gets angry at me for calling? What if it is a bad time for them and I'm interrupting something? I'm even worried that I won't be able to stop talking when I'm supposed to."

"I understand. It is a bit different than how you have always been told to pursue a new job. However, what is the worst thing that can happen?"

"I won't get the job. Maybe the hiring manager will think I'm a bad candidate. I'll feel like an idiot. I don't know."

"My father, a retired Army Colonel and a distinguished combat veteran, has a little saying that always puts things in perspective for me. Whenever I'm feeling frustrated or worried about something he'll ask: 'Is anyone shooting at you?' In most cases, the answer is no, well, okay, in all cases so far. That's perspective. Nothing bad can happen on this call if you listen and learn. Remember some time ago I told you that I always look for binary responses, yes or no. If I hear 'yes or no' I know what to do. It's when I hear 'maybe' that I get stuck. If you call someone like this director and ask him about the things that are important to him and to his company going forward with the idea that you are interested in helping and he is abrupt, rude, or for some reason angry that you called, then this call is productive in a different way. You, like me, will end this call knowing that this is not someone that you would want to work with."

"How can you say that and be so sure?"

"Because not only are there millions of potential opportunities out there, but also we've put in enough effort to know that we are bringing value to the right place and potentially the right person. We are not blindly selling ourselves to just anyone. Instead, we are trying to learn and increase our ability to help in specific and relevant applications. We are not wasting anyone's time. We are doing good things. There are a lot of organizations looking for help and they have to compete for talent in much the same way that we have to compete for jobs. We don't need to burn our time trying to work with people who don't want our help. We can move on. Think of the benefit of having this information now as opposed to finding out you that hate your boss six months after taking a job."

"That sounds so harsh to me though."

"It's okay, it probably won't ever happen. You'll be surprised how easy it is to talk with people. Better still, once you've done it a few times, you'll be even more surprised how productive it is to listen. The most important things are to be genuinely interested in what they have to say, letting them say it and responding intelligently."

"So what happens after you have this conversation with the director? What do you do next? And, what should I do?"

"Well remember this is just a first short call and he said he thought it could be up to six months before they are ready to hire. The call is important but it is not going to get Tom a job right now. However, if done right, it will satisfy my tactical goals and establish an opportunity for further communications. Hopefully I'll learn a lot more about what is happening and improve my rapport with the director as well. On top of all of that, it's also just good practice to call people and talk no matter what happens.

I go into these things very open minded about the possibilities and with confidence that if I do enough good quality work something will pay off eventually. I can't predict all of the good things that can come out of developing a contact like this. More than once, people I've had nice but seemingly unproductive conversations with have sent my name and number to other people they know who might need help."

"Are you going to send Tom's resume?"

"After the call, I'll review everything to see if Tom is still a good fit for a potential job there or if I have other candidates who might be a better match. Then I'll call Tom, share what I learned, see if he's still interested and if we want to make any updates to his resume. Most likely, after all of that we'll send it."

"Is that it?"

"For now probably yes. If the call is as expected, then I will have learned a lot about what's happening at the company, developed a rapport with the hiring manager and sent Tom's resume. Finishing up, I'll do some quick research to see if there are other applicable candidates and tag them for future contact. I'll stay in touch with the director and maybe ask a question or two via email in a few weeks. Beyond that it's time for me to move on to the next contact."

"Most of that sounds like it would work for me too. Is there anything else I should do that would be different? Should I send my resume?"

"If you liked what you learned and are still interested, then review your notes, if helpful, add things to your resume or in the body of your email and send it. Per your tactical goals, you will have established a dialogue so it will be okay to email this contact in a few weeks. When you do, keep in mind that it is very good to be able to demonstrate that you've taken some initiative and done some reading as well. Investigate some of the needs that were discussed during the call and see if you can reveal that you've done some homework in a thoughtful question or two. Again, this is just one result and it is tenuous at best so it's good to do all of these things but you have to keep going too. You will need a lot more results like this to end up with a job."

"What if I don't get him on the phone the first time? Or, if I'm going to make calls like this, are there good times or bad times to do it?"

"It is important to consider the time of day and day of the week before calling. I'm not going to call first thing on Monday morning for example. Getting people like this director on the phone is probably one of the hardest things about my job. These people are busy. They have meetings, they travel all the time and they have a million things going on at once. It helps me to think about their priorities versus mine."

"I thought we just talked about priorities and goals."

"No, this is something different. I'll explain. You and I are searching for jobs. That's all we are doing. These hiring managers may be searching for potential candidates but it is not all that they are doing. In fact, of the things that most of these hiring managers are doing, looking at resumes, talking to candidates, having interviews and actually working to fill their open positions are often not the most important things. That's part of why it sometimes takes months to fill the jobs I'm working on. They are going at a different pace than we are. For us, job search time moves fast, for them sometimes it doesn't."

"How do I deal with that?"

"We adjust to their pace. Remember this is about them, not us. We are patient with each contact individually but maintain a sense of urgency for our overall search. This doesn't mean we stop and start or wait and see. Instead we compartmentalize each situation and keep moving."

"Right, I get it. Ideally I'll be able to create a lot of situations where I can call someone and then develop a list and work through it getting people on the phone as I can."

"Exactly. Getting back to your question about when to call, there's no perfect answer. I said previously that I'm not going to call first thing on Monday morning. Ideally I like to try to avoid times when I suspect there may be meetings or other conflicts. The best times to call and hope to get someone are early mornings before regular working hours since a lot of senior level people come in early to get some quiet time work done, and just after hours for the same reason. Friday afternoons can be good because the week is wrapping up and you might catch someone winding down. If there is an assistant or someone that picks up the phone it is a good idea to ask them about when to call back. In the end you get people on the phone through persistence."

"Do you leave messages or voicemails?"

"Most of the time, no. Not only is it really hard to leave a cold-call message that will generate a callback but it also cedes control over to them. I don't want to wait on someone to get back to me. Of course, you have to analyze each situation individually. For example, if I've been referred and have permission to use someone's name, then I can leave a message that establishes credibility. That might generate a call back. Or if there is an administrative support person working with my contact, I might let them know that it is easier for me to call back and ask about a good time. Persistence is great but being productive also means being polite and thoughtful and not bothering people."

"Altogether, this sounds pretty hard. There's so much to think about. I am not sure I can do it, and I'm still not sure what will happen."

"All you can do is try it and see. You have nothing to lose. In the end, you will spend less time actually trying it than you will spend thinking about all of the reasons to either try or not try it. After you make a few calls and talk to people, you'll find that the planning for each call goes faster and the conversation becomes natural for you. Your confidence will grow and you'll do better. Have fun with it, just like the emails before. There are a lot of good things that can happen and very few, if any bad things."

The rest of our conversation was about the emails Karen has started to send and the replies she's received so far. She has gotten a few and they break down into similar categories as mine. She has a couple opportunities to make calls too. I think she's going to do it and I'm very curious to see what happens. We are planning to talk again soon.

I've gone through 98 of my first 100 emails. So far I've gotten a handful of new contacts, some general referrals, one potential future job and a few candidates. There's nothing that I can use to buy groceries but it's more than I had in the beginning. Any one email can change what happens. I'm only looking for one job for Tom. I could get my lead after sending one or five hundred emails and the scale of the reward still justifies the effort.

For variety, when I first created Tom's marketing list of companies and because his target is Houston, I included a few very large oil producers. These are companies that operate exploration and production businesses. They are big and hire a broad variety of supply chain people. One trend in the industry that I've noticed over the last couple of years is that some of these big oil companies, often known as either "upstream producers" or in the case of very large ones, "super-majors," are bringing in more and more supply chain people from outside the oil industry. Over the course of a few hard to get conversations with a couple of senior VP's, I learned that a lot of energy company executives are starting to pay attention to the money that can be recovered by having world class supply chain organizations. One VP explained things to me very plainly once by saying: "In the past we've just made so much darn* money that nobody cared." Now though, because some of these companies have gotten so large that the potential savings represent billions instead of millions and because the industry has become much more competitive, things are changing.

The second of my last three replies that fit into "potential position" category was from a director at a super-major. It was a long shot since, on paper, Tom's experience didn't directly apply to what they do but, per my theory about changes in supply chain in the energy industry, it seemed worth a try. Surprisingly, the director I contacted said she thought that they might be interested in someone like Tom. She didn't have a specific opening right now but said they were hiring people all the time. She told me she would love to have his resume for her file if I could get my firm qualified as a vendor and get assigned a human resources person to work with. She gave me a contact to pursue and said to use her name.

Because of their internal hiring process, I can't just send her Tom's resume. A lot of very large companies have specific procedures for managing recruiting agencies, just like they do for job seekers, and sometimes you have to work within their system. Like before, I need to call Tom, let him know who I spoke with, that she wants his resume and that there may be a position. Then I'll see if I can get in touch with the human resources person the director referred. From a process standpoint this is a much more round-about way of trying to get a candidate into a company but it does work sometimes. Also because this company is so large there's no other way to work with them. As before I'll invest a little time and see what happens. If I make progress then I'll invest a little more time. We'll see. The process for my company is different than what you would experience as a job seeker but again, not that different. You don't have to become a qualified vendor but you may have to apply through their system in addition to communicating with a hiring manager.

If you get a reply from a potential hiring manager in which they say that there may be a potential position opening up and that you should apply through normal channels, then do it. As soon as you've done it, email them back, thanking them, saying you did it, suggesting they look for your resume in the database and offering to send them a copy directly if they would like. This is also a good time to ask a question or two about the areas in which they most need help. Even though you've been directed to apply through their website and human resources, you've still gotten a reply from a valuable potential hiring manager contact and can still develop a rapport. Remember there are no rules for communicating with people and it pays to take some chances if you've done your homework.

This is less of a call opportunity than the previous reply because the director is referring me into a defined process. It would be self-interested to call her before completing the process she recommended. The current openings are probably on their website and there may be no way to apply to upcoming openings. The best option might be registering on the career section of their site and creating an automated search if possible, checking back regularly and staying in touch with the director.

In my case, if I can reach the human resources person she recommended and get my company setup as a supplier, then I will get back in touch with the director, provide her with an update and ask some of the same needs oriented questions that a direct job seeker might ask. Regardless of the process, it is still important to develop a relationship if possible.

This brings me to the last reply out of my first 100 emails. By now, I'm already well into generating a second list of another 100 contacts and sending out emails. I have only just begun my campaign with Tom and when measured against the possible reward, it remains a very worthwhile endeavor.

My last reply came from a Director of Raw Materials Procurement at a very large and well known manufacturer of oil industry equipment. He said that while he does not need someone like Tom in his department right now, he believes that one of his colleagues might. He goes on to request that I send him Tom's resume and says that he will pass it on to his colleague. I've never worked with this company before and so far all I know is that they fit the basic parameters of the type of company that might need someone like Tom.

It seems redundant but again my first step is to call Tom and explain things. Again I'll ask permission to send his resume and tell him where it's going. I do this every time because I think it is important to keep people apprised of what's happening. As well, from a business perspective, I want Tom to know I'm investing time in helping him. Hopefully, if he has faith in my abilities at this stage, not only will he trust me later when it's time to negotiate, but also, he might rely on me more and not work with as many other recruiters.

Again, it would be great to know more about what's happening at this company and why they need people before sending Tom's resume. Also it is worth noting that this director said he didn't need someone like Tom on his team right now but, like before, he may still need help. In addition,

I don't know anything about his colleague, the needs of the other department, or the specifics about the potential position yet. I would also like to have the name of his colleague and be able contact him or her directly. So, there are several pieces of information that I'd like to get before emailing Tom's resume and my notes. This is clearly another call situation.

What are the differences in this situation between what I want and what Karen, Anthony, or you should want?

There aren't many. There is still a potential position and a good reason to call to learn more. The only difference is that since the director said he didn't have a position for you but that his colleague might, it makes less sense to question him about his needs. Of the pieces of information that I'd like to get, there are three that are also useful for direct job seekers. Wouldn't it be good to know more about his colleague, his colleague's department and some of the specific details about the need or position? Calling in this situation is not self-interested because the purpose is to get more information in order to make sure your experience is relevant before sending your resume. The approach is always about making better use of their time and helping.

Like before, it took just a few moments to get the director's telephone number. However it took nine attempts over four business days to get him on the phone. It was late on a Thursday evening when I got him, almost 7:00 PM Eastern Time, 6:00 PM for him in Central Time. Despite the fact that he was packing up and about to walk out to his car, he picked up his phone, asked for my number and called me back on his mobile phone. I got close to ten minutes of his time, five minutes longer than I hoped for, and an excellent result. The director's name is Paul and our conversation went exactly like this:

"Hi Paul, thank you for taking a moment to speak with me, I appreciate the callback. Before sending you my candidate's resume, I wanted to see if I could learn a little bit more about the situation there."

"No problem Kurt. I've only got a couple of minutes now but if you have a quick question or two, fire away."

"In your email, you mentioned that you didn't have anything for my candidate, Tom, but that one of your colleagues might. What department does he manage and what's happening?"

"Okay, so I'm responsible for global commodities sourcing, raw materials only, like steel, concrete, plastic resins, specialty metals, etc. My colleague is responsible for manufacturing, global logistics and inventory management. We're growing and I think he needs to find a new Senior Procurement and Materials Manager to support two very large manufacturing locations in the USA and possibly one in Asia. The person who had the job was recently promoted internally. I'm not sure of the status of his search, or even if the job is still open, but the guy you described sounds like he might be someone worth looking at."

In that one answer I got two of the four pieces of information that I wanted and a few other bits of information that might be useful later. I now know the title of the position and why they are looking. The things I already knew about the company include their products and manufacturing style, raw materials needs and size. With my supply chain knowledge and experience, I know what the director is talking about and can make some estimates about the specifics for the role.

I don't ask permission to ask my questions, nor do I apologize for asking. I didn't say "if you don't mind, would it be possible to tell me about…" My questions were direct because we are two people having a conversation and there's not much time. I wouldn't apologize or ask permission to ask a question in a normal conversation so I don't in this one. Looking at how this conversation is presented in text it is easy to see who is doing most of the talking so far. Here's a clue: it's not me.

"That job does sound like something my candidate, Tom would be interested in. How would you like to handle things? Should I contact your colleague directly to learn more about the details?"

"I'll give you his name and title but I'd prefer it if you send your candidate's information to me and didn't call him directly. I'll make sure he gets the resume. The job is not posted but I believe there is a job description somewhere. If I can find it I'll send it to you."

"Okay, no problem. I'll get Tom's resume and my notes out to you as soon as we finish this call."

At least I'm getting the colleague's name and title, it's Carl and he is the Vice President of Manufacturing. His title tells me more about their organization too. Instead of reporting to a Director of Materials or Logistics, this job will report right to the VP. That means it is more senior and potentially better for Tom. I am not going to contact Carl directly because I was asked not to. The surest way to make this process fail would be to disregard Paul's instructions. If he wants to be the point man, then I'll follow up with him. I will do some research to see if I can learn more about Carl though and use that information to brief Tom. This has gone pretty fast so far but I still want to know more.

"So Paul, you said that you guys are growing, how is the growth impacting what you are doing in raw materials and commodities sourcing?"

That's a good question. It showed that I'm listening and that I know a little about supply chain management. I know that while growth is good, it also increases raw materials needs, puts pressure on the supply chain and can create situations that require compromises.

"It is definitely a challenging time right now. We are struggling to keep up with manufacturing needs and product orders. Growth is great but it really stresses the supply chain. In my group we seem to be continually running behind and end up making shorter term arrangements with suppliers or having to identify additional sources at the last minute, both of which result in higher costs."

"Are some commodities more difficult to manage than others?"

"We are competing globally for limited supplies of raw materials and prices are rising as a result of demand. The toughest commodities to manage specifically are concrete and steel. We are up against companies in rapidly growing areas like China and India and everyone is after the same stuff."

"If you could get help for your team, where would you need it the most?"

"We're pretty well covered but I tell you what, I don't have an open requisition right now but I would love to know about a good steel sourcing person with just a few years' experience and some exposure to Asian suppliers."

Bingo! This was the last piece of information I was hoping to get out of this call. Paul does in fact have a need on his team. It's not a job yet but he did say that if he had a good candidate in hand he is pretty sure he could get approval to hire because they are growing. He gives me some more details and we wrap up our call. I promise to send Tom's resume as soon as possible, tell him that I have a couple people I can speak with about the potential steel job and that I'll be in touch in a few days. He says he'll pass along Tom's resume to Carl and get back with me via email if there's any interest. Usually calls like this result in a small amount of uncoordinated dancing around my office. Then of course, I immediately get back to work.

Not bad at all for the 100th out of 100 emails sent. Again, there's nothing here that means I'm going to get paid so I won't stop any of my other efforts. However to sum up, I did get a good opportunity to send Tom's resume into a potentially viable, though unadvertised job through a new contact and I got a lead on a second job. I won't get to contact the specific hiring manager on the job for Tom but Paul and I had a good conversation and developed a rapport. I believe he will get back to me whether they are interested in Tom or not. In the meantime, I'll talk to a couple of people about the steel job for him, and see if I can identify any other candidates for the materials management job with Carl, just in case it doesn't work out for Tom.

How in the world did I get Paul to share so much information with me on this first call? One word: Credibility. I was able to establish credibility very quickly.

First, I make calls like this all the time so it's comfortable and even somewhat informal partly because of practice. Like I explained to Karen previously, these things get easier with repetition. Experience helps but it is not the only or even most important thing. I am also genuinely curious about Paul's business and what's happening at his company and it shows in the way I speak with him. However there's still more.

Notice, our call got specific quickly. Within just a few minutes he was admitting to me that his company was struggling to get good prices for steel and concrete. At first glance, this seems like insider type information but the reality is that at that time, everyone was struggling with raw materials and it was all over the news. Even so, what made Paul feel okay about telling me all of this?

Credibility. Let's go back and look at everything that led up to the call. All of the things I did and said were meant to establish credibility in order to create an opportunity for Paul to share information. The first things I did were research based, learning about Tom's background, experience and applicability (value), then about Paul's company (potential needs), and finally identifying Paul as a contact specifically. In my original email to Paul I demonstrated that I understood who he was in his organization and what his company did in the way I summarized Tom's experience:

> "The candidate I'm working with is a Materials Manager for a well-known utilities infrastructure manufacturer in the southeast. He's purchases about $250 million per year in steel commodities, is responsible for inventory management at two facilities and has been promoted repeatedly. He has an MBA and a BS in Engineering. I am trying to help him find a new position in Houston so he can be closer to family."

Paul's company is based in Houston; Tom wants to be in Houston. Paul's company manufactures oil exploration and production equipment for global customers; Tom's company manufactures utility infrastructure equipment for global customers. Both require large amounts of raw materials from a global supply base in order to support manufacturing needs around the world. Lastly, Paul is in a position where he might be responsible for hiring people at Tom's level or will at least have some knowledge of his company's current needs.

Why are all of these things important? And, how do they contribute to this being a successful call?

Well, it is not as if Paul is in Des Moines and I'm asking him about Houston. I'm not trying to get Paul's advice about someone who has no experience in raw materials or supply chain management or is in a completely different type of manufacturing. And, I'm not going over the top. Paul is not an Executive VP who would be way above these types of decisions. All of these things seem really obvious now, after doing the research, but we know what work went into it. Paul also knows which is why he responded in the first place.

Most people like to keep their doors open to possibilities, whether the possibilities are about opportunities for themselves (because I'm a headhunter) or about opportunities to hire someone, meet someone, or be in contact with someone. Very few people will refuse easy information. People who get into management positions often get there because they keep their eyes and ears open for opportunities. They are curious, want to know about things and ask questions.

When I contact the right people at the right time, I can generate some interest just by introducing myself as "an executive recruiter specializing in supply chain management positions within the energy and manufacturing industries." Normal job seekers can't do that but you're not going to charge them a big giant fee either. Regardless, if you get to the right people, a worthwhile percentage of them will want to know why you are calling or emailing.

When I ask a broad question seeking an expert opinion: "What is your opinion of the market in Houston for people with his (Tom's) skills and experience?" I show that I am interested in their viewpoint. It is a compliment, whether or not they actually answer the question. Notice, Paul didn't.

All of these things led to my last question, seeking specific guidance, the one that Paul answered in his reply: "Who do you know that hired someone like this recently or may still be looking?"

Paul replied to my email and took my call because I established credibility and got the timing right. We had a good conversation because I was able to ask a couple of insightful questions and didn't push or sell too much.

Out of 100 emails, only two resulted in me being able to have useful telephone conversations and develop new contacts, and only one resulted in the possibility of a job for Tom right now, though not through my target contact, Paul, but rather from a lead to his colleague, Carl.

The research and work that went into the other 99 emails was the same as the work that was done to find Paul. Our conversation and the progress that was made could have happened with any of the others, and might still. The only difference with Paul was that the timing was right. While I don't control timing, I do control how many people I contact and the quality of the message I send. The thinking is simple: Contact enough people over a long enough period of time and the timing will be right for at least one of them.

So it is not as if I found an opportunity for Tom with a single email and phone call. No, the progress made with Paul is the result of several weeks of work.

Reviewing everything, you may be thinking to yourself that my experience with Paul, both via email and on the phone is radically different than what you as a job seeker would experience. It's not. We all did the same preparation work in the previous chapters. Despite our different positions, if we go back and analyze the emails that Karen and Anthony sent for example, we can see how they might also arrive at the same place, ready to make this call.

Karen's emails will be going to people like Paul but within her own discipline. Remember, she is a Customer Marketing Manager for a wireless network services provider who is contacting director level people in marketing in similar or complementary industries with titles like "Director of Global Marketing." If she has done her homework, and I think we know enough about Karen to know she has, then some of the things she writes about in her brief summary will resonate with the people she has selected to contact. Statements like "I'm responsible for organizing and managing technology presentations to enterprise customers and end users" will mean something to the people who receive her emails. The replies she gets will reflect this. It is highly likely that Karen and her contacts will share some of the same areas of responsibility. Again, this shows. Karen demonstrates relevance and establishes credibility in the effort she has put forth both in her research on companies and potential contacts and in the way she describes herself.

Karen also asks for opinions based on her contact's viewpoints. Because Karen targeted companies outside of her specific industry, a lot of her questions had to do with transition from one industry to another. This can be a very personal and insightful question for contacts who have changed industries. One set of Karen's questions included the following:

> "What challenges did you face when you first moved
> into the handset manufacturing industry?
>
> Was it an easy or difficult transition?"

These questions not only ask for an opinion but also imply Karen's interest in making a change. If she is reaching out to appropriate contacts who changed industries and they read a little about her background, she may get replies about potential positions. Other questions that Karen might ask could include:

> "How could someone from outside your industry help
> you the most?"
>
> "What skills and experience would you like to have on
> your team but don't now?"
>
> "What is the most important experience someone can
> bring in order to help you meet your goals?"

Many of these are variations on a theme. The idea is to get the contact talking a little bit in order to learn more about what's happening and see if he or she needs help.

Again, Karen, like me, may not get a direct answer to any of these questions. A contact might read between the lines and simply come back with something like what I got from Paul, an email that requests a resume and mentions that an internal or external colleague might have a need. Or she could get one like the one I received from the first of the last three directors saying that they may have a position open up in a few months. The possibilities are endless and some of them will result in calling opportunities. If Karen sends out enough emails, she'll get replies just like I did.

For Karen, getting an email like mine from Paul, presents an easy call opportunity. In fact, the call might be even easier since the contact would not be a potential hiring manager, instead the "Paul" in Karen's case would be a networking point or maybe a peer. Karen is calling to learn more so that she can do a better job of providing information for the contact's colleague. She can open the call by saying, "Before sending my resume, I wanted to see if I could learn a little bit more about the situation there." Her first question on a call like that would be very similar to the one I asked Paul. She could ask, "In your email reply you mentioned that one of your colleagues may be looking for help. What department do they manage and what is happening there?" Then, just like me, she should stop talking, listen, take notes and potentially ask another question or two. If Karen is in the right place the conversation will make sense. She will understand things and have insights and opinions that can result in good thoughtful questions without scripting.

It is important to be able to visualize yourself in conversations that involve things that you've done and know about. If you find that you don't know something, ask questions. If you are really lost, then you're probably not in the right place. It is okay, it just means you need to do more research and recalibrate.

How does someone like Anthony, with less experience than Karen or Tom, identify and approach a call situation? Should he also make direct calls like we did?

In his initial email, Anthony introduced himself as a recent college graduate with a degree in Human Resources Management and a little less than a year of experience with a small executive search firm. Because he is just out of college and has little experience, it is both expected and acceptable for Anthony to seek advice from people who have the types of jobs he wants and from potential hiring managers. Anthony's ideal role would be an entry level type of position in Human Resources. He is not restricted by any specific industry or expertise. As a result his questions can be more general and he can reach out to a much wider audience.

Anthony really is seeking advice. The things he would most like to know and act upon have to do with how someone like himself can make a real contribution, what companies want from people who are just starting out and what others who have progressed from being recent college graduates to being employed experienced along the way. When he sent out his emails he included some of the following questions:

> "What are some of the challenges you faced when you first started out in Human Resources?"

> "What was the most important thing you did to get where you are today?"

> "How can someone with my level of experience help an organization the most?"

The questions he included asked for broad opinions and personal experiences. While he, like Karen, didn't say "I'm looking for a job" the implication is the same. Why else would Anthony be emailing potential hiring managers and contacts currently in human resources positions?

140

Again, as with Karen's emails or mine for Tom, Anthony's recipients may not answer his questions directly or even at all. Those who reply might just skip to the bottom line, recognize that Anthony is looking for a job and respond accordingly.

The responses to Anthony's emails will also very likely fall into similar categories as the responses to Karen's initial emails or my emails for Tom. The specific results may differ; for example, Anthony may get more general guidance replies where people either offer advice on how he might better prepare himself for the job market or anecdotal advice about their own experiences. However there is a very high probability that Anthony will get emails with specific referrals to other contacts that may need an entry level person. He may also get replies that are about potential jobs and represent resume sending opportunities. In the same manner that I am doing for Tom and Karen is doing for herself, Anthony will need to analyze his replies to determine if there are situations that might merit a call.

Do the two situations that prompted me to make calls for Tom make sense for Anthony to call on as well? In both cases there were potential positions, one that might open up in six months and another with an internal colleague. Should Anthony want to get some of the same information that I wanted for Tom? Yes. What are the differences in how Anthony might approach his calls versus me or Karen?

My first call was in response to a resume request for a director who told me that his team was expanding and that he might have a position opening up in the next six months. When I got him on the phone I said:

> "Hi, thanks for getting back to me about the candidate
> I mentioned in the email. Before I send his resume I
> wanted to learn a little more about the situation there.
> As your team is expanding, where do you think you
> will need the most help?"

It is just as plausible that Anthony could get a similar response from a Human Resources or Talent Acquisition Manager who requests a resume pending an upcoming position. He emailed them seeking advice and guidance, they recognized that he is trying to learn what he needs to do to get a job, appreciated his initiative and requested a resume. It happens all the time. Just like me or Karen, Anthony could simply reply and attach his resume or he could try to call and learn more before sending it. Again, there's nothing wrong with reaching out to thank someone for replying and ask for a little more information ahead of sending a resume. In this situation, the very first thing that Anthony is going to say to his contact when they pick up the phone is "Thank you." How can that be a bad thing? The rest of his call will be very similar to mine. Anthony wants to do a good job, he wants to provide the most useful and efficient information possible. He wants to learn. Calling in to get more information only furthers that effort and benefits both parties.

In the case of the "potential job six months out," Anthony's goals are just like Karen's, both tactical and strategic (ultimate). He would like to develop a dialogue if possible in order to increase his chances of being remembered and seriously considered when the job does materialize. He can learn a little bit now, send in his resume and then follow up sometime later with a new question or two based on doing more research about his contact's company and the topics covered in their first short conversation.

Anthony can handle the second call situation, the "internal colleague with an open position," exactly the same way I did for Tom or how Karen might. He can just as easily call and seek advice on what is most needed, show a true and genuine desire to learn and help, then send in his resume and follow up later.

So what happens next? Well, I sent Tom's resume to Paul for him to forward to Carl. Then I called Tom and told him about my conversation with Paul. Being resourceful, the last thing I asked Tom was if he knew of a good commodity management person with experience in steel sourcing in Asia. He referred me to someone who used to work for him, Ron. Obviously the very next thing I did was call Ron. We'll get into what happened with Tom, Paul, Ron and Carl in the next few chapters.

In the two replies out of the first 100 emails that resulted in call opportunities, was calling the only or best way to accomplish the intermediate goals? Could any of us have done the same things via email? Is calling really so important?

Calling is important. It is what begins to make people real. The difference this makes is immeasurable. Putting a voice together with a name, an email and a resume adds an important dimension to filling out who you are as a candidate or who I am as a recruiter. In terms of modes of communication, calling is just behind meeting in person and ahead of email. When people speak they have the opportunity to consider responses and reply in real time; unlike email, which, despite the speed of the process, is still writing to someone instead of speaking with someone. Calling and speaking is human with all of the inherent positives and negatives. Out of all of the pieces of paper with names on them scattered on someone's desk, the person who called is real. Where the rest can be crumpled up and thrown away without regard, the one with the voice is different. The reader, hiring manager, networking contact or advice provider cannot purposely disremember the voice connected to the name connected to the resume on his or her desk. Some of the things that influence hiring decisions the most have little to do with the list of qualifications on a piece of paper. The resume, experience, research and targeting will get you to the right place but it's not all that's required to open the door. Identifying opportunities for, creating, developing and maintaining relationships are what make the difference. Relationships may exist via email but until they are reinforced by a voice or in person, they are not real.

Calling is worth the risk. Not everyone will do it. It takes a little courage and practice to do it well and we all make mistakes doing it, but when it works, it is an act that separates us from the blind resume senders and the others who are only names on a screen or in print.

Calling the right people and asking questions with the intention of listening, learning and doing a better job demonstrates a kind of confidence and initiative that is very attractive to the majority of hiring managers. Calling also provides an opportunity for rapid and sometimes unexpected escalation. When people talk, ideas flow freely and things can happen.

Here is an example: A few years ago I took some time off from recruiting to do other things, some undefined until I started doing them. One of these other things became a full time job for almost ten months. It all started very humbly, I was at my parent's house eating breakfast and reading an article in the local newspaper about a homeless services organization that ran a café that was also a school for culinary arts. Their aim was to provide homeless people with marketable job skills and culinary arts certification in order to make them more employable. According to the article, even though they had a very good graduate employment rate, they were running out of funding and would soon go out of business. I commented about how it seemed like such a good idea and that it should not go out of business. My mom, with a subtext that meant you need to find something to do, said, "Why don't you go see if you can help?" I found the main telephone number and called. To my very real surprise, the woman who answered put me through to the president of the organization. We chatted for a few minutes. I told him I was interested in learning more and seeing if there was anything I could do to help. He invited me to lunch. It was an interview from the first moment.

Two more interviews and I was offered a job as Director of Marketing and Business Development. In the ten months I worked there I met some great people, learned a lot about non-profit organizations, operating a café, and culinary arts education. The café team, including a pair of energetic chef-instructors, various project managers and myself devised and executed a series of plans to make the café more self-sufficient as a working restaurant. In less than one year we increased revenue 300%. The café, instead of closing, is still there today, nine years later.

When I look back on that experience I am happy to have had it and there is no doubt in my mind how the opportunity came about. One cold phone call and a couple of questions started the whole thing. There was never an advertised job. There was however a recognized need that had not been codified and an opportunistic hiring manager. On the phone that day, later at lunch with the president of the organization, and with his staff in the interviews that followed, we defined how their need could become my job.

Again, how could I do it? How can anyone just pick up the phone and call? Aren't there all sorts of bad things that might happen?

Regarding the situation at the café, sure there are some potential negatives but not really. What if I had not gotten through to the president? What if I had left a message and nobody returned my call? What if? Who can say? Maybe I'd still be at my parent's house reading the newspaper and maybe the café would have closed or succeeded another way. In the end, it's irrelevant. I did call and things did happen. They happened because we made them happen.

If that opportunity didn't work out, I would have found another. A much more important call was the one with Paul reviewed earlier. There were risks involved with that one. However the only risks I care about are the ones I can control. How much I talk and what I say are up to me. I decide which questions to ask, which not to ask and when to listen. I determine my angle of approach. As I said earlier, I am genuinely interested in what Paul does, his challenges and where he perceives needs. I want to help. Obviously I don't control Paul, how he reacts to my call or what he might say or do.

If I do everything I set out to do on a call and do it well and the call still fails then, as I said to Karen previously, it tells me that I am not in the right place or dealing with the right people and that the best thing to do is to learn what I can and move on.

Not every call goes well. Paul could have been uninterested, or bothered that I called instead of replying via email. After hearing my questions he might have felt they were too intrusive or gotten offended that I asked. He could have decided right there on the phone, after hearing my voice for a single second, that I was not someone he wanted to work with. All of these things are possibilities and they do happen. Even so it will have only taken a few minutes for me to find out. The only baggage I carry with me from failed calls are the things that I believe I can do better. I make notes and try to learn in order to improve.

Chapter 4 started with this paragraph: "Every time you speak with anyone during your job search the conversation you are having is an interview. Every email you send is an interview. Every phone call, every introduction and every handshake, these are all interviews. This is important."

It is still important, and in fact, this idea, that every communication you have along the way to getting a job is an interview, dovetails with the concept about who is in control of what you say on a call. These calls take forethought and practice. Opportunities to call someone and have a conversation like the ones discussed are valuable and should be treated that way. I call a lot of people, sometimes as a result of an email, other times just cold, so I practice a lot. I still think about every person on every call, who they are, what I'm doing and how I might add value and help. I do this so that I can have as many chances for a success as possible.

Speaking with people live is the best way to rapidly move from email to real interview, whether it is another telephone call, a quick meeting for coffee and a handshake, or a full blown, come to the site and meet everyone interview. It can also be the most efficient way to eliminate a company or organization as a prospect. This too is something you control.

In the next chapter we are going to get into interviews both telephone and in person. Hopefully we'll get a chance to practice what we learn. Before we move on though, let's review a few basics about what we're doing.

To be clear: We are pushing outward, doing research, contacting people, asking questions, sending emails, making phone calls and moving. Every piece of information we get along the way has some value, whether it is a positive or negative, everything we learn helps us steer. We are eyes and ears absorbing and applying information to reach a specific goal. Every contact we develop is a source, potential guide and, most importantly, a person, just like us. It is important to remember and keep track of how we are moving forward and with whose help, and to be appreciative. We are asking questions to learn, to leverage opportunities, gather information and build a foundation that will support moving up to the next level in the process.

Chapter 7: Breaking Through

Several weeks ago I predicted that Anthony would come floating into my office one day and say something like: "Today must be my lucky day!" When we originally talked about it, I went on and on about how much I dislike the concept of luck. The point I was making at the time was that Anthony shouldn't forget all the work he did to get his lucky breaks, and, more importantly, that he doesn't rely on luck going forward. So of course Anthony's greeting this morning was totally expected:

"Today must be my lucky day!"

"I know you said that just to get to me. What's up? Did something happen?"

"I've been invited to interview for a new position."

"Fantastic! Tell me everything. How did you get the invitation?"

Anthony has been doing a lot of good work lately. He just finished the temporary project he was working on for his friend's company and he has been networking aggressively, sending out emails and getting some responses. He hasn't tried many calls yet but he has sent out a few resumes in reply to potential future job openings and other opportunities. Even though he doesn't have a job yet, he is feeling pretty good about things because he's hitting his daily numbers, generating emails, spending time doing research, adding names to his lists and contacting real people. He's taking regular satisfaction from doing the work and starting to build up momentum.

Anthony is building a critical mass of activity. He is exerting energy outwards. The energy he exerts and the inertia he produces will cause movement, create reactions and ultimately bring results.

Interview invitations are a product of this type of effort. They may come in a logical planned way, at the end of a telephone call, in reply to an email, or because of a referral. Or they might come in an unexpected way, through a chain of contacts and communications that result in a timely introduction. Is that luck? No, it's rain, like in the storm analogy earlier.

I asked Anthony to walk me back to the very beginning of the chain of communications that led to his interview invitation and explain everything that happened along the way. We talked about some of it before but reviewing it again is helpful on a couple of levels, first to further illustrate the point that Anthony worked hard to earn this interview opportunity and to force him to think about every step so far and what can happen in the next steps in order to prepare.

One of the people Anthony sought advice from was a woman who has a similar education background, including both the degree and university, but had graduated a few years earlier. Diane, his new contact, is now a Human Resources Project Manager with a large local non-profit organization. She started as a Human Resources Assistant two years before and was recently promoted. Anthony found her profile, saw their common education background, some information about her current position and how she got there, and concluded that she would be a good person to contact. In his introductory email he referred to their shared degrees and said he liked what she was doing. Then he asked her advice. She replied and a conversation developed.

Anthony didn't ask Diane for a job, or if they were hiring. Over the course of their emails, he asked her about what she was doing and what she thought was important for her organization. He asked her about the challenges she faced, her accomplishments and future goals. He asked her if she liked her job. He asked her about the organization's structure and how her work impacted everyone else. As their discussion progressed, Anthony was able to ask her opinion about what he could do to bring value to an organization like hers, how someone with his level of experience and education could help. All of this took place via email over about a week and a half. Even though Diane wasn't in a position to offer him a job, their email exchange was a great learning opportunity for Anthony. Because there was no real hiring pressure or even defined goals, other than learning and networking, Anthony thought there could be a good opportunity to have a real conversation. Since Diane's office was not too far away, he asked if they could meet in person instead of just talking on the phone. She thought that meeting would be fine.

Anthony called me before meeting with Diane. The first thing I told him was that asking Diane if they could meet was a courageous and proactive thing to do. While their meeting was not a formal interview, I suggested that Anthony treat the opportunity very professionally and really think about what he's doing, not so much in the way he dressed, business casual, but rather in the way he presented himself, focused on listening and learning, not self-interested but confident, positive and knowledgeable but not assumptive. Before their meeting, Anthony did some additional research to understand more about Diane's organization and what they do. He made a couple of notes but didn't want to rely on them as much as just let the conversation flow and ask a few questions.

They met at her office at lunchtime, went to a nearby coffee place and basically continued their email conversation in person. Anthony asked questions about her experiences, opinions and ideas and then he listened. He brought a couple of copies of his resume in case she asked but she didn't and he didn't offer her one. This was just a conversation. Even though he's never actually said it, Diane knows that Anthony is trying to get his career started and is looking for a job. Right now though, he's not asking her to give him anything other than advice. His approach keeps it easy for her. When they parted about a half hour later Diane mentioned that she would be happy to let him know if she heard of anyone looking for help and that it would be okay to stay in touch. He thanked her for the opportunity to meet and told her he really appreciated her advice and ideas. That was it.

Anthony left the meeting with a couple of contact referrals to add to his list and a better understanding of one possible career trajectory from someone who started out just like he is now. He also took home more knowledge about some of the challenges people like Diane face regularly and how they help their organizations the most. Lastly, he and Diane developed a rapport and can stay in touch. Even if nothing else ever happens, this has been a very productive experience for Anthony. Including research time, emails and the meeting, he has only invested a couple hours networking with Diane and he has added a lot more detail to his understanding of this type of job. Hopefully Diane will value the experience as well. Her career is progressing and eventually she may need to hire someone like Anthony or she might hear about a position with one of her peers and can help everyone by making a good referral. Any number of things can come from a meeting like that.

To actually get a job though, Anthony has to keep going and develop more conversations that can turn into relationships with more people like Diane. After the meeting he sent Diane a short email thanking her again. Then he wrote down his notes, composed emails to the contacts she referred and got back to the work of doing research, finding new contacts, sending emails and following up.

Ten days later he received an email from Diane. She said she wanted to check in and let him know about an upcoming event that might be of interest. She included an invitation to her non-profit's annual open house. The open house is a family-day type of event, it's casual; employees meet with the public and the executives meet with community leaders. It is held at their campus every year in the late spring. Diane said she would be there with her family but would be happy to introduce Anthony to some of her coworkers. Obviously this was a great opportunity so Anthony accepted. Being invited to a social event was a lot different than what Anthony expected would happen when he first contacted Diane. He mentioned this to me when we spoke.

"This is totally different than what I expected. I thought, if anything maybe a job would come up sometime and she would remember me if we stayed in touch. What do I do now? We haven't talked about something like this. What do you think is the best way for me to handle it?"

"First off, you're doing great. One of the things that almost makes searching for a job like this fun is that the kind of networking and exploring you are doing can result in all sorts of positive possibilities. We couldn't predict that you might be invited to an open house but here it is. What do you think about it?"

"Honestly, I am not sure what to think. I know it is a good opportunity but it is not a meeting or an interview. I don't want to be that guy who only talks business at the party and turns people off, but I do want to meet people and make connections and I still want as many people as possible to know I'm looking for a job."

"Did you ever specifically tell Diane that you are looking for a job?"

"No I never did."

"And yet your conversation with her really developed didn't it? I'm willing to bet she figured it out. This is a social event though and it is always important to consider the venue. You may be on a mission but again, this is not about you. Since you described this as an event where employees and executives meet with the public and local officials, there probably won't be too many opportunities for in-depth conversations. However you will get a chance to meet a lot of people. Probably the most challenging thing will be keeping track of everyone. If you can, get business cards, and at least remember names and write them down as soon as you get the chance."

"What else? Is there anything I can do to let people know I'm interested in working there?"

"Are you really interested in working there? You don't know much yet, do you?"

"Well, I'm interested in working somewhere and I like what I learned from Diane."

"That's a start. This can be a great chance to speak with other people like Diane and learn more about what they do, allowing you to form a much more developed opinion of their organization and the types of needs they have. Maybe after this you'll really know if you want to work there or not. What do you need to do to get more information? How did you do it with Diane?"

"Well, I just asked her questions about what she did, how she impacted her organization and if she liked her job. As she gave me answers, as I learned, I asked more detailed questions and our conversation kept going."

"Perfect. So when Diane introduces you to people at this event, you might ask them how they know Diane or if they work together regularly. It's better to ask a question like that than the typical: 'What do you do for the organization?' Or 'What's your title?' You'll most likely get the same answers but it sounds better. Then you know the rest."

"Yes, listen and don't talk too much!"

"Well, yes, that's basically it. Ask a few questions when you can. Don't sell yourself, keep your expectations in check and move around. Don't shadow Diane or linger in any one conversation too long. Take cues from those around you and mingle. There's probably free food too."

"That's it?"

"This is another not-an-interview interview situation. There are plenty of opportunities to blow it. You don't want to be that 'Anthony guy from the open house who…' and is remembered negatively. So be conservative and think about what you say and do. Don't push things, just go with the flow. There is very little chance that you will leave the open house with a job but there are a lot of other ways an event like this can contribute to your overall job search."

After we talked about it, Anthony went looking for even more information about Diane's non-profit, including reading about all of the different divisions, their missions, executives and team members. He read everything on their website and checked out recent press and news articles on other websites. Through all of his research, Anthony referred back to the specifics he learned from Diane about her role, considered how her team in Human Resources supports the rest of the organization and what their goals might be.

Anthony went to the open house out of curiosity, to explore and learn, with a desire to meet more people to follow up with later. Because it was a social event, he managed his expectations. To be sure, when he replied back to Diane accepting the invitation, he asked about the venue and dress. I told him that it was not clumsy or socially awkward to ask. In fact, it is far better to ask and know than it is to guess and be wrong.

The open house was pretty crowded but Anthony was able to find Diane and her family shortly after arriving. They spent a moment catching up then Diane introduced Anthony to some of the people in her department, a mix of her direct peers, other Human Resources Project Managers and a few more entry level people who would be more like

Anthony's peers, Human Resources Assistants, Talent Acquisition Specialists and others. When he got chances he asked questions. Sometimes he asked people how they first learned about the organization, if they liked it, and if they had similar education backgrounds to his and Diane's. He asked their opinions about some of the recent articles he'd read online. He didn't ask all of his questions at once or ask the same person every question; he just went with the flow. He paid attention and listened for opportunities. He didn't do anything to indicate that he was looking for a job; he just gathered information and participated in the conversation. By asking insightful questions he was able to demonstrate that he was familiar with their organization, had read about some of their current challenges and was genuinely curious.

Later Diane introduced Anthony to a couple of the division managers, her boss, a Division Project Manager, and one of his peers, Gerald, another Division Project Manager. Diane actually introduced Anthony as a "sharp recent graduate with a degree in Human Resources Management who is interested in what we do." Diane didn't prepare Anthony or share any additional information about either her boss or Gerald, it was just an opportune time for her to introduce him in passing. It was a very short introduction but Gerald, being direct, looked Anthony straight in the eyes and said, "So are you looking for a job?" Anthony didn't miss a beat and replied, "Yes, yes I am," then stopped talking. He didn't whip out a resume or ask any questions but instead waited for Gerald to finish or provide more information. Gerald did just that. He gave Anthony his business card and asked him to send his resume first thing Monday morning. That was it. Diane and Anthony moved on and Gerald and Diane's boss continued their conversation.

The first thing Anthony did on Monday morning was spend a few minutes online looking for information about Gerald's background. Then he composed a short email and sent his resume. He told Gerald that it was great to meet him, that he's looking forward to hearing back and would be happy to provide more information. The only other things included in the email were Anthony's contact details. It is worth noting that Anthony didn't add a lot of extra material, any self-interested details like salary information or even a cover letter summarizing his greatest accomplishments or areas of interest. Remembering something he and I talked about previously, Anthony decided to wait before providing more information than what was requested. He didn't know if there was an appropriate position on Gerald's team yet because there were no job descriptions posted online. Gerald's resume request wasn't a good calling opportunity since they met in person and Gerald gave Anthony specific instructions. If Gerald wanted Anthony to know more or if he had other questions, he would have continued at the time. The best thing for Anthony to do was to follow Gerald's instructions to send the resume then move on to other things.

It was Friday before Anthony got anything back. Gerald forwarded his email and resume to the Senior Human Resources Manager on his project team, Tonya, and asked her to get in touch with Anthony. In her reply, Tonya mentioned that Gerald is responsible for forming a team to manage a new project and that there were several open positions. She is looking for help to work on identifying and screening candidates to fill the open jobs. She already has a Talent Acquisition Manager on her team but they still need another Talent Acquisition Specialist. Based on Gerald's suggestion, she thought it would be good to have Anthony come in for an interview with both herself and the Talent Acquisition Manager, Jeff. She attached a brief, fairly generic job description and included some available dates and times.

After bringing me up to date on everything that happened at the open house and afterwards, the very next thing Anthony said was:

"What do I do now?"

Despite his initial reservations, Anthony has developed a trust in this process. Even though he is not officially my candidate and I have no relationship with Diane's non-profit, I want to help. So Anthony and I are going to spend some time getting ready.

Lately, Anthony has been really thinking and working hard on his job search. He is staying disciplined and being creative. For example, identifying Diane as a potential contact was smart because they received the same degree and she is in a position that genuinely interests him. Unlike Karen or Tom, Anthony is being less industry specific in his search. This is both a good thing, in that it opens up all sorts of company or organization types and potentially a bad thing because of the potential for information overload. By taking his search for contacts beyond just looking in companies that interest him; Anthony's plan to filter for common education backgrounds, not only refines his search but also creates a good way for him to introduce himself.

Anthony is doing a great job of staying in the moment too. He's not creating yes / no situations. He's not asking anyone for a job or if they could hire him now. He isn't trying to skip ahead in the process for the sake of his own agenda. He's not passing out resumes and cover letters to everyone he meets. He is demonstrating real interest and enthusiasm, backed up by reading ahead and asking thoughtful questions. He is listening in conversations, is genuine and is not just focused on what's in it for him.

Now, because of his efforts, stemming from that first advice request email to Diane, Anthony has a real interview opportunity. Things just got serious and Anthony is a bit nervous. Because he has only been on a few interviews in his career and really does need a job, this interview, like every real interview is very important.

Before we dig into serious interview preparation, it is important to reiterate that while it seems like this interview opportunity came about fairly easily, the reality is that it is but one tangible result out of hundreds of emails sent. In retrospect the chain of events that led to it is simple enough: Anthony contacted Diane, they developed a conversation via email and eventually met in person. She invited him to the open house where he met Gerald, learned about an open position and was invited to interview. What is not described are the hundreds of other emails that Anthony wrote and sent; the ones that never got any reply, the ones that got replies but were closed conversations, the open conversations that didn't progress past one of the typical reply scenarios, the other leads, paths, contacts and every other shred of information Anthony has chased down that didn't go anywhere. Anthony got this single interview opportunity as a result of all of the work he's done to date. As he was doing the work he didn't know which, if any, of the emails he sent, calls he made or leads he developed would turn into a real opportunity. He worked them all confident that if he built up enough momentum something would happen and it did.

I have prepared a lot of people for a lot of interviews and many of them have done very well. Without saying that the process is the same everywhere or every time, I will suggest that the thing that is a good interview is consistently similar and the preparation that I go through with candidates is applicable to a broad variety of interview types and an even wider variety of job types. With Anthony, we are going to start at the very beginning.

What is a job interview?

Here is what a job interview should be: A person, a candidate, you, Anthony, Karen, Tom or anyone else meets with potential hiring managers, potential peers or potential colleagues to discuss how everyone might be able to get to together and agree on a way to solve a problem or pursue a goal.

Interviews are pre-qualified meetings in most cases, meaning that the participants are selected based on experience and education, usually after a resume has been submitted. The expectation is that the interviewer(s) and job seeker will speak the same professional language. The interview process is about details and fit. It is an imperfect process.

Remember the definition of a job from the first chapter? "Jobs come as a result of a goal or problem, a need, which an organization wants to address." A good interview is one where everyone learns as much as possible about how to address a specific need in the time allotted, and enough information has been exchanged to be able to make clear decisions about the next steps. A bad interview is one where one side asks all the questions but doesn't address the need and the other side provides answers that are designed not to be wrong. This is true regardless of interview type, whether it is a telephone interview or a face-to-face interview, given as behavioral, informational or structural.

In any setting, interviews are important. Consider that after a first interview, which could last from a couple of hours to all day, or might include little more than a single hour with a potential new boss and may or may not lead to a second interview; a candidate might get the opportunity to make a decision that will impact the rest of his or her life, including not only their job and future career but also the possibility of relocating, selling a home and finding a new one, changing kids' schools, helping a spouse find a new position and much more. Just describing it makes for a long sentence but it really is a lot to have to think about based on such a short interface.

The process is difficult from a hiring manager's perspective too. This new hire may be the only chance to add staff to help round out a likely already short-staffed team. Comparing good candidates is sometimes like comparing apples and oranges; different people bring different strengths and weaknesses and understanding priorities is crucial. Every hiring manager wants to get the perfect person for the job while knowing that perfection is impossible. Making the right hiring decisions is absolutely critical and people are often watching.

Given the ramifications of getting it right or wrong for both parties, what can be done to make sure interviews are engaging rather than confrontational? How do we move both parties to the same side of the table and put the needs on the other side in the spotlight? Is it even possible? If so, where do we start?

The first thing Anthony needs to do is to assemble everything he knows, including the job description, all of his notes about the organization, any information he has about Gerald's background and department, and a list of all of his contacts. He has already confirmed the interview date with Tonya and Jeff. That part was easy, he's unemployed so his schedule is pretty flexible. We've got four days to get ready.

Now that he has an actual job description and title, Anthony can do some research into other positions with similar titles. He can find other job descriptions and look at how other companies and organizations describe Talent Acquisition Specialists. He can look up all the unfamiliar terms on his job description. He can get back on LinkedIn.com and search for people using that job title and see what they do, how they describe their roles and what they cite as accomplishments. He can look for people who work in similar types of non-profits or expand and look for people who work at a variety of company or organization types. Anthony needs to get a handle on what it is that a Talent Acquisition Specialist does and the language used to describe it. Again, since he has little experience and has never been a Talent Acquisition Specialist, Anthony has to work a little harder than Karen or Tom to get a good understanding of the job. Learning the language and terminology used to describe the responsibilities of a Talent Acquisition Specialist will help Anthony understand the needs that created the position and how the role functions within an organization.

Once he's put all of his information together with the research he's done on Talent Acquisition Specialists, Anthony needs to consider all of the things that might happen during the interview, including the questions he'd like to ask, the questions he thinks they might ask and how the overall process might flow. While he may not guess correctly about everything, he can start mapping out the steps along the way in order to form his own strategy. There may or may not be a second interview if this interview goes well. He may or may not get to ask all of the questions he wants to ask and they may or may not ask him everything he thinks they will. Based on the information Tonya sent, Anthony is not sure if he will meet with Tonya and Jeff individually or together. The actual agenda for the interview was not revealed either. Anthony doesn't know if they interview based on a set of standard questions, whether questions will focus on his background, experiences and education, or if they will be behavioral and focus on how he might respond in certain situations based on both his personality and their anticipated needs. He doesn't know if there will be an opportunity to really discuss the position and their goals. Lastly, he doesn't know when they would like to have the position filled or, if there are other candidates scheduled for interviews. He can ask about some of these things before or during the interview, like timing, but for the rest he will have to wait and see. He can, however, prepare for almost everything.

Thinking about and understanding the interview process will help Anthony know when to ask certain questions and what to say at certain times. For example, if he learns that he might be invited to a second interview if the first one goes well, Anthony can expect to get more details later and doesn't have to try to get all of the information at once, including the most self-interested things about salary and benefits. Process timing is critically important in interview situations. It takes confidence to do it well and confidence comes from knowing, even speculating about what will happen. In this sense, confidence means trusting that all of the answers will be provided eventually if you play the game correctly. There is a very specific time and place for every question. Everyone wants the answer to every question right now, however it is patience and trust that separates the candidates who get offers from the ones who don't. Really knowing and trusting the process allows for candidates to avoid big mistakes. We'll get into specific do's and don'ts later but first let's break down what Anthony knows so far, the questions he might want to ask, what he can find out about before the interview, and what he will have to prepare for without having all of the information.

Anthony is skipping the telephone interview and going right to a first on-site interview. He is going to meet with two people to start with, Tonya the Senior Human Resources Manager and Jeff the Talent Acquisition Manager. Organizationally, both Tonya and Jeff are on Gerald's Project Team. If Anthony were hired, he would report to Jeff, who reports to Tonya, who in turn reports to Gerald. The position is Talent Acquisition Specialist. Based on what he's read in the job description he received and what he's seen in both other job descriptions and the backgrounds of other people who do that job, Anthony has a pretty good idea of what a Talent Acquisition Specialist does. He's hoping to learn more of the specifics at the interview.

In order to prepare, Anthony can ask himself questions and use his notes and research to consider answers. The most foundational question Anthony might ask himself and think about is "What would make Jeff happy?" It sounds really simple but it isn't. What we're really talking about here is trying to figure out what the Talent Acquisition Specialist can do to make Jeff's job easier as Talent Acquisition Manager, which should make him happy, as well support Tonya and ultimately Gerald, who will have even more senior internal customers to satisfy. The question "What would make Jeff happy?" is a lot different than "What can I do to be successful?" or even "What are the expectations for someone in this role?" The first question focuses on Jeff, while the second two are self-interested.

Taking it further, the question can be broken down into parts: "What are Jeff's short term goals?" and "What is Jeff's vision for his team in the long term?" Notice again, these questions are different than "What are the short terms goals for the position?" or "How would you define success in the long term for someone in this role?" Taken to the next logical step, Anthony should also consider the things that Jeff has to do in order to make Tonya happy. He can also ask Tonya about her short and long term goals. In this interview, all of the questions they will ask him and that he will ask will be related to the main question: "What would make Jeff happy?" because Jeff's happiness is also Tonya's and Gerald's. Even questions about Anthony's education, experience and how he might handle specific situations are ultimately tied into the core question about what would make Jeff happy. Anthony has to think about the things he's done and have examples in mind that he believes will address Jeff's needs.

Anthony will be more successful in the interview process if he is really thinking about and focusing on how he can help Jeff instead of what happens if he does, or what's in it for him. There will be a time for both of those thoughts and plenty of questions, but that time is not now. Being selfless at this stage of the process is very important. The temptation for any candidate, including Anthony, is always to want to know how all of this will benefit them.

Very few of us go to work for fun. The vast majority of us work because we have to in order to earn a living. We look for jobs in order to either find work or find work that is better than the work we do now. A better job typically means that it pays more in either cash or benefits, is easier, allows for more opportunities for growth, or is in a better location. Even though this is straightforward enough, candidates often go into interview situations acting as if this is a big secret. It's not, everyone knows that people seek better positions in order to improve their lives in one form or another and that their motivation is largely self-interested. This should be treated as fact and common knowledge.

Because everyone knows that people seek new positions in order to improve their current situations it doesn't need to be brought up in interviews. In fact, in Anthony's case, talking about what he wants at the interview is pretty much the last thing he wants to have happen. Really knowing and taking to heart the idea that if they want to hire him they will have to pay him is liberating. It is not as if they can force him to accept an offer. If all goes well and he eventually gets an offer he will have ample opportunity to ask questions and negotiate when the time is right. There should not be any huge surprises if an offer is forthcoming either. Going all the way back to the very beginning, Anthony has done the value analysis, he knows where he might fit in and at what level, he's identified the types of positions he should be pursuing and established contacts with people who own those types of roles. The job he is interviewing for is at a level that can make sense for him. Because he knows this he can afford to put all of his self-interested thoughts aside and focus on learning as much as he can and figuring out how and if he can really honestly help Jeff, Tonya and Gerald.

The goal of the first interview is not to answer every question about whether or not this is the exact right job for Anthony right now. Rather the purpose of this first interview is to gather information, demonstrate value, interest and enthusiasm and be invited to participate in the next step of the process. Achieving the goal means understanding the process and respecting the timing. In addition to the goal, I'm giving Anthony a specific mission, the same one I give to every candidate I work with. After the interview, we're going to debrief and I'd like Anthony to be able to tell me if he is interested in this job and why. It's an essay question. I want Anthony to be able to explain what Jeff and Tonya need in terms of both tactical and strategic support, if he can do the things they are looking for and if he wants to do them. I expect him to be honest in his evaluation of both the job and of his capabilities and be able to provide examples. Hopefully he'll get a chance to ask enough questions to be able to form an opinion, or at least know when he will get an opportunity to ask more questions in the next steps.

Before that though, Anthony and I need to take his thinking and general research and turn it into questions and answers, both for the things he will want to ask and for how he needs to answer their questions. He should also send an email to Diane to thank her again for the invitation and introductions and provide her with an update. He can ask her a question or two as well, or perhaps see if they can schedule a call. He doesn't need to push it too much with Diane or ask too many questions but in the general course of conversation he can say that he's excited about the interview opportunity and ask her what she thought of her interview process a few years ago. Hopefully, she'll talk about it and reveal more information about how they do things.

My next meeting with Anthony is a morning brainstorming session. I've got some time before work so we're going to try to figure out what Jeff is thinking. I ask Anthony to imagine that he is in Jeff's position, with his goals, challenges and responsibilities. Putting himself in Jeff's place should help Anthony imagine both the types of questions he'll have to answer and ones that he'd like to ask.

"What are the main things that Jeff will want to know by the end of this interview? Think of it on the simplest level."

"I guess if I were him, I'd like to know if I could do the job."

"That's it. Jeff will want to know if you can actually do the job. He will want to know if you can do this one and potentially the next one too. Hiring is expensive so he is thinking ahead. Along with those things he's wondering if you will fit into the team and the organization in general, and if you'll be interested and like what you're doing. At the most basic level, Jeff is wondering if you will make him happy as a member of the team and make his job easier, not harder. He may not quantify it in terms of happiness but the things he views as important all add up to making him happy."

"I don't suppose he is going to say it like that though is he?"

"I don't think so, though I imagine that it sounds like this in his head:

Can Anthony do this job? Can he do the next job? Can we afford to hire him? Will he fit in with the culture of the organization? Does he want to do the job? Is he interested, enthusiastic, knowledgeable, and motivated? Will he continue to learn and improve over time? Will we lose him to another company too soon? Will he be a low maintenance team player with initiative and creativity that gets the job done and makes my life easier? Will he make me happy?"

"How do I deal with this?"

"If you were Jeff, and you needed to figure all out of these things, what types of questions would you ask a candidate who is in for an interview?"

"Well, if Jeff is the Talent Acquisition Manager, based on what I have read, he's responsible for developing and implementing a strategy for recruiting all of the people who will be required for Gerald's project team. I think he works on all of the positions and with all of the departmental team leaders. He reports to Tonya who is responsible for all of the human resources functions within Gerald's project team. I have never spoken with him but based on everyone else I met at the open house, it wouldn't surprise me if Jeff is like them."

"What do you mean?"

"The other people I met and spoke with all had college degrees, were all smart, very energetic and really seemed to like not only what they are doing but the organization itself. Everyone said it was a fun place to work."

"That's really good. It sounds like you're getting a feel for their culture and have some understanding of what Jeff does. How will a good Talent Acquisition Specialist be able to Jeff help out?"

"The job description says that the Talent Acquisition Specialist will be responsible for things like assisting in completing and publishing job descriptions, reviewing resumes and applications submitted, making first contact with potentially viable candidates and scheduling telephone interviews for Jeff and the hiring managers. There is also some reporting to other hiring managers and progress reporting to Jeff. Some of the other descriptions I read said similar things or added additional responsibilities like database management or ad placement."

"Jeff and Tonya will want to know if you can perform the functions described in the job description. One or both of them will probably review your background with you, going through your job history and education to see if you have done any of the things listed. They will ask for examples looking for details and any information that reveals that if you did do some of these things, how well you did them. They will probably ask you to describe specific situations and your role in them. All the while considering your answers in the context of what they know they need from a Talent Acquisition Specialist.

Going further, let's imagine what it would mean to be able to do each of the things in the job description well, and additionally, what types of problems might come up. For example, would you say that it would be important for the person who is responsible for publishing job descriptions to have an eye for details? Or how about the ability to work under pressure; do you think a Talent Acquisition Specialist has to be able to work with hiring deadlines and managers who need help immediately? How about communications skills? Do you think that it is important for the person who will be making first contact with potential candidates to have good communication skills? Would having these abilities make for a better Talent Acquisition Specialist?"

"Yes, I see how you're thinking. I need to look at the job description line by line, consider all of the responsibilities and the difference between doing them and doing them really well."

"You can go even further than that. What kinds of problems do you think Jeff has? It's okay to speculate, to guess even and think out loud about this. Write them down and really think about how you can help."

I sent Anthony off with a bit of a homework assignment. He's got a few days before the interview so there's plenty of time to really think everything through. He's going to email and then, hopefully, call Diane so perhaps he'll get more information from her too. His homework is thinking and writing down potential questions and answers. He's not going to be memorizing anything, rather this exercise is about becoming familiar with what might happen and being prepared. In our brainstorming session we covered how we think Jeff and Tonya might approach this interview. Now Anthony needs to consider specific questions that they might ask and how he might respond. He needs to really think about all of the projects he's done both while completing his degree and at his previous position, and what things he can cite from his own experience that address things like attention to detail, working under pressure or with deadlines, and having good communications skills.

There are also different interview styles to consider. Anthony may get the chance to ask questions or he may not. The questions he is asked may be specific to this position or they may be behavioral.

For example, Jeff and Tonya might ask Anthony questions like "Have you ever worked with databases and spreadsheets?" or "Have you ever conducted interviews, either in person or by telephone?" In both cases they want Anthony to have a specific answer, yes or no, and to be able to explain and add detail, but not too much. These questions apply to what they are doing now and what they need a Talent Acquisition Specialist to be able to do. They will evaluate how Anthony might handle a specific task or project and question whether or not he has done anything like it previously. They will also compare his experience to the other candidates they are interviewing.

Jeff and Tonya may also ask questions like "How do you handle meeting tight deadlines?" or "Describe a situation where you were working under pressure?" "Have you ever had to resolve a conflict?" "If so, what did you do?" "Describe an experience where you worked on a team to complete a project." "What was your role on the team?" "How do you respond when confronted with a policy or position you disagree with?" These are behavioral questions. They are looking for experiences in Anthony's past that might reveal how he will handle similar situations in the future. The things they will ask about will be more general and represent situations that are likely to come up on the job but don't necessarily describe them specifically.

How should Anthony handle these types of questions? And how can he find opportunities to get to the questions he would like to ask them?

Of the two types of questions, the questions that are more about specific tasks or responsibilities will be easier to work with in terms of creating an opportunity to have a real conversation about Jeff and Tonya's needs in Talent Acquisition but he can use a similar approach for both types. The strategy is simple: Ask a question at the end of every answer. It is easy to ask for immediate feedback or if the interviewers would like more details, clarification or if your experience is applicable to their needs.

Why is this tactic both necessary and helpful? If Anthony is answering their questions correctly asking a question after his answer is necessary because initially his answers will be concise and not overly detailed. As such, he can easily ask if he has provided enough information or if they would like more. This is helpful because being concise, conservative, spare or direct when answering questions allows for opportunities for secondary questions, keeps the conversation moving and contributes to creating a conversational exchange. This is different than the interviewers asking a relatively short question and a candidate going off on a ten minute story. Remember one of the goals of the interview is to maintain a balanced conversation and create an exchange of information.

Imagine this scenario, the interviewers ask a candidate to "Tell us about an experience in your past where you led a team on a specific project." An answer to a question like this could easily develop into a long narrative which might shift the balance of who is doing most of the talking onto the candidate (who could get into details that are boring, too revealing or not applicable). This is particularly true for positions that are very technical or with candidates who have a lot of potentially applicable experience.

The strategy of asking a question after every answer is what I call a "check / balance." The idea is to prevent yourself from going too long on an answer or getting off topic. It is a useful thing to do for candidates who know they tend to talk too much in interview situations and for candidates who worry that they don't talk enough. In most cases, the best answers will be as short as possible while always containing the following key components: A concise description of what was asked about; information that specifies the scale, scope or time involved; a plan of action and lastly, measurable or tangible results. At the end of an answer like that it is easy to ask something like "Does this make sense for what you need to do here?" or "Would you like more details?" One of two things will happen after asking a question at the end of your answer, either they will request more information or they will move onto the next question. Either way, they are talking so information is again being exchanged between both parties.

Getting back to Anthony, let's imagine that Jeff or Tonya do ask him to describe an experience where he led a team to complete a project. Since Anthony has thought about his experiences and accomplishments he should have a ready example without necessarily anticipating that specific question. In fact, Anthony did once lead a team on a project. During his nine month position at the recruiting firm he was assigned a search for a large automotive parts manufacturer. The company wanted to hire a Program Manager who could lead the division level team responsible for starting the manufacturing of a new plastic part. Anthony was tasked with directing the search, including communicating with the client, making sure ads were written and published, supervising the research specialist, screening and presenting candidates, scheduling interviews and ultimately helping negotiate any offers. The client wanted someone hired and on board in 60 days. Anthony's team exceeded expectations by identifying, recruiting and delivering two highly qualified candidates in less than 30 days. The company was so pleased they hired both of them resulting in two commissions instead of one, doubling the firm's estimated revenue. It was a solid accomplishment and Anthony can relay the story quickly, provide significant details and cover all of the components required in a good answer. Afterward he can ask if they would like more information about any of the details, like how they recruited the candidates, how many they interviewed, or anything else. He can also ask if Jeff and Tonya have similar hiring deadlines or if they run recruiting projects in the same way.

Notice, that in his answer, Anthony can avoid getting sidetracked or go off on any tangents while still providing a lot of relevant information. There is always a huge temptation to give more information than is required. Like it would be for most people, this is an important interview for Anthony. They, we, all of us, want to do well and be looked upon favorably. We want to do as much as we can to impress and please the interviewers. We want them to know everything about just how good we are. Often, this typically benevolent desire ends up being part of what contributes to making the interview conversation a one sided affair that goes wrong. How could this happen in the scenario described above? Well, if Anthony was very proud of the way he led the recruiting research part of the project he could very easily be drawn into going over every detail of just that part stretching out his answer and likely providing not only more information than what was requested but also potentially boring the interviewers or appearing overly self-interested.

Sticking to the major points; the description of the project, the scale, scope or time involved, the actions planned and taken, and the results attained keeps things moving and keeps Anthony on target. Asking if Jeff or Tonya want more information afterward or if that situation is applicable to their needs creates the opportunity for Anthony to go back and add detail if they want it. Again, the reason for answering questions this way and asking a question at the end of the answer is to control the length of the answers, make sure that the conversation stays on track and to both elicit feedback and to cultivate a true exchange of information during the interview. By asking questions at the end of most answers, a candidate also continually refocuses the conversation back on the interviewers and their needs.

Before I started suggesting this approach, many of my candidates would call me after interviews and tell me that they didn't know how to ask their questions or that there wasn't really any opportunity to ask them. Because of this, in many cases, the candidates didn't feel like they learned enough about the positions, which, in some cases, made them less interested, excited or committed about making a change. Sometimes they also felt like they did all the talking. Results were mixed, some interviews like that went well and others didn't. However things definitely changed when I started suggesting that candidates try to keep their answers as tight and brief as possible and ask questions immediately after answering. Now, a higher number of candidates come out of interviews feeling like they learned more about the needs and position, and that the conversations were more engaging. Additionally, they are better able to answer my interview debriefing questions. Clients seem pleased too since my interview to placement ratio improved after starting to suggest the check / balance concept to my candidates.

We've talked about when to ask questions, now it's time to discuss which questions to ask and how to ask them. People don't think about it as often but a lot of information is revealed not only in the answers they give but also in their questions, both in how they are asked and what's asked about. A good question well asked can demonstrate knowledge, reveal that a candidate has done their homework and keep the conversation focused on the interviewer's needs and goals. Asking the wrong questions in the wrong way might suggest too much self-interest or cause the conversation to drift away from needs of the position. Ideally, questions should be structured to accomplish two things; first, to gather information about the role and second, to reinforce your enthusiasm, interest, qualifications or value proposition.

In terms of what to ask about, the main areas to explore for almost any job are the relationships: managerial, internal or external customers and organizational structure, and the needs and goals of the team and team managers, both short and long term. Understanding what is hoped for and needs doing, who is involved and how everything and everyone are related means understanding the job.

For example, Anthony knows the basic requirements of the Talent Acquisition Specialist position from reading the job description and doing some homework online. Since he did some research and found job descriptions and profiles of people who are Talent Acquisition Managers he also has an understanding of what Jeff does. Based on these two things he can see how a Talent Acquisition Specialist might support a Talent Acquisition Manager. However there are a lot of details that he doesn't know like if there are other Talent Acquisition Specialists on Jeff's team and if so, how many; or, how Jeff's work is divided up among Talent Acquisition Specialists and the other people who report to him. Anthony doesn't have any real information on the broader impact of Jeff's team either, like how many hiring managers their recruiting efforts support or how Jeff's role functions within Tonya's area of responsibility. Building a picture of how the organization works, how the Talent

Acquisition Specialist fits in and contributes and how everything is supposed to operate is critical, especially for Anthony because he has so little work experience. Asking questions about the organizational structure, who supports who and how everything works will also demonstrate that Anthony is really thinking about the position and that's a good thing in an interview.

A good opportunity for Anthony to ask an organizational type of question would be at the end of an answer about something he did at a previous job. The example described previously where Anthony explains how he led a team assigned with recruiting a candidate for an automotive manufacturer is perfect. At the end of his answer, depending on whether or not more information about that experience is required, Anthony might be able to ask a question about who the Talent Acquisition Specialists work with there. Since he worked with a research assistant and an advertising person, he can ask if he would be working with similar staff members there. He can ask how they work with the various hiring managers, which may be similar to how he worked with outside clients as a recruiter. He can add to those questions by asking about some of the challenges or problems Jeff faces working with all of the different parties involved.

Ideally Anthony will be able to ask Jeff about all of his internal and external relationships, who his customers are and how a good Talent Acquisition Specialist can fill in the gaps for Jeff, both short and long term. Hopefully Anthony will get the same opportunity with Tonya and, when speaking with her, can recall what Jeff said and add that to the conversation.

Asking questions about the needs and goals gets to the heart of why this job exists and what the company or organization wants to do. Everyone recommends asking about the goals or expectations for a position in interviews. It is common advice. While it is always good to suggest asking about goals, the language used is very often wrong. We have all seen interview guides that recommend asking questions like:

"What are the short term goals for this position?"

"What can I do to be successful?"

"What are your expectations for someone in this position over the long term?"

"How do you measure success for someone in this role?"

What is the problem with all of these questions? The language is self-interested. The person asking them is really asking about themselves and what they have to do: "What can I do to be successful?" It may not seem that way at first glance but asking how the hiring manager will measure success for someone (me, me, me) in this role focuses back on the person in the position, not on the mission or the team. Even a question as innocuous and common as "What are the short term goals for this position?" puts the emphasis back again on just that position. Subtle? Yes, but also palpable. People notice. The questions you ask, just like the answers you give or anything else you do, give off ripples that affect everything they hit. You can control this and you can control the feelings and perceptions of the people you speak with by changing the language. Asking questions like this reveals that you are mostly thinking about you, not everyone, the team or the mission. Questions like this keep this discussion in interview mode which separates you from them.

What is a better way to ask about the goals, challenges and needs of an organization or company? Again, why does this job exist? The job exists because Jeff has a need, goal or problem he needs help to resolve. So instead of asking about the needs or goals of the position, it is far better to ask Jeff what he needs:

"What are your short term goals?"

"What is your vision for the team?"

"What types of problems or challenges are you facing?"

"What do you want to accomplish over the longer term?"

The subtext of all of these questions is "How can I help you the most?" Notice all of the questions ask Jeff what he wants to do. None of them ask about the success or goals for the position. Questions like these recognize that there is a team and that the team shares a mission that is owned by the team leader, Jeff, and that is where the focus should be. Structuring questions like this engages and positions candidates as solution providers. These questions are not about impressing people by setting up opportunities to describe past experiences ("I did that..." or "I did this..."); instead, questions like this lead to conversations.

When this works, hiring managers open up and talk about what they need and what they want to do. And what happens next? A real discussion takes place between a candidate who is genuinely inquisitive, wants to learn and help and a hiring manager who has needs. The idea is this: If you can engage hiring managers and get them to share what they really want to do, you can almost physically join them on the same side of the table so that you are both facing the same set of problems, challenges or goals and talking about ways to address them together. Again in Anthony's situation he can not only ask Jeff what he wants to do but also he can ask Tonya what she would like from Jeff's team and what she wants to do. He can ask both of them how their teams support the big picture goals that Gerald is trying to tackle as well and form an even larger picture of what is happening.

This approach, asking questions from the position of a solution provider, saying essentially "I am here to help," is a large part of what changes an interview from confrontational to engaging. The "I am here to help" point of view is aligned with the mission of the interview in that to be able to help you have to know what needs to be done both short and long term, who contributes and who benefits.

Candidates who are there to help are both selfless and confident. Their selflessness comes from confidence. It sounds counterintuitive but if you go into an interview with a good understanding of your value proposition, its market value and the level of the position, then you should be pretty confident that if everything goes well and you receive an offer it will probably make sense. Even if you don't know the level of the position specifically, understanding your value proposition is enough. At this stage the amount of any offer is not nearly as important as demonstrating a willingness to jump in, get involved, contribute, be a team player and help! In fact, doing all of those things will not only improve the chances of getting an offer in the first place but also likely improve the offer itself. Think of this as a first business meeting and not an interview. There's a job to be done and you're there to get the details in order to determine if it is a job you want to bid on. Be a solution provider.

Even the language that Anthony uses can demonstrate his interest and enthusiasm. Where possible, Anthony, particularly in his questions, should try to use inclusive language. What does that mean? Mostly it's about pronouns. Instead of saying "I," Anthony should say "we." Instead of saying something is "his" or "my / mine," Anthony can say it is or was "ours" or "our." When referring to things that he did at previous positions, using both "we" and "I," instead of just saying "I," gives the impression that Anthony is a team player. If they ask what his role was on the team and he led it, he should say "I led the team," but when talking about what the team did, "we" is better. When asking Jeff a question about how things work there, Anthony can say "Is that similar to how we would do things here?" Or when asking an organizational question about internal customers, Anthony might ask "Who do we serve?" Or, "Would our goals be similar here?" if comparing the new project objectives with the goals at his previous positions.

Using "we" and "our" instead of "I" and "my / mine" inserts Anthony into the equation and puts him one step closer to actually being there. This type of language not only helps him see himself there but also helps get them to see him there as well. By continually avoiding "I" and "my / mine," Anthony takes the spotlight off of himself, the candidate who is looking for a job, and keeps it focused on the people who need help and the team's mission.

Additionally, by listening to the language that Jeff and Tonya use he can get a sense of their level of engagement with him. Are they saying "we" or "our" in one-on-one conversations with him? If they are then they might be visualizing Anthony working there too.

Using inclusive language, asking a lot of questions about the organizational structure and asking about Jeff and Tonya's specific needs are assumptive interviewing techniques. The assumption that Anthony is making by using this language and asking questions in this way is that he is confident he can really help and that this meeting is more than an interview, it is an opportunity to begin to get involved. He is not being overconfident, instead he is trying to keep the conversation focused on what needs to be done. This is similar to the assumptive sales technique that sales people use to ask potential customers where they might put an item in their home or which color best matches their other stuff well before the potential customer has even thought about buying it. This technique encourages visualization. By using it, a sales person can get a potential customer to visualize a product in a familiar place, making the actual buying decision easier to process. In interviews, it moves the conversation past the big decision, in this case, "Who is the best person for this job?" and into how everyone (including the candidate) can put their heads together and actually do the job.

The mental image this creates is of two or three people sitting around a circular table, leaning inward with their arms on the table, heads together, engaged in a conversation where everyone has something to share and the focus is solving a problem or chasing a goal. This is counter to the image of a more standard, confrontational interview where the parties are on opposite sides of a rectangular table with one if not both parties sitting up and back in their seats, coolly interviewing the other party, not engaged, almost interrogating. Which of these types of conversations will have a better chance of everyone agreeing on something? While this may not seem obvious during the interview, these subtle changes in language and attitude will resonate with the interviewers long after the interview is over.

Anthony and I have covered a lot of ground. We spent so much time because Anthony really doesn't have much experience interviewing and this is so important for him. Most of what we've talked about so far has been strategic. We haven't spent any time on the basics yet and it is always a good idea to do that as well. In the next chapter we'll talk about some of the more detail level do's and don'ts in interviews that apply to everyone, not only Anthony but also much more experienced candidates like Tom or Karen.

Chapter 8: How to Get It Right

One of things that Anthony and I did in the previous chapter was to establish a foundational point of view: "I'm here to help" or "I am a solution provider." Now we need to use that for more than the strategic things like how to answer and when to ask questions, but also for our attitude and emotional responses. We need to control ourselves in interview situations to avoid making simple mistakes. This means not getting nervous, not saying the wrong things, or revealing too much too soon. It also means sticking with the pace and program, and having discipline. It's easy if you know what to do and what not to do. It is also universal, everyone needs to think about these things.

This is in the book because it needs to be. It is discussed with every candidate before every interview, to be sure even though many may know these things already. Remember, one mistake can kill an interview and turn several weeks, if not months of work into total waste. There is a good chance someone will make a mistake in this process. It would be better if it were not any of us!

Everyone needs to review the basics, even people like Tom and Karen, both of whom have years of professional experience. Why? Tom for example, has only worked with a couple of companies in his whole career. He has been promoted repeatedly and has probably been through several sets of internal interviews, however he has much less experience with external interviews.

Believe it or not, it is often the most senior level people who not only ask for my help preparing for interviews but also appreciate it the most. While they may have twenty plus years of career history and have interviewed candidates themselves repeatedly, many, like Tom may have only ever been an interviewee a few times. They know that interviews are important and most want to take time to get prepared. However, not all of them know how to prepare. As a headhunter, in a decent year, I'll setup over thirty interviews with top candidates for very well-known companies. It is the feedback from all of these interviews, year in and year out, good news and bad, both from candidates and companies that is the basis for everything I tell candidates now, including Tom.

It's been about a week since I sent Tom's resume to Paul, the Houston based Director of Raw Materials Procurement at the large oil equipment manufacturing company. In the meantime, I've continued to market Tom to other companies. I'm not just sitting around waiting to see if Paul replies. I need to make as many people aware of Tom as possible to improve my chances of placing him. I won't stop marketing Tom until we're done. Sure enough though, early in the week I received an email from Paul. He passed Tom's resume on to the Vice President of Manufacturing, Carl. Carl liked what he saw and wants to setup a telephone interview with Tom. Good news! We're moving to the next step.

When I tell Tom, he says that he definitely wants to have a preparation and review session. He hasn't interviewed in years. Since we first spoke, Tom has taken time to read some of the press and other materials about the company so he is more familiar with them. He'll spend some additional time now to see what other details he can dig up. I'll help out as well and send Tom notes on what I know about Carl, including a profile I pulled off of LinkedIn.com. We schedule a preparation call a few days out so Tom has a chance to do his homework. He says he wants to brush up on the basics and has a few questions too. For example, what should he say if they ask about money? Or if they ask why he is looking? Is a telephone interview a good time to bring up new ideas? How can he best highlight his accomplishments? Can he ask them about benefits or vacation? What about the relocation policy and moving? How can he ask about his long term career prospects?

As with Anthony, Tom and I also talk about the strategic goals of the interview. He has thought about some of the challenges a company like this might face and he's considered how he and his team have addressed similar issues in his current role. He believes that, based on what he knows right now, there is a good chance that he might be able to help. For the interview, Tom is more concerned about the details, any trick questions or anything else that might hurt his chances if done incorrectly.

"What if they ask me why I'm looking?"

"Why are you looking?"

"Well, when we originally spoke I told you that I am primarily interested in moving from Memphis back to the Houston area. My job here is fine, I do have questions about the long term future, but mostly I want to be closer to family. I'd like to get with a good company that can provide opportunities for my future. However I'm not in a hurry and I don't want to just jump ship or make too many sacrifices. I don't think this is what I should say to Carl though. It doesn't feel quite right."

"I understand and agree. Before we talk about how to answer the question, I want to note that it is always important to be very honest with these types of questions and answers. You can and should include some of what you said in your answer."

Tom doesn't need my advice regarding honesty. He'll be fine. For everyone else, the bottom line is that it is always important to tell the truth. That means not exaggerating, misleading or withholding important details. Why? Because there is no way to recover after getting caught in a lie. That's it. Game over. The interview process will end right there every time.

Why is Tom looking for a new job? Or, why is Tom considering leaving his current company? Tom said it was because he wants to move to Houston and that's okay. He said that there is nothing wrong with his current company, and that is better than okay. Tom's interest in moving to Houston is an opportunity for Carl's company. This is still a dangerous question though. What if Tom's current job wasn't good or if he had other reasons for wanting to move? It would be very easy for Tom to say more than he needs to here, even potentially including something negative. Ideally, Tom will want to keep his answer short and to the point so he can finish by asking a question and refocusing the conversation back on what Carl wants to do. The answer he should give is:

> "My current job is fine however I have family in Houston. When the recruiter called and told me that your company might need help in purchasing and materials I became interested and wanted to learn more. Tell me, what are your most important immediate goals?"

That's it. Full stop. That's the whole answer. It says everything that Tom needs to say. For most people who are currently employed an answer like that is sufficient. If there is no relocation involved, even the second part of the answer is fine. If there is no recruiter involved, probably again for most people, then the last part, "I became interested in your company and wanted to learn more" or "I couldn't pass up an opportunity to speak with you," is good. An answer like that says you like the company and value the opportunity to speak with them. It is a compliment. It is positive. There is no need to elaborate further almost regardless of circumstances. This is one of those times where it pays to stop talking and let a pause happen if it is going to happen. If there is a pause and you're done, the interviewer will eventually say something. Anything else that is added is unnecessary. If it helps, remember your favorite police show and think about Miranda Rights – "Anything you say can and will be used against you..." Okay so it's not that bad but the point of this is to shift the focus back to them.

On the long list of things nobody wants to hear in an interview are sour grapes or negativity. Never say anything bad about your current employer or any previous employer. Like everyone's mother always says, "If you don't have anything good to say, don't say anything at all." Definitely do not say: "I want a new job because my current boss is an (insert preferred expletive)."

Your current situation is most likely not important to satisfying their need so these details are not important to the conversation. Who is this interview about?

What if Tom was unemployed? What if he got laid off and that's why he is looking for a job? It's okay. People get laid off. The idea that companies don't lay off good people is a myth. The decisions that result in regular people losing their jobs are often made in bulk many levels above. The important thing is to keep the answer short, to the point and then move on. The right answer is:

> "My company decided to make some changes and myself and several others were laid off."

Again, stop talking. Those are the facts and that is all that is necessary. Definitely don't say anything negative about the layoff, the severance or your personal situation. The temptation for anyone asked why they are looking for a job is to justify and explain. That's a mistake. The quality and brevity of your answer is more important than the quantity.

Compared to the motivation question, "Why are you looking?" the rest of the questions are easy as long as we remember to keep the answers short and stop talking at the right time.

"How much money are you looking for?" or "What kind of salary are you seeking?" Easy! "I am currently earning or was previously earning (give the specific amount per hour, month, or year)" and stop talking! If they ask what it would take for you to join them repeat your current or previous compensation level and say that you are looking for a long term career opportunity and would be very excited for a chance to review an offer after the interviews. Then what? Stop talking! The key is to keep the answer short and direct, then try to move the conversation back to their needs and goals.

The same goes for benefits, vacation or any other forms of compensation. The best answers simply state your current situation, reaffirm your interest in the process and nothing more. Don't justify, explain or add more information than is required. Regarding benefits it's not necessary to get into specifics yet. It's easy to get bogged down in benefits details when these types of questions come up, however, before an offer is made it is not really helpful. There will be time for all of that later. If things go well, you can make time.

Some interviewers will go through a candidate's entire career history and ask about why they made every change. In each case, it is best to use the same strategy as above and keep the answer honest, short and to the point. "I was recruited over by an old colleague." "The company reduced headcount and my position and several others were eliminated." "The new position was a great opportunity and an increase in responsibility."

The confidence to keep these answers short, to delay exploring things like compensation, benefits, vacation or to explain and justify all the changes in a career history is the same as the confidence that we are applying to every stage of this process. The time to find out and ask about the self-interest items like compensation structure, benefits and vacation is after an offer is received. For now the only goal is to get to the next step. In Tom's case, the next step, after this telephone interview, if it goes well, would be a trip to Houston for an all-day set of interviews.

Even though we spent a few minutes talking about the basics, chances are not much of this will come up in during his conversation with Carl. His call with Carl should be very on message in terms of what Carl's company wants to do and where they need help. Carl has seen Tom's resume and knows that they should speak the same language.

What Tom really wants to know ahead of his call with Carl is how to bring up his own ideas or highlight specific accomplishments. He is rightfully worried about talking about himself too much but he has been able to do some good things in his current position and feels like it would be helpful for Carl to know about some of them. We talk about the check / balance approach and I suggest Tom try to frame his ideas and accomplishments in the form of questions. First, keeping in mind that this will probably only be a thirty to forty-five minute call, Tom needs to understand that he probably won't get to cover everything or ask every question. If he can get Carl talking about some of the challenges he is facing, the easy way for Tom to bring up his ideas or previous accomplishments is to simply ask Carl if they have tried (x)? If Carl asks for more details, Tom can say, "We did (x) and it we got good results. Would like to hear about some specific examples?" Without saying "I" too much or running on and not engaging Carl, Tom can bring up things that he has done if he feels like they are applicable to Carl's situation, while still allowing Carl to direct the conversation. In doing this, Tom simply has to remember that he's not there to sell anything. He's there to listen, learn and see if he can help.

Telephone interviews lack the visual signals that come in face to face meetings so Tom has to pay attention for other cues. This means actively listening. Pauses in the conversation can feel more amplified on the phone and unnatural in the conversation. As a result, the urge to keep talking to avoid a pause is even greater. Again, this is where the check /

balance approach can be very helpful. Stop telling stories and ask a question. Candidates should continually ask for feedback, ask questions and engage their interviewers instead of going off on long soliloquies and having to stop and check if the other person is still on the line. This is especially true for people like Tom who work in complex environments and have years of applicable experience. The temptation is to keep adding detail and talk right through the pause. This is dangerous. The last thing a candidate wants is to sense that they have lost the interviewer somewhere, that he or she is actually doing something else while passively holding the phone to their ear. The way to avoid this is to engage, stop talking, check in and ask questions.

The check / balance approach doesn't go both ways though. Interviewers are not obligated to avoid speeches or long explanations. One thing that is critically important in any interview is staying in the moment. This is especially true of telephone interviews. Be in the interview during the interview. Listen actively and acknowledge the details. Don't type or read emails, don't look at or do anything else, and don't schedule telephone interviews while you are driving! Focus all of your attention and energy on the voice on the other end of the phone. If it helps, close your eyes. My own trick is writing everything down. Often people really stumble in interviews when they step out of the moment and try to construct their next question or answer while the interviewer is still speaking. That is not listening and it will show. I suggest to all of my candidates to not only stay in the moment as best as they can but to also not try to preselect answers or questions or even draw conclusions about the job during the interview.

I'm not too worried about Tom. I've done the homework to know that everything looks good on paper. Tom's background matches the kind of experience we anticipate Carl needs on his team. We talked through everything. Tom is genuinely curious to find out more about what's happening at the company and what he can do to help. He is going to focus on learning about Carl's mission, his organization, vision, and some of the challenges he is facing. Tom is going to keep his own answers short and direct. He's going to try to bring up his accomplishments and emphasize his expertise by making his questions insightful. And if Carl asks him any self-interested questions, Tom knows what to do.

The last thing we talk about is process and perspective. Just like with Anthony, Tom and I want to map out what we think will happen so that he can get an idea of what to do when. We know that if this telephone interview goes well the next step would be for Tom to fly out to Houston to meet with Carl and his team. That's our goal. No matter what, at the end of this call, we want Carl to be interested in inviting Tom to come to Houston. When I say this to Tom he asks:

"What if, at some point during the call, I decide I'm not interested in the job?"

"We would still want them to invite you to interview in Houston. We can always decline. More importantly, it would be better if you could, both in your mind and in your actions, wait until the call is over before drawing conclusions about whether or not you want to continue. Thinking about it during the interview will show. Remember stay in the moment. There will be plenty of time to analyze the results and figure out what to do after the interview."

"Okay, that makes sense. How should I close the interview call? What should I say to Carl to let him know if I want to come in for an interview?"

"The best thing is to be direct. I would suggest thanking Carl for the opportunity to speak with him and telling him that you are definitely interested in continuing the process."

"And then stop talking, right?"

"I think you're going to do really well on this telephone interview Tom. Please don't forget to call me after so we can debrief."

What I told Tom about closing the interview is pretty straight forward. In his case, particularly since I am managing the process, we already know what the next step will be so there's no need for Tom to ask. The key things that Tom needs to do are to show his appreciation for the opportunity to speak with Carl, state that he is interested in continuing the process and be enthusiastic about the possibilities. He doesn't need to overdo it, but Carl does need to get the sense that Tom is genuinely interested in moving forward.

However, the reason I'm writing this book is because most people are not working with recruiters. They don't have someone who can get involved after the interview and follow up, get feedback, coordinate next steps or stop the process. Most people have to do all of these things on their own. So how do you do it? What don't you do? And how come everything takes so long?

First, like I said to Tom, the most important thing is to make sure that there is no doubt in the mind of the interviewer about the level of interest in the position. Tell them. Be enthusiastic and positive. It is also okay to ask about next steps. The simplest and least self-interested way to ask is to be direct. It is okay to say, "If you feel like this conversation went well, what would be the next step for us?"

Doing any more can appear self-interested. One of the most difficult parts of this process is dealing with the unknowns. Tom and I spent a few minutes talking about this as well. He asked me if I knew if there were other candidates interviewing for the position or if I had any sense of the timing. I told him that I don't worry about the things I can't control, including other candidates and timing. All we can do is give our best and see what happens. The way we hedge risk though is by continuing to look at opportunities with other companies.

There is really nothing more Tom and I can do ahead of his interview. Hopefully everything will go as planned and we will move on to the next steps of the process. That's not always the case though. Sometimes interviews don't work out. In the next chapter we'll talk about some of the things that might happen during an interview, what happens when interviews don't go well and how to think about the results.

Chapter 9: When Interviews Go Wrong

Not every potential match is perfect and sometimes the weight of a failed interview can really impact how a candidate continues their job search. Interviews that don't go well hurt. That's true even for me. However, after setting up so many I know that a bad interview is not always the candidate's fault or even my fault. In fact, *fault* is rarely an applicable term for any party involved. It sounds like a really simple observation but most people who have worked hard to get an interview only to see it go poorly will blame themselves instead of considering other possibilities.

Karen was pretty upset when she called. I could hear a quiver in her usually very confident voice. Something was wrong. It had been a couple of months since we had spoken. Karen is a busy person. She lives the classic paradox shared by a lot of people who are looking for new jobs; a large part of her motivation is that her schedule is brutal. However, because of her schedule finding time to search for a new position is really hard. She's been doing it though and has made progress. In fact the reason for her call today was to tell me about the highs and lows of her efforts so far.

It was Friday afternoon. Karen had taken the day off because she had a job interview. Since we last spoke, Karen has filled as much of her spare time as possible doing research, identifying contacts and sending out emails. She's sent out a few resumes on request and was feeling pretty good about the momentum she was building up. At this point, Karen is being even more precise in her email marketing. She is identifying companies that interest her and have relevant positions posted. Then she is finding contacts who might be potential hiring managers for the open jobs and contacting them directly. She isn't applying for the jobs or even admitting to the potential hiring managers that she knows about them. Instead she is sending them the same type of introduction and advice request emails she might send to other potential hiring managers or peers and letting them make the connection, if there's one to make. In these situations, because she knows that they might be looking for someone like her, she believes that her rate of replies will be higher. So far, she's been right, even for a couple of the companies that were well outside of her industry. In fact, she mentioned one of them to me when we first started talking about her job search.

Originating from a set of introductory emails sent to a potential hiring manager contacts, a big, very well-known sports apparel manufacturer invited her to interview for a regional business-to-business marketing management role that she found online. She never applied for the job; instead, she identified a few contacts, emailed them to introduce herself, express interest in what they were doing, and seek some advice. It just so happened, as Karen planned, that the first contact she emailed knew the hiring manager responsible for the open job. Karen got an introduction, there was a short dialogue via email, a request for a resume and then an invitation to come in for an interview. She was super excited. She couldn't help it. Based on everything she had read and heard about this company she thought it would be a great place to work.

She didn't get a chance to call me ahead of time for preparation but she did a lot of the right things on her own. She told me that she called the company before the interview to get the names of a couple of the interview participants and then figured out who the others might be based on finding profiles on LinkedIn.com. In all, she found profiles for eight different managers who could have been panel members. Only four would actually be on the panel and she had the names of two already but she figured it couldn't hurt to know who some of the other players were anyways. Then she scoured the internet for information about this company. She read product reviews, press releases, executive biographies, mission statements, financial data and everything else she could find. When she was out shopping she made a point to look at their products and their marketing. She even looked up past marketing campaigns so she could think about the evolution of their corporate identity. She read everything she could about their top three competitors and how they fought for market share. She spent time thinking about the challenges of marketing in the sports apparel industry and how or if it might be related to wireless communications. She recalled and noted accomplishments in her past that might be applicable to some of the issues this company could be facing. She anticipated questions, both that she would like to ask and what she thought she might have to answer. She thought about what she would say, how she would handle self-interested questions and how should get her own ideas across. Her goal was to bring a lot of positive energy and knowledge to this interview, to learn about the needs of the position and managers, show how she could help, demonstrate interest and enthusiasm and hope that she could make it to the next level. In typical Karen style, "ready" was probably an understatement.

The interview took place in a meeting room at a popular hotel. The panel members were mostly from out of town and had traveled in for a series of meetings and interviews. Karen was on time but had to wait a little while for the interview to begin. Within minutes, Karen sensed that something didn't feel right. The introductions seemed to go okay, though Karen noted that one of the panelists didn't really make eye contact with her and had a weak, if not disinterested handshake. Then as the interviewers started talking they didn't seem that prepared. The hiring manager spent the first few moments looking for and then reading the job description out loud to Karen. Then the Human Resources Manager read some information about benefits and things. After that the hiring manager started asking Karen questions from a printed list, reread her resume and walked through her background while the Human Resources Manager took notes. The other panel members didn't seem involved at all. One was even looking at his mobile phone. While the hiring manager was asking questions, Karen noticed that he seemed tired and was kind of slouched back in his chair. She tried to compensate by leaning in and making eye contact. She tried asking questions between her answers and his questions. She sought feedback about whether or not he thought her experience was applicable and she asked about some of their challenges. She had guessed correctly about one of the other two interview participants so she knew who she was speaking with and tried to engage him as well. It didn't feel like anything was working though. Both of the other two seemed like they were only there to observe and neither really said anything. The hiring manager kept reading questions from his list and the Human Resources Manager kept writing things down. At one point he even said, "We really just want to learn about you right now, so if we could, let's go through the questions on the list. If we're interested you can ask questions later."

Karen told me that she felt like they just didn't like her, that they had somehow already decided that she wasn't a fit and were just going through the motions.

"It was the longest 40 minutes of my life and that was it. At the end, the hiring manager stood up, thanked me for coming in and said they would be in touch. He didn't even offer to shake hands again. He just looked at his watch and turned to walk off. The others followed. I felt really terrible and had no idea what I did that was so wrong. I really wanted this to go well. I love this company and they hated me. I tried so hard."

"What else happened? Did they ever really talk about the job or what they wanted to do?"

"You know, I am not even sure what else happened. I think I'm still processing everything. I am pretty sure I won't be hearing from them though. What did I do that was so wrong? I wish we could have spoken before the interview. I feel like such an idiot. I really, really wanted this."

"First, based on what you told me about your preparation, I'd say you did a good job. I don't think I would have suggested anything different. It sounds like you made a good effort in the interview too. So I'm not sure you did anything wrong at all."

"Well, this was a train wreck of an interview, so clearly I did something."

"Let's take it apart and see if we can figure it out. You said, right from the beginning, that the energy didn't feel right. How did it feel?"

"I went into this with a lot of energy and enthusiasm but they just kind of sat there. It didn't feel like an even match for sure."

"How about the job, did you learn anything new when they went through it with you?"

"Like I said, the hiring manager basically read the same description that I originally found online. He didn't add any real detail and wasn't responsive when I asked questions. Based on the description, the job sounded like something I could do. I was familiar with the general requirements. I wish we could have gotten into the details though."

"When you say the job seemed like something you could do, did it seem challenging? Or did you feel like it would have been easy?"

"It's hard to say since I didn't learn much about the size of the job. I guess it seemed like a lateral position to me, maybe even lower than my current job."

"When you first read about it what was it that appealed to you?"

"Mostly I liked the company and the industry. I told you, I'd love to try something new and sports apparel feels like it fits my personality. It seems like there would be a lot of energy. I imagined that they would have a young, athletic culture and that I would be really happy working there. I love their marketing and image."

"How do you feel now?"

"Like they sucked the energy right out of me!"

"What about the people you met with? Would you want to work with them?"

"I don't know, maybe if they got to know me better it would be easier. I really don't know."

"The initial impression you got wasn't very good though was it?"

"No, not really, but I'm sure that has more to do with me. I must have done something to make them uninterested."

"Sometimes there just isn't a match. I know you did your best to make this a good interview and I know you well enough personally to be sure that you did a good job preparing. You have a history of doing good work and a series of accomplishments to back you up. Based on how you described the interview, it sounds like you were not the one who was unprepared."

"What do you mean?"

"When I asked if you wanted to work with them, you didn't give me a real answer. You said that maybe it would be better if they got to know you. The truth is that you really wouldn't want to work with these people. They didn't give you a warm feeling and in fact took more energy from you than they gave. For you to work with them would be a compromise. Maybe they had a bad day, maybe they don't represent the culture of the whole company, maybe any number of reasons. You felt it almost immediately though. Sure, if you didn't already have a job and there was enough of a connection for them to offer you the position, you might take it but I think we know enough to know it is not where you belong."

"Maybe but I really love this company."

"I think you love their shoes and their marketing but you have to remember that you are interviewing them as much as they are interviewing you. It is important to be objective. If this were to progress to the next levels, then ultimately, you might have some serious decisions to make. Up to this point, we have spent a lot of time talking about things like value and understanding how you can satisfy a company's needs or help them achieve their goals. We have gotten specific too. I told you that all of this research, from figuring out your value proposition to identifying and communicating with really relevant contacts would give you confidence, the kind of confidence that says, 'I am in the right place and I've done the work.' It is also meant to empower you to be objective after the interview is over so that you can truthfully look at what happened and adjust or make decisions."

My aim here is to try to get Karen to look at the process honestly and objectively. It's not an easy thing for anybody. Karen loves this company's products and went into this interview imagining how great it would be to work with them and now she feels like she got punched in the stomach. Her enthusiasm and energy are gone. We already went through her preparation and the interview itself. Now she has to back out of her vision of working there and compare it to what really happened.

There are only a few possible results from any interview:

- Both parties are interested – The process moves forward

- One party is interested, one isn't – The process stops

- Neither party is interested – The process stops

If both parties are interested, that's great, but why? Why does the company seem to think it would be a good fit? Can you really help them? What is appealing about the position? Why would this position be a good move? What are the long term prospects? What is the personal impact? Is it a new location? Are there family or other considerations? Is there enough information to answer these questions yet?

If you are interested and they are not, why aren't they? Is it based on skills or experience? Is the position too senior or junior? Is something specific missing? Is there too much of a difference in industry, company, culture, potential compensation or personal chemistry? Where does this match fall apart? Is it something that can be improved upon or changed? What can you do better next time, from selecting the contact, company or industry to preparing and going through the interview?

If they are interested and you aren't, why aren't you? What is wrong with the position? Was it this company specifically? Was it the industry? How did you feel about the hiring manager and other team members? Is it because of the level or size of responsibility? Was the title inaccurate? Should you move on to other industries or companies? Should you adjust the types of positions you are seeking based on titles? Interviews don't come easily so it is important to see if there something you can do to avoid this situation in the future.

If neither party is interested was it because the specific position is not a fit? Or are there other reasons? Are there other potential opportunities at this company? Were there any positives to this meeting? Did you get along with the hiring managers and other interview participants? Where was the disconnect? Was it the wrong level, location or compensation? Was it because of the company specifically, the industry in general or something else? Why did this interview happen in the first place? What went wrong during the initial communications? How can this also be avoided in the future?

The answers to these questions will help us calibrate and figure out what to do next. Your job search, like any of my candidate marketing campaigns, is all about time, and managing it well. It is critical to look at everything to figure out ways to improve going forward. So, what is the most honest assessment of what happened in Karen's interview?

"So if I look at the possible outcomes from an interview, like you explained, and figure out which one is most likely what happened to me, how do I really think about and apply the results?"

"I go through this after every interview. Here's an example: I just had an interview with what I thought was a perfect candidate and one of my long term clients, a Fortune 250 company with over $24 billion in annual sales. The position was for a strategic sourcing person to find and buy hundreds of millions of dollars of different types of steel from a global supply base. My candidate has experience doing exactly that for two of the top five automobile manufacturers in the world. He also has an engineering degree and an MBA. He's very interested in this company and the job is a top prospect. He is at the right salary level for the company to efficiently hire him and they like his background. Sounds good, doesn't it?"

"Yes, from what I understand, this does sound really good. What happened?"

"At first things progressed really well. We had two telephone interviews, both with Vice Presidents. Both said they really liked my candidate and everyone involved thought the conversations went great. The personal chemistry and management style seemed to match as well. Then a month went by and nothing happened. I know that everyone has tough travel schedules but there wasn't any real direction or communication either. That's fine. I can manage it with my candidate. These things take a while sometimes. Then, after six weeks of waiting and getting nothing, the Human Resources Manager sent me an email informing me that they want to fly my candidate in to interview next Monday – it was already Thursday. Again, we can handle that. My candidate is very interested and despite the long wait, he definitely wants the interview and can make it happen. The interview is scheduled to last a total of eight hours with a one and half hour lunch break in the middle. Through the course of the day my candidate is setup to meet with seven different people, including his potential hiring manager and two other Vice Presidents, a couple of people who would be peers and a couple more that would be internal customers. We get all the information and prepare. When he gets there for the interview some things have changed and he has to meet with a few different people and in a different order. That's fine too, we're ready for anything. What we didn't know was that the hiring manager, a Vice President with global responsibilities, was preparing a major presentation for the executive management team and was behind schedule and stressed out. For some reason, after six weeks of waiting, they setup my candidate to interview the day before the VP's big presentation. Again, these are stressful jobs and there is always something, so my candidate could handle this too. The thing that might have been the straw that broke the camel's back was the fact that the Vice President, who was normally pretty easy going, at least on the phone, couldn't stop using the F-word during the meeting. My candidate told me that he must have said it twenty times during the interview!"

Karen laughs.

"The guy has twenty years in the automotive industry so he's okay with bad language. He told me he stayed focused during the interview and didn't let the VP's mood affect him. We talked about all of the interviews. Of the seven people he was scheduled to meet, two were out. A couple of the others were called into the interview that morning and weren't ready. He told me that the level of disorganization and chaos really turned him off. He said that the hurry-up part of the telephone interviews, then the six weeks of nothing, then the hurry-up for the on-site interview, combined with the stress of the interview itself was enough to make him really question if he wanted to work there at all."

"Wow, things went from great to terrible pretty quickly. Did you hear from the company? What did they say about the interview?"

"The company told me that they really liked my candidate and wanted to move forward with the process. However, during the six weeks of waiting, my candidate interviewed with a couple of other companies too. He told me of course, and I used that information to try to get my client company to move faster but couldn't. In the end, one of the others was quicker and they made a good offer first. Their whole interview process was better managed and my candidate thought that was a good indicator of what it would be like to work there. So, he accepted the other offer."

"Did you tell your client about the other offer and why he decided to take it?"

"Yes, because it is important for all of us to understand why this process failed. But remember, I'm just one recruiter and they are a giant corporation so they may or may not be receptive to my comments or make adjustments."

"Right, so what are you going to do now?"

"I'll do the same thing I suggested that you do, analyze what happened and make adjustments. Good interviews are hard to come by and I put a lot of work into this one. I trusted that the company would be prepared to hire someone and I invested a lot of time in recruiting. They have been a client for years and we had a good track record. In this case I was wrong, something had changed. From a review standpoint, this process started out with both parties interested and quickly changed into one party being interested and one not. The who's who part is pretty easy to figure out as well as the cause. The company mishandled the process, my candidate lost interest and I lost an opportunity to earn a nice commission.

When it was all said and done I took a good hard look at their hiring process to try and figure out if it made sense to continue working with them as a client at all. Good candidates are hard to find so the question I asked myself was, 'If I keep sending them my best candidates, will they be able to hire them?' The conclusion I came to was that my time would be better spent marketing my best candidates to other companies, companies that could manage the process more effectively and actually hire people, like the company that just hired my candidate!"

"So you stopped working with that company?"

"Yes, after considering how likely it would be for them to change their processes, it seemed like the best thing to do. Based on what I told you, do you think I made a good decision?"

"I don't know, it sounds like a tough call. But I get the point. In your situation, working on commission, you have to manage risk. So I guess if you think it is too risky to work with a company than you can choose not to, right?"

"Exactly, it's a difficult decision though. Now, how does this apply to your situation? Of the three examples of the types of results that can come from interviews, which one really happened to you?"

"Well, as you explained it, at first I thought my result was that I was interested and they were not. But when I really thought about it, I figured out that I don't really know their position at all since they didn't say anything specific. The only cues I got were negative but they didn't tell me directly that they were not interested, so if I'm being really objective, I have to say I don't know how they feel."

"That's smart. Interview time seems to go by very quickly and in hindsight sometimes it is hard to remember exactly how everyone responded. I can't tell you how many interviews I've had where candidates have come out thinking that they made mistakes and that the company wouldn't be interested, only to find out later that they did well and the company is interested. What did you think about next?"

"I tried to really consider what you said about working with those people and I thought that maybe my result is that they might be interested but I shouldn't be. Or, maybe neither party is interested."

"Why shouldn't you be interested?"

"At first, before the interview, I really did daydream about what it would be like to work for them. Maybe I'd have a nice office, get to go to all sorts of great events and work on big campaigns. It's funny, but I pictured myself wearing their shoes to work, going to their health club and everything. Now though, after the interview, I want to be more objective. I've been with my current company for years. I've been promoted a few times and I've done pretty well. If I take a position with another company I want to be with them for a long time too. If I make a move, it has to make sense, beyond just being a change for the sake of change or just to do something new. When I really thought about the team I met and if I wanted to work with them for several years the answer I arrived at was no, I don't think so."

"Why not? What made you change your mind?"

"I was disappointed in the way they conducted the interview. After talking about it with you, I really think I did a good job on my part of the interview. I mean, if we're trying to have an honest assessment and I think if I didn't prepare, if I wasn't qualified or simply didn't do a good job, I would want to be able to admit that to myself so I could try to do better next time. However after reviewing things, I think I did pretty well in this interview."

"That's a big departure from how you felt when we first started talking. What made you go from being in love with the company and blaming yourself to being disappointed with them and how the interview was conducted?"

"They didn't let me ask questions. They didn't provide more information or do anything to get me excited. In fact, they shut me down when I tried to learn more. I don't think what I tried to do was out of the ordinary or unprofessional. I would do it again. When I left I was discouraged and tired. I was not excited or really enthusiastic anymore. They took away my energy. And, worse, before I really considered everything that happened I thought it was my fault and that made me wonder if I was good enough to do anything.

Once I figured out that I really did okay on my part of the interview and that the negative feelings I took from the experience came from them more than me, I knew that this was not the right job for me. I'm not blaming them or condemning the whole company. I might even approach them again sometime. I'm simply not the right person for this particular position or this specific team."

"What can you take from this experience and apply going forward?"

"One thing is that I want to feel differently when I leave an interview, especially one that I've really prepared for and feel positive about. I want to feel excited about the opportunity as I'm walking out the door. It is important for me to feel encouraged by the people I might be working with instead of discouraged. From now on, I'm going to really think about how the interviewers make me feel and what they put into the process the same way that I analyze my own performance before, during and after an interview."

"How about your confidence?"

"What do you mean?"

"We just reviewed your interview experience from preparation to conclusion and didn't find a whole lot that you could have done better. This analysis is useful not only to understand what happened and what you can improve upon, but also because you may never get any constructive feedback from them and you need to be able to go into your next interview with confidence. For example, if in review, we found things that you could do better, you would do them and that would make you more confident going forward. Or, as in this case specifically, where we really didn't find things that you could fix, the review should at least help identify what really went wrong and allow you to maintain your confidence. Does that make sense?"

"Yes, I think so. I was really down when I called you but now I am thinking about it differently. I know that I was prepared for the interview and that I did as well as I could. I worked hard to get ready, was attentive and engaging and knew what I was doing. And now I know that even though the interview didn't go well it doesn't mean that I didn't do a good job."

Post review, Karen also now knows that had she ended up working there, there is a good chance she wouldn't have liked her boss. Then what? The good news is that she learned how to analyze what happened and form her own conclusions now, before going to work there. Maybe it was just that team or just that position. Maybe she'll get a chance to look at a job with that company again and it will be different, for now though, this has been a fairly efficient process. In total, Karen spent some time finding the position and contacts, traded a few emails, put in a couple of hours to prepare and then attended the interview. In terms of results, Karen knows that she can indeed start from scratch to identify an opportunity, communicate interest, demonstrate value to the right contacts, and get invited for an interview. She also knows that she can analyze the results and form her own, independent conclusions. More importantly, if she can do it once, she can do it again and again, and she can do it with even more confidence. The last thing Karen learned is that a good interview takes a solid effort from both sides. One party can't carry the entire process. Despite the fact that Karen's interview didn't seem to go well, it was still productive.

Interviews are always somewhat experimental. Everything may look great on paper but nothing is certain until real people get together and talk. All of us will have good and bad interviews. The important things are to do our best to adjust and ensure that any mistakes we make don't happen again, and to understand that we are not the only ones who make mistakes.

Chapter 10: Getting Ready for a Trip

"Looks like I'll be making a trip to Houston."

"That's fantastic! Did you guys discuss any potential interview dates?"

"It will be a week or so before we can do it. Carl has a trip to a key supplier and we have end of quarter reviews here. He said he'd be in touch and have someone from HR call you."

"Okay, sounds pretty standard. Tell me about the call. What did you guys talk about?"

"Well, first off, Carl told me he only had about 30 minutes but I'm pretty sure we ran about 15 minutes over. It seemed like we could have kept right on talking."

"It's great when interviews run overtime and always one of the things I like to hear. How did the conversation start?"

"The first thing Carl asked about was my motivation. 'Why was I looking for a new opportunity?' I answered the question like we discussed, I told him that you and I were talking about my long term desire to move back to Houston and when you told me about a potential opportunity at Carl's company, I couldn't pass up the chance to learn more. When he asked me why I wanted to move back to Houston specifically, I told him that my wife and I were from Houston and we really wanted our kids to be close to their grandparents. He asked about the kids' ages, talked about his kids, who are just a couple years older, and added a little about where they lived in the city. It was friendly.

Then we started talking about work, some of what's happening in the steel market, how we're dealing with inventory and parts issues, and stuff like that. Our two companies don't compete in any product lines but we both buy various types of raw metals and processed steels from all over the world so it was no surprise that we are facing similar challenges. He asked me some questions. I was able to ask him some questions. It felt like a good exchange.

After that Carl started asking more specific questions about my current position. He wanted to get a sense of the size of my responsibility, our operating environment and level of sophistication. I made a mental note to try to keep my answers really concise like we talked about and ask questions after replying. That helped. As he was asking me questions he was also telling me about some of what he needs there. I could tell that he was kind of thinking out loud and gauging the similarities and differences between the two work environments."

"How did you guys finish out the call?"

"At some point, Carl looked at the time and said he was late for his meeting. He continued and said that he'd heard enough and asked if I'd like to come out to Houston. I told him that I'd really like to meet him and his team, thanked him for the chance to speak with him and said I'd wait to hear from you about arrangements. Obviously asking about next steps or anything like you and I talked about before was unnecessary so that was it."

While Tom was talking, I was listening, acknowledging, making notes and just letting him tell me about the conversation with Carl in as much detail as he remembered. I wanted to hear about the things that made enough of an impact in Tom's mind for him to want to bring them up during our call immediately afterwards.

Based on the way Tom opened the call to me, enthusiastically saying that he'll be making a trip to Houston, I have a pretty good idea which of the three possible interview results we're looking at: Both parties are interested – The process moves forward. I still want to ask Tom some more questions to make sure there really is a good potential fit though.

The questions I'll ask will help us determine whether or not there is a match in terms of the type of organization, size of the job responsibility, the structure of the internal relationships, and chemistry. What does Tom think about the company? Can he visualize himself in this role? What about Carl? Did he learn enough to consider if Carl was someone he could work with long term? Does the job represent a move forward in his career? Is he really interested? If so, how much?

We talk about personality types, energy levels, language and conversational engagement. At the interview stage, in positions like this, after resumes and biographical notes have been exchanged and people are actually talking to each other, personality fit becomes one of the strongest positive determining factors. Do Tom and Carl have similar personalities or styles? Will they meld or clash? What can I learn about Carl from how Tom describes him?

All of these questions are based on our belief that the results show that both parties are interested. If we felt like the interview went any other way, we would have worked with questions from one of the other results. Tom couldn't answer all of the questions yet, it would be difficult for anyone to be able to initially, but we got through a lot of them. We already knew the answers to some of the questions and we'll find out the answers to a few more as the process continues.

All I'm doing in this conversation is posing questions and letting Tom steer us to the conclusion with his answers. If Tom knew the questions or had thought of it this way he could do this himself. I am just prompting him to talk to himself and work through the interview conversation to identify and organize what he learned with me listening. This is important because the next step means investing time and money for both parties. Tom doesn't need to know absolutely for sure that he'd take a job with Carl's company just yet. However, he does need to honestly attempt to figure out if he learned anything that would make him definitely uninterested. It is easy to be excited about being asked to continue to interview. Good analysis afterwards should tell you whether or not it really makes sense to keep going. There is always the possibility that Tom's conclusion might change from being "Both parties are interested" to "One party is interested, one isn't." If it does, the sooner everyone knows the better. It is a lot to attempt to extract from a forty-five minute telephone conversation but the more we can figure out now, the better I can help both parties either continue to move forward or switch to other prospects.

How is what I'm doing similar to what you need to do for yourself?

Just like the debriefing and review that Karen and I did after her interview, Tom and I are also working to justify our opinion about which of the three possible interview results occurred and why. Our conclusion will be different than Karen's but the approach is similar. One difference, in Tom's case we already know what Carl thought, he's interested and he invited Tom to come to Houston and interview.

Telephone interviews are a lot different than face-to-face or on-site interviews. They can be more intimate and more distant at the same time. In Tom's case, this was a one-on-one call with Carl, the hiring manager for the position. Carl did not put Tom on speaker phone – candidates should never use a speaker phone during an interview but sometimes interviewers might – and there were no interruptions on either side. They were essentially speaking directly into each other's ears. While there was a physical distance, the conversation itself was very direct. This was a very good interview situation. It's not always like that though. Sometimes there will be more than one interviewer on a call, maybe together sharing a speaker phone or in different locations. Sometimes telephone interviews will be very short, conducted just to put a voice with the resume. Other times they will be almost administrative and done by a human resources person who only needs to get basic information or describe the process. The goal for the candidate is always to get to the next step. Depending on the type of call, it won't always be possible to evaluate the position yet, but the goal remains the same.

Again, Tom got forty-five uninterrupted minutes of fairly intimate telephone time with Carl, the hiring manager for the position. That might be more time than a candidate would get alone with a hiring manager at an on-site interview. It is definitely more time than Karen got with any one manager from the panel that interviewed her. Anthony only got thirty or forty minutes each with both Jeff and Tonya in his interview. So as a valuable step in the process, I would rate Tom's experience very highly. It was definitely a real first interview.

The interview process goes quickly and people on both sides will make big decisions based on relatively small amounts of time spent together. Hopefully Tom was able to get a sense of whether or not he would be seriously interested in this job and can back up his initial enthusiastic opening statement: "Looks like I'll be making a trip to Houston."

We already knew the answers to all of the questions about the impact of a move like this on his personal and family life. Tom and his family like Houston and want to move there. Based on what Tom learned about the size and scope of the position, the reporting staff and other details, he believes that this job does represent a larger responsibility than his current position. He also thinks he can help Carl. While they didn't get into enough detail to talk about actual solutions during their phone call, Tom was able to learn about some of Carl's challenges and he has ideas. There is a lot more to learn, but in our review, nothing jumped out that suggested we should stop the process.

Carl didn't bring up money during their call and obviously Tom didn't ask. When I originally submitted Tom to Carl I included his compensation information in my notes. Remember, I work for the companies so that's part of my job. In doing this, I assumed that Carl knows he will have to improve upon Tom's current compensation in order to hire him. Most of the time, this is the way the world works. I expect that Carl will have considered this and can manage, otherwise, there was no point in scheduling a call with Tom in the first place and definitely no point in flying him in to meet in person. Sending in a candidate's current compensation information is an efficiency tactic for me. If Carl looked at Tom's current compensation and got sticker shock, I would find out very quickly and with little investment of time. Then I could choose to move on or suggest alternatives.

Tom and I spent the last part our call reviewing the things that we'll need to do while waiting to get the Houston interview setup. I told him that I would send a short email to follow up with Paul, provide some feedback and reiterate Tom's interest, something like this:

> "Hi Paul,
>
> I wanted to let you know that I was able to speak with Tom after his telephone interview with Carl and he was very positive. He told me that he thought the call went well and that he is definitely interested in continuing the process. He mentioned that Carl invited him to come to Houston to interview.
>
> I'll wait to hear from someone regarding the details of Tom's interview trip and we'll get everything setup. Please let me know if you have any questions or need more information.
>
> Best Regards, Kurt Schmidt"

I also made sure that Tom had Carl's email address so he can send him a quick thank you email. Candidates should always send thank you emails or notes, even for telephone conversations. Not only is it courteous but it also sets up a chance for Carl to respond directly to Tom and for their conversation to continue during the interview coordination time. Tom's email to Carl should go like this:

"Hi Carl,

I'm glad we got a chance to speak earlier and I really enjoyed our conversation. I'm definitely interested in continuing and I am looking forward to meeting you and your team in Houston.

Please let me know if you need more information or have any questions. Otherwise, I'll wait to hear from the recruiter to get things setup. Thank you.

Best Regards, Tom Brown"

If, on the other hand, Tom concluded that he was not interested in continuing to interview for this position I would send Paul an email indicating as much and withdrawing Tom from consideration. Depending on why Tom wanted to withdraw, I might try to help identify other candidates for Carl. Even if Tom wasn't interested, it is still very important for him to email Carl directly and thank him for the opportunity. Again, it is always good to maintain and cultivate relationships through small courtesies. Replying, thanking people, writing and sending short notes of appreciation is easy and only takes a moment.

The only thing left to do after sending out our follow up and thank you emails is to wait for Paul or Carl to get back to us about the interview. We know that it is going to be a week or so before we can plan the trip, so I'll put this project aside and continue marketing Tom to other companies. I suggest that Tom continue to read and do research about the company while we're waiting. There's no way he, or any candidate going into an interview can know too much.

Will I really continue to market Tom? Yes, absolutely. The fact that Tom is continuing the interview process with Carl and his team doesn't guarantee anything. If I want to earn my commission, I need to see it through and market Tom until someone hires him. By continuing to build new connections and seek opportunities for Tom I am reducing risk and increasing my possibilities for success. Anyone looking for a good job should do the same. There is no downtime until the goal is achieved, even while we are all excited and waiting to schedule interviews.

As expected, about a week later I received an email from Sheila, a Human Resources Representative at Paul and Carl's company. Together, we organized the interview. We exchanged dates until we found one that worked for everyone then she provided me with their travel agency information so Tom could book his trip. More importantly, once the date and travel were confirmed, Sheila sent me the itinerary with the schedule of interviews and the names and titles of each person that Tom will meet. With this, the notes that Tom and I made from his conversation with Carl and our base of research into the industry and company, we can get ready.

When I called Tom to explain the process and provide him with Sheila's information I left him with a couple of questions to think about ahead of our next conversation: Why do you think you were invited to interview in Houston? What did Carl hear that made him want more?

To do well on the next interview, Tom and I really need to think about the answers to these types of questions. What do we think it was that made Carl want to fly Tom in to meet the team and see the company? Was it Tom's knowledge of the supply chain challenges inherent in sourcing and managing global steel inventories, similarities in internal processes, Tom's way of thinking, the scope and size of his current role, a personal connection, or a shared experience or style? All of the above? Some of the above? What's the most important thing for Carl? What did Carl identify as Tom's strengths? What about weaknesses?

Since I marketed Tom into Paul and not Carl, and Paul wanted to remain my point of contact, I will never get a chance to ask Carl what he's looking for, what he liked specifically, how many resumes he's seen, candidates interviewed, or even how long he's been looking. The only intelligence I have, beyond my initial research, is, in Paul's words, that "Carl really wants to hire exactly the right person, someone who can hit the ground running." Normally, I can get some direct feedback from a client between interviews so that if there are areas in which my candidate was weak we can improve. In this case though, the advantage of being a headhunter is gone and Tom and I have to speculate based on the clues he got from his conversation with Carl. This is very similar to what anyone would have do on their own without access to direct feedback, and again, why our initial debriefing call was so important.

By having our debriefing call right after Tom's interview with Carl, we were able to capture Tom's immediate impressions and document much of what he learned while the conversation was still fresh in his mind. Making notes about the interview as soon as possible is critical and really pays off while preparing for the next round.

Part of our preparation process involves seeing if we can figure out if Carl emphasized any specific needs over other desires. For example, people repeat things that are important to them. During their call, did Carl talk about any particular issue more than once? Was there anything that Carl discussed at length, went into a lot of detail about or really stressed? Did he mention any other names, departments or locations of particular interest or need? Did the pitch or tone of his voice change at times? How about the speed or intensity of his speech? If so, what was he talking about when it did? Were there any topics that seemed to make him more passionate or emotionally involved? If Tom really listened we should be able to pick out the two or three things that are really important to Carl.

What about during Tom's responses or while he was asking questions? Did Carl give any clues as to how he felt about any of what Tom said? Did Tom hear any affirmations or anything that might be the equivalent of nodding his head if it were a face to face conversation? Did Carl recognize and acknowledge any of Tom's experiences or accomplishments? If so, which ones?

Does Tom know which key things lined up between his experience and abilities and what he learned about Carl's needs? How can he expand upon the things they talked about and form questions that he can ask some of the other team members using his conversation with Carl as a foundation? How does what he learned begin to fill in the blanks about Carl's organization, Carl's role, the internal and external customers and their challenges or goals? Does Tom have a sense of which departments and teams he'd be working with and what they need? Will the issues that are important to Carl be important to the other people Tom will meet?

Before moving on in our preparation it is worth noting that if Tom had not been invited to interview on-site we would still want to ask ourselves many of the same questions. Going forward, it's always important to figure out how or if it is even possible to improve. If Tom wasn't invited to continue to interview it would be helpful to know why. Part of that analysis would also include emailing Paul and Carl for direct feedback. Of course there is a chance they wouldn't provide anything useful. So, it is important for us to work back through the first interview to see where things didn't match up. At Tom's level, and as it is with most of my projects, jobs tend to be extremely specific. While, personality and chemistry are very big determining factors on the positive side, most often it is detail level skills that end up making the difference on the negative side. For example, what if Carl repeatedly mentioned that his company is focusing on developing raw materials sources in central Africa? That might be a determining factor if Tom has never been on the ground in central Africa. Carl knew that Tom had global experience and Tom knew Carl had global needs but it wasn't broken down to specifics until the interview. Enough details like that and the job is not a match. It's not anyone's fault, in that example, Tom simply had qualifications and experience that were different from Carl's specific needs. This is why we have interviews.

Alternatively, we might be able to tell from reviewing Carl's responses if there were things that Tom should have done or said differently during the interview. For example, if based on Tom's recollection, Carl responded to a lot of questions or acknowledged Tom with single word answers and then moved on to another question or changed the subject, maybe Tom was talking too much. This was something Tom and I discussed so we knew it was possible. It would be rare for a hiring manager to tell me that a candidate talked too much during the interview so we have to figure it out. Again, going back through the first interview and really looking at what Carl said will give us clues as to what happened, positive and negative.

By the time we confirmed all of the travel arrangement details, I had already been able to do some research to get background information and basic employment history on most of the people on Tom's interview list. Just like in the earlier chapters, I did this research online using websites like LinkedIn.com. The itinerary that Sheila put together includes one-on-one interviews with six different people over the course of the day. Tom will fly into Houston the night before and return to Memphis in the evening after the interviews. This will be his only set of on-site interviews and the agenda is pretty typical for these types of jobs.

Tom and I will talk one more time before his interview. In our last preparation call we'll go through the names on the list and review what we know about each participant. For example, Carl is the Vice President of Manufacturing responsible for manufacturing operations at two large facilities, one in Houston, the other in Malaysia. He works with several Director level people who may or may not report to him and are responsible for individual departments like Supply Chain Management, Quality, Sourcing and a few others at both division and corporate levels. The Directors have Managers who report to them and so on. My main contact, Paul, is the Director of Sourcing for the whole corporation. He's on the itinerary. The corporate Director of Supply Chain Management, Laura, will also be participating in the interview. Between them, they are responsible for sourcing raw materials, parts and components (Paul) and managing the inventory levels, availability of parts and supplier continuity for all of the business units (Laura). Two of the manager level people who report to Paul and Laura are also on Tom's interview itinerary; Deborah a Commodity Manager who reports to Paul, and Scott, the Logistics Manager who reports to Laura. Deborah is responsible for identifying suppliers and negotiating long term agreements to purchase a specific commodity for all of the business units, in her case, steel. Scott is responsible for arranging transportation suppliers to move raw materials and parts from the supplier locations to the manufacturing locations in a certain region, for him, Asia. The last person on the list is Sheila, the Human Resources Representative. She's actually first up on the schedule but last on our list.

Why were these people selected to be on the interview list? Who are they and how do their jobs relate to Tom's potential position? Where would he fit in?

Tom is interviewing to become the Senior Procurement and Materials Manager. He would report directly to Carl and work very closely with Paul and Laura. He would also have a team that would report to him. Based on Carl's description during their call, Tom understands that the Senior Procurement and Materials Manager is responsible for identifying and qualifying suppliers, and ensuring the cohesiveness of the supply chain from the suppliers to the factories, including local inventory management. This is similar to the way things work with Tom's current company. In Carl's business unit this includes the manufacturing facilities in Houston and Malaysia. Tom would work with Paul because Paul, as Director of Strategic Sourcing is responsible for identifying and qualifying suppliers for all of the company's business units, including Carl's. Tom would need to work with Laura because in her role, she is responsible for overall inventory levels and supplier logistics for all of the business units. Deborah and Scott, who support Paul and Laura respectively, would work directly with various team members on Tom's staff.

How do Tom and I know so much? First, these types of manufacturing companies tend to have similar organizational structures. Also, Tom's experience and my own helps us fill in the blanks. Both of those things are bolstered by our research. Remember there were a lot of reasons why Carl and Paul's company originally made it on my marketing list for Tom including the size of the company, type of industry, raw materials used, operating locations and more. We didn't arrive here by accident. In addition to all of that, the fact that I was able to find out some background information on almost everyone on the interview list means Tom and I can form a pretty good picture of how things work.

Trying to figure out how things function leads us to considering the types of goals organizations like this have and the types of problems they might encounter. Everyone on Tom's list has a stake in the success or failure of the new Senior Procurement and Materials Manager. Why? What are some of the challenges we think that each of the people on the list are facing? What do they need help with and how do their needs relate to the Senior Procurement and Materials Manager? What would Tom, as Senior Procurement and Materials Manager, need from each of them?

Do we have any clues? Going back, did Carl mention Paul or Laura? Can Tom ask Carl about them specifically in their next conversation? It would be good if he did, it would demonstrate that Tom is thinking about the different departments and the scope of his potential role. Getting Carl's impressions of Paul and Laura's needs can provide some insights for Tom that can also be useful when he interviews with them next. Even though the order of interviews is out of our control Tom can still be thinking about questions he might ask in the early interviews that can provide insights into things that might be discussed in the later interviews.

Keep in mind, Tom is currently a Materials Manager with a large electrical infrastructure manufacturer. There is a Vice President of Manufacturing and Directors of Sourcing and Supply Chain Management at his company too. The products, customers, some suppliers and locations are all different but it is still large complicated global manufacturing and Tom is already responsible for a significant piece of it. Without making any assumptions, this similarity is part of the reason he's here and belongs here and some of their challenges will be very comparable.

For example, what if Carl mentioned that they are having issues with high inventory levels in both Houston and Malaysia and that he'd like to see inventory levels reduced and more accurate forecasting of material requirements? The Senior Procurement and Materials Manager owns inventory management locally but at a corporate level, it is part of Supply Chain Management and would come under Laura. What does she think of this issue and how can she and Tom work together to address it? What has she done so far? Has Tom tackled similar challenges in his current role or in a previous position? If so, what did he do to solve the problem? Or if Carl said he'd really like to see them develop steel suppliers that are closer to their manufacturing locations and can provide cheaper raw materials, then Tom would need to seek help from Paul and Deborah. In the interview he could ask them about how they think they can all work together to meet Carl's goals.

Like in the first interview, Tom wants to create opportunities for exchange conversations and get beyond the basic questions and answers.

This is even more important in a second interview but it is also easier if we use what we learned in the first interview. For his second interview, Tom and I are developing a strategy that considers the organization, the individuals and teams within, the needs of each and how each position supports the other en route to achieving the overall goals. We are trying to be specific where we can, based on our research and experience. By thinking about who's who and what kind of things each of them have to deal with individually and as a team, we are building a foundation that will allow us to form questions, summon experiences and consider solutions in a similar way to how we prepared for the first interview but at a much more detailed level.

These are the mission critical second interview points that Tom and I will cover during our call.

- Recall and research the things that were identified as important from the first interview and be prepared to discuss them with both Carl and the other people on the itinerary

- Review any potential weaknesses or issues that you might have identified in yourself during the first interview and consider how to address them

- Learn about every member on the interview team and be prepared to ask about their needs, goals, challenges, backgrounds and why they like the company

- Develop questions that show that you remember names and have thought about the relationships inside and outside the company

- Show that you understand where the position resides in the organization and the impact it has overall

- Demonstrate that you have considered the needs of every stakeholder, internal and external customers and the challenges they face or goals they would like to achieve and how those things relate back to the mission of the Senior Procurement and Materials Manager

- Create opportunities for more specific exchange type conversations by keeping answers concise and following up with questions or eliciting feedback

- Be sensitive but assumptive and show that you want to take ownership and accept responsibility for accomplishing the mission

- Remember, this is still about them, focus on their needs, goals and desires. Don't sell yourself, instead, selflessly offer to help and be able to provide solutions

- Don't rush the process when it comes to your own needs. Be confident that if you do well on this part there will be time to discuss everything as things progress

We will also spend a few more minutes on typical do's and don'ts, which in summary, are very similar to what we talked about for his first interview. Tom needs to focus on them, avoid discussing compensation unless he has to, engage every member of the interview team, be on time, dress conservatively and professionally, demonstrate interest and be genuine. Then we'll review the directions again to make sure Tom knows where he's going, how he's getting there and when things start. To repeat, interviews are about them not us. They might start late, there might be changes in the itinerary, anything can happen. Regardless, it is our job to be in the right place at the right time no matter what.

The last thing Tom and I are going to talk about is how to end the interviews with each person. First it is important to keep in mind who's who. Carl is the hiring manager, Paul and Laura are indirect managers, and Scott and Deborah are peers to Tom's potential staff. Carl is the person who is going to make the decision about who to hire. Paul and Laura will have significant input but are not the decision makers and Scott and Deborah will contribute their opinions.

As he finishes the interview, Tom needs to tell Carl that he believes he can help. He needs Carl to know that he is interested in joining the team and wants the job. What if Tom isn't sure yet or maybe thinks it is not a fit? The message should be the same, that he's interested. Ultimately, we want Tom to have options, to be in control and to end up in a position where he's the one who gets to make a decision. Since we know this is the only interview, if it goes well, the next step would be for the company to indicate their intent to make an offer. Even if something happens, during or immediately after the interview and Tom becomes uninterested, the interview is not the place to reveal it. That can be done later after we hear from the company regarding their level of interest.

Because this is their second conversation, Tom might also ask Carl a question or two about the remainder of the process. It is okay for Tom to ask Carl what to expect going forward as long as he frames the question selflessly. For example, Tom can ask Carl when he hopes to have someone on board and working.

Paul and Laura need to leave the interview feeling that Tom is capable, interested and enthusiastic about joining them. His capability will hopefully show in the interview itself and he can reinforce his interest and enthusiasm by saying as much when they part. It is important that both Paul and Laura are supportive of the idea of Tom coming on board. Neither of them will make the decision to hire Tom but a negative opinion from either is probably enough to eliminate Tom from consideration. The same is true of Deborah and Scott. Both of them need to have a positive opinion of Tom for him to get hired.

As I've said repeatedly, companies tend to be very conservative when it comes to hiring. It is normal for my clients to only hire someone when everyone is in agreement. Even one negative opinion could end Tom's candidacy.

The last thing I want to reiterate to Tom is that he needs to try as hard as possible not to draw conclusions or figure out if he really wants this job during the interview. It is better to reserve that thinking until everything is done. To do well on this interview, just like in the last one with Carl, Tom needs to stay in the moment. He and I will debrief again afterwards and he will be able to tell me what he really thinks.

On a personal level, I still get a little nervous when I hang up the phone and send someone off on an interview like this. Tom is about to get on a plane and there's nothing more I can do. Sure, I have a large commission at stake so there's always worrying about the money. However there is something more. Curiosity is part of it, as is a desire to help. So, for the next couple of days, while Tom is flying out, interviewing all day and flying back, I'll worry a little bit about whether or not we did enough. It's natural. I won't be sitting around looking out the window watching planes go by though. Nope, I've got other projects going, and not only for Tom. As always, the best way to make this time go by is to focus on another project and work on increasing my chances to earn a commission.

One of the reasons that I do my job the way I do, spending a lot of time with every candidate ahead of every interview, gathering and researching as much information as possible, and doing my best to get everyone ready, is that I believe if I'm committed and really show it, the people I work with, the candidates that I send on interviews and the companies that I conduct searches for, will respond in kind. I wouldn't keep doing it this way if it hadn't ever worked. I would change or starve. It does work though and the proof is in the fact that Tom really did call me right after his interview in Houston.

Chapter 11: Twists and Turns Along the Way

Anthony left his interview feeling pretty good but with doubts. He doesn't have much interview experience and the interviews with Tonya and Jeff were very formal in terms of process, questions and structure. They were both very friendly, great to speak with, and interesting; and while Anthony ended up feeling okay about his performance, there were no clues about the next steps and he really didn't get any immediate feedback.

Like in many interviews, Jeff and Tonya finished by telling Anthony that it was great to meet him, that they had other candidates to interview and would be in touch. That's all they said. They didn't reveal the next steps or provide any other real information. Anthony made a point to demonstrate interest in the position and said he's looking forward to hearing from them and that was it, the interview was over.

"I have no idea how it went. They finished by saying that they said they have other candidates to interview and would be in touch. They didn't tell me if there would be a next interview or if this was the only one, or really what would come next."

"How did you reply?"

"Things seemed to wrap up quickly so all I could do was what you suggested. I thanked them for the opportunity to interview, told them I was very interested and said I'd look forward to hearing from them. I didn't know what else to do."

"Did you get business cards or any contact details so you could follow up?"

"I got Jeff's business card but I didn't get Tonya's. I did manage to ask a receptionist for Tonya's contact details on the way out though."

"Nice job. What are you going to do now?"

"I'm not sure, I mean, of course, I'm going to email Jeff and Tonya to thank them again and reaffirm my interest but I'm wondering if there's anything else I can do. They didn't tell me much leaving the interview so I have no idea how I did. To be honest, I feel a little deflated thinking about them interviewing other candidates and everything. Is it bad that they told me they have other candidates to interview? It kind of sounds like something they would say if they weren't interested."

"Don't read too much into that. First, it is very common for interviewers hold off on giving any feedback during or immediately after an interview. In situations where candidates meet with the interviewers separately, the interviewers will want to have a chance to review the interviews together before giving feedback. Additionally, they probably really do have other candidates lined up to interview. If the other candidates' interviews were scheduled already then certainly they are not going to cancel them, right?"

"Sure that makes sense. I didn't really ask any questions when they said it. Should I have asked them how many other candidates they will meet or how I did compared to others they've already seen?"

"I wouldn't have. Asking how many others there are or when they will be finished interviewing sounds a little insecure. It's great if they volunteer the information but it doesn't much matter. The only thing that's important is whether or not you'll move forward and you'll find out soon enough."

"Okay, so I'll just send the thank you emails and that's it then?"

"Yes, for now. If they are interested, they will call. Regardless of the outcome, all you or any other candidate can do is make sure you give your best at the interview, be courteous, professional and interested in the follow up, then move on to the next thing. It is important to do the things you can do, do them well and not worry about the rest. You can control how well you do on your part of the interview through careful preparation. You did that. You can control how and if you follow up after the interview and what you say in an email or note. You are doing that too. How they respond and when, is really out of your hands so you should get on with your search while you are waiting."

Just like it is for me with Tom, the absolute best thing that Anthony or anyone can do to make the waiting for feedback time go by more quickly is to go right back to work doing research, networking and looking for new contacts and opportunities.

Anthony and I talked a bit more about his interview. He told me what he learned during the interview and how the preparation and research really helped him anticipate their questions. The interviews were similar to what we imagined. Jeff and Tonya asked about some of Anthony's previous experiences, both at his job and during his education. They also asked a few situational questions. While Anthony didn't have answers memorized and the questions weren't exactly like we predicted, just the fact that he did so much thinking about possible questions ahead of time helped. Anthony was armed with some experience items in mind to offer as answers and a method of answering that we thought would forward the conversations. In both cases, Anthony thought our strategy worked. He was able to give specific examples then seek feedback or question the applicability of his answers to get Jeff and Tonya talking. This helped create good exchanges of information in both of his interview conversations. Anthony learned a lot more about Jeff's specific needs because he was familiar with the role of Talent Acquisition Specialist based on his reading and could ask insightful questions. When Anthony met with Tonya, he was able to get her to explain her role, how Jeff's team supported her mission and how both impacted the organization overall. Because he was able to ask questions, share information and get new details in return during the interviews with both Tonya and Jeff, Anthony was able to learn enough about what they want from a Talent Acquisition Specialist to compare their desires to his abilities in an honest, objective way. Based on everything he learned, Anthony thought he could do this job and would enjoy it. He is very hopeful for the opportunity to continue.

Nobody mentioned compensation in Anthony's interview. Neither Jeff nor Tonya asked about his previous salary level or expectations and Anthony didn't bring it up. Even so, if he receives an offer, he is not expecting a surprise. He looked up the average salaries for people in positions like this and is hopeful that any actual offer would be similar to what he found during his research. If it is, then for Anthony, at the very beginning of his career it would be a nice start. For now, Anthony is going to keep working to find more opportunities, while crossing his fingers and hoping he made it to the next step with this one.

"Do you think I should send a quick note to Diane or give her a call to tell her about the interview?"

"Definitely, but make sure you consider the context and your message. You wouldn't want Diane to think that you're looking for her help in navigating the interview process, would you?"

"What do you mean?"

"You should tell her that you thought it went well and thank her for introducing you to everyone and helping out. You want to maintain your relationship with Diane and I'm sure she'll be curious about the interview. The important thing though is to make sure you don't ask her for anything. Report, be thankful and tell her you'll get back to her when you learn more. Oh, and one more thing, if you call her, which I think you should, be sure to smile when you talk."

"On the phone? You think I should smile while I'm talking on the phone. That seems weird. Really?"

"Trust me on this, just do it. In fact, do it all the time."

"Okay I will. One question, what if she starts telling me more about her interview experience?"

"She might. Let the conversation flow but remember to manage your level of self-interest. You have spoken with Diane several times now so you know her personality better than I do. This is not her job or interview process so you can't be perceived as asking her to influence it. You can absorb information and listen of course. I would guess that she is probably also hoping you get the job, so she might be willing to share. Just be sensitive about the relationships involved."

"You're always trying to think of everything, aren't you?"

"If only I could. I do try to think about the relationships and the conversations a lot because it's all we've got at the interview stage. All of the decisions that everyone will be making, positive or negative, are a product of the short amount of time we're sharing right now, so it's worth thinking about."

Two things popped out of the email I got from Anthony a few days after our conversation. He called Diane and they had a nice chat. She was pleased to hear that Anthony thought he did well on the interview and wished him luck with the rest of the process. Then she threw him a curve ball, she told him that she had to take a standardized personality test as part of her interview process. She said they required every potential new hire to take the test, and while it is not a pass or fail type of test, they did consider the results in the context of the personality of the organization. If there was ever an email that reeked of anxiety this was it! I could tell from Anthony's typing that he was worried.

The other thing that Anthony wrote was that five days after the interview, he still hadn't heard from Jeff. Knowing him pretty well by now, I could picture him pacing around his living room burning a path in the carpet trying to figure out what to do, in between searching for more contacts and job leads of course.

In my reply I reminded him that our time, job search time, is different than corporate or hiring manager time. In addition to finding help, Jeff and Tonya have to do their jobs. We, on the other hand, are only doing one thing and spending all of our time on it. We're moving a lot faster than they are. About the personality test, I figured Anthony might want to talk about it so I told him to stop by if he got a chance. I think he was at the front door before I finished clicking send.

"What if I don't have the right personality? Or better, how do I make sure I have the right personality?"

"As far as I know, there are no right or wrong results, only indicators of potential traits. I've never taken a personality test as part of an interview process but there are examples online you can take for fun. You might try one."

"Other than looking for a couple of tests to try online, is there anything else I can do to prepare? What do you think they are looking for in candidates who take the test?"

"I've had clients who use personality tests and I have done some reading on the thinking behind them and a bit about how to take them, and I can break down what I tell candidates in three words: Honesty, Decisiveness and Consistency."

What I'm telling Anthony is simple and true. He can't really prepare for a personality test. Nobody can. It is helpful to know a little about the structure of the tests but most of us are already familiar with true or false tests, multiple choice tests and sliding scale tests so there won't be any surprises there either. I have no experience analyzing the results of any personality tests or discussing how they are used with any of my clients, and frankly, I'm not sure I'm smart enough to know how to use that information even if I had it. The tests are designed to catch people who try to outsmart them so there's little point in taking chances or trying to manipulate answers. Getting caught, which in this case might mean having inconsistent answers on the test, is probably not going to help you get a job.

Instead of trying to figure out how to prepare, when I speak with candidates about personality tests I suggest they consider how they might use the opportunity to take the test as honestly as possible in order to potentially benefit from the results themselves. Honestly answering each question means reading the question and answering decisively, using the first logical response that comes to mind and sticks. Honestly taking the test means being consistent, treating each question the same way, and not going back through your answers to make changes or try to manage the results. Personality tests are designed to be non-judgmental in that they don't define any personality type or combination of traits as good or bad, rather the results are more about whether or not someone may or may not fit a particular situation based on parameters determined by the potential employer or test administrator.

If an honestly taken personality test ends up being what stops an interview process from continuing, the candidate might be better off. For example, I once read about a young woman who was required to take a personality test for a chemist job at a pharmacy and was admittedly not hired because of her results. As the story goes, her answers suggested the potential for traits like stubbornness, argumentativeness, willfulness and individualism. Because of this, the potential employer determined that she wouldn't fit in and didn't hire her. Fortunately, the woman in the story later selected a career path in which her natural disposition could be better used. She entered politics. It was a good choice and we all know the name Margaret Thatcher because of it.

The point is that if you have to take a personality test for an interview and decide to do so, the results of the test belong to and can be used by you as well as the potential employer. That brings up another point, the word "decide," what does that mean?

I once had a candidate who refused to take a personality test. He told me he felt that the company didn't need that information in order to determine whether or not he could do the job and he didn't feel like providing it. His position was that it was none of their business. It was a killer. He had just interviewed on-site with a mix of potential managers and peers and everyone loved everyone. On paper things looked great, the company could afford to make him a good offer and the position was a clear move up. Both the company and I considered the personality test a formality and were already talking salary. When I told my candidate that the company wanted him to take a personality test, he said he wouldn't do it. I informed the company and they told me that the test was mandatory. If he didn't want to take it, the process would stop. I called my candidate and told him that we would be unable to continue if he didn't take the test. We talked for a while and he explained his objections. It wasn't complicated, he simply didn't believe that he should have to take a personality test to get a middle management job at a large manufacturing company. I had to respect his decision. On a personal level I kind of agreed with him and if he's willing to pass up the job because of the test, there's nothing I can do. We will all have choices to make during the course of our careers and we are allowed to make them.

Why do companies use personality tests? Is that kind of information really helpful or even necessary for filling most jobs? There's a lot of debate about using personality tests to screen candidates for employment. While usage is increasing, the validity of the results is still questioned by the scientific and psychological community. Even so, like many things, the creation, administration and management of personality testing has become an industry in itself. Products and services are designed and sold as tools to help streamline the hiring process, which fits into the efficiency mindset of many large organizations. Additionally, increased exposure and usage has become self-perpetuating. The thinking is: If thousands of other companies are using them, they must be good, so we'll use them too!

The tests themselves are in fact not about you. They are another of many tools designed to create standardized, objective data that can help human resources departments eliminate candidates. The idea is that if every applicant takes the same test then they can all be evaluated the same way. By creating a set of parameters that defines those to be included or excluded, a part of the elimination process can be effectively automated.

The most popular personality test is the Myers-Briggs Type Indicator which uses approximately one hundred multiple choice style questions and statements to help identify one of sixteen combinations of personality types as defined by Carl Jung and refined by Myers-Briggs. There are no right or wrong answers. The test has been widely accepted as an evaluative tool, though its true validity is somewhat unproven. For some people the test can be useful in order to learn more about themselves. Again though, for potential employers, it is largely a way of screening candidates that can be automated, outsourced or simplified for efficiency.

I'm not a big fan of this type of testing as part of the hiring process. I believe it objectifies people and, in some circumstances, doesn't contribute to the goal of getting someone hired. Personality tests don't seem very personal when it comes to the potential relationship between an individual manager and a future employee. The bottom line remains the same though. If a personality test is part of the interview process and you decide to take it, the best thing you can do is to focus on being honest, decisive and consistent.

There are other types of tests that can be useful and it is worth noting because these too might see wider adaptation. A couple of years ago one of my key clients went through a major restructuring and team development phase within the supply chain organization for several business units they were merging. The company is a very large, well known global oil and gas exploration and production company. The businesses involved were what they called "downstream operations" and included things like refineries, pipelines, distribution channels and product marketing. Each business unit had a separate supply chain management team performing functions that some of them actually had in common. The company's goal was to unify these teams into one larger, centralized and more strategic group and remove redundant elements. Doing this would allow them to combine similar spend categories, consolidate suppliers and make larger, more favorable longer term deals with the remaining key suppliers. To build the new centralized team they would need to hire a variety of people, both at the staff and management levels. Because there were so many openings and because newly hired managers would have to staff up their own teams, the senior management wanted a tool or system that would allow them to try to objectively evaluate and compare the supply chain skills of each candidate. The solution they came up with was to partner with a supply chain management consulting firm, design a specific skills test and have the consulting firm administer and grade the tests independently. This was not a personality test. The questions were designed to test each candidate's specific knowledge of the types of supply chain management and strategic sourcing practices the company wanted. There were multiple choice questions, true-false questions, short answer questions and even a couple of situational essay questions. The test was timed and monitored in a controlled setting for consistency. Excluding the essay questions, which were evaluated for communications and problem solving skills, the remainder of the test could be graded objectively using a simple key. In this case, and again, because of the number and varying levels of the open positions, having a skills evaluation tool that could be used by both the current senior management and the newly hired managers to measure and compare the specific supply chain management skills of potential new hires turned out to be a pretty helpful thing.

From a recruiting standpoint, when I was first told about the skills test I worried that this additional step would make it so hard for applicants to get through the process that making placements would be extremely difficult. The company thought of this though and provided some preparation material so that we could set some expectations for candidates and screen them ourselves before submitting them. The preparation materials were available to all applicants, not just recruiting agency candidates. Also easing things a bit was the fact that the skills test would only be administered to candidates who successfully completed the first on-site panel interview. From my perspective, I was sure that any of my candidates who got through the first round would be strong enough to satisfactorily complete the test. The company's view was similar but more about managing costs. The test was expensive so they didn't see value in having every applicant take it, just the ones they were serious about after the interviews.

I went through a pretty thorough debriefing session with the first of my candidates who took the test and was able to harvest enough material to make sure that I could prepare the others. Since the test was similar, but not the same, for each applicant, the preparation could be consistent as well. Regardless of the preparation the candidates still had to perform, and from what they told me, the test was really difficult. Even so, knowing what was coming probably gave them some advantage. In the end, I placed four people in great new jobs and helped my client identify candidates who could make an immediate impact. Great for all of us but what does this have to do with you?

Skills tests like this are not applicable for every type of job but may become more commonplace for certain types of positions. It is a question worth asking during the normal course of finding out about the interview process. Learning that a skills test is a part of an interview agenda should not be a panic inducing event. Knowing about anything ahead of time is good. Once you know, well, you know what I'm going to say now: Do some research so you can figure out how to prepare. While it might not be advisable to grill your contacts about the specifics of the test during the interview, it probably isn't too hard to research the types of tests used for your particular industry, skillset or application, to read about them or even try one. The thinking is similar to any other interview preparation exercise. We may not be able to guess exactly which questions will come up in an interview but by drilling down into the needs of the job to figure out what's important, we can think about a range of potential questions and proactively anticipate what will happen. The same is true for standardized skills tests. The questions to ask are:

- What skills are important in this field or for this job?

- What types of questions could be asked to measure or evaluate those skills?

- Are there any existing tests that I can find to practice?

- Are there organizations that create and administer tests like this for my position, field or industry?

- Are there specific certifications, licensing bodies or other entities involved in the testing?

- Who can I ask to learn more?

It's been ten days since his on-site interview and, outside of a short email yesterday to tell me about an upcoming telephone interview, Anthony hasn't said much. I know he's pacing around and thinking about it but he is being pretty patient, and with another upcoming telephone interview, he's continuing to make progress and increase his odds too. It's not an easy thing to do, to put an unfinished interview process aside and really focus on lining up more prospects. It takes discipline.

I'm curious about Anthony's interview as well. Since becoming interested and helping him prepare, I too want to know how it went. Fortunately, I also have plenty of things to keep me busy, including waiting to hear how Tom did in Houston.

That's when the phone rang, as it always does. It was Anthony and he just finished a call with Jeff. His tone was mixed. Jeff told him there was another candidate who had two years of experience as a Talent Acquisition Specialist working on exactly the same types of recruiting projects that would be required for this job. She interviewed two days after Anthony. Her current employer is reducing staff, and while her job is secure, she wants to be proactive and find a new opportunity. Jeff explained that because of the urgency of his recruiting needs, he really needs to hire someone who can make an immediate impact. Anthony was out. The news stung.

Jeff wasn't finished though. He told Anthony that they really liked meeting with him and that both he and Tonya thought it would be great to have him join the team. Better yet, and the reason it took ten days for him to get back to Anthony: There's another job. Before calling, Jeff explained that he wanted to meet with the other hiring manager, Kyle, to tell him about Anthony and suggest they schedule an interview. Kyle agreed and wants to meet. The position on Kyle's team is similar, also a Talent Acquisition Specialist, but instead of recruiting very specialized types of candidates for technical positions, Kyle's projects are more

238

general and don't require as much specific experience. Jeff thinks it would be a good match.

Some companies require two interviews before being able to make a hiring decision, some only need a single interview; some companies do panel interviews and others conduct sets of one-on-one interviews. There are no rules that specify how interviews should be structured. Regardless, there are typically four decision making components that an interviewer or interviewers will want to investigate: Qualifications, Experience, Personal Chemistry and Peer Approval, usually in that order.

Without previously defining it, we've spent most of our time focused on Qualifications and Experience. We've worked on fine-tuning our Qualifications and Experience since the very first chapter in order to be able to demonstrate to the right people in the right language, that we can help. We will need to continue to demonstrate our Qualifications and Experience from the beginning to the end, from the initial value research, to resume writing, advice seeking, contact development, telephone interviews and ultimately on-site interviews and beyond. Qualifications and Experience will get you in the door, and in the end, are what will enable you to create value for your employer. Properly approaching the next two components, Personal Chemistry and Peer Approval will help close the deal and keep you there.

What is Personal Chemistry? Personal Chemistry is the potential for a positive working relationship between a hiring manager and a candidate. It's conversational, cultural, mission oriented, style influenced and a million other subtle and not so subtle things that people consider both consciously and subconsciously when trying to determine if they can be productive and work together. In any social situation, parties evaluate each other to discover if there is Personal Chemistry. In an interview situation having or developing Personal Chemistry with the hiring manager is critical to getting an offer. Again, hiring is a big responsibility and a largely unpleasant process for hiring managers. Hiring someone who doesn't work out is expensive and damaging. Getting along is important to getting things done. Personal Chemistry is not one-sided though. Candidates need to evaluate potential hiring manager relationships just as carefully. Nobody wants to dread going to work every day because they hate their boss.

Personal Chemistry or, a lack of, is discovered in the first and in every following interface between a hiring manager and a candidate. The amount of time it takes to measure Personal Chemistry can be as long as an entire one-on-one conversation during a telephone interview or as brief as a handshake at the beginning of a panel interview. A candidate can't really prepare to like or not like a hiring manager. In terms of preparation the most important thing to consider is attitude. Remember, this is not about you, this is about showing the ability and desire to help. Demonstrating enthusiasm, interest and motivation will go a long way towards creating Personal Chemistry.

What is Peer Approval? Peer Approval is the support from peers, colleagues, supervisors, team members and other involved staff that helps a hiring manager make a hiring decision. In the interview process, from a hiring standpoint, Peer Approval is insurance and a sharing of responsibility.

Peer Approval is necessary in most cases, because no hiring manager wants to hire someone that his or her other team members won't like or be able to work with. Additionally, no hiring manager wants to hire someone that doesn't work out for the company or organization. Team building is a key management skill and poor hiring decisions lead to ineffective teams which ultimately lead to changes in management. Peers, whether they are more senior than the hiring manager, more junior, team members or colleagues from other departments, may not have the final decision but it is extremely rare for a hiring manager to act counter to peer opinions. Fortunately the preparation for doing well on the Peer Approval part of the interview process is exactly the same kind of attitude management required for the Personal Chemistry component.

Putting forth a good effort in order to establish Personal Chemistry with a hiring manager and making a good impression with the team to garner Peer Approval are necessary but neither, alone or together, will generate an offer without continually demonstrating Qualifications, Experience and a desire to dig in and help.

Most interview processes will consist of at least two actual interviews, a telephone interview or on-site interview with a hiring manager, and peer interviews, usually on-site and either in a series or a panel. There may be other pre-interviews beforehand, like a telephone interview with human resources focused on very basic qualifications, experience and availability. There could also be additional interviews afterwards. Typically though, two is sufficient.

Qualifications and Experience are always the first things reviewed by a company. It's your resume and hopefully it's in the right hands. If it isn't, there's a good chance that the reader won't be able to discern your value proposition and you'll get passed by. If the right person is reading your resume they are looking for specific experience and applicability to the immediate need, appropriate career level, necessary or desirable education or professional certifications, and anything else that will help them decide to include or exclude you from the remainder of the process. Remember, it's always faster for recruiters, human resources staff and hiring managers to exclude rather than include candidates when a job has well defined requirements.

If your resume is in the right place at the right time and your Qualifications and Experience match a current need, the next step is to see if there is Personal Chemistry with the hiring manager. For efficiency, Personal Chemistry usually comes before Peer Approval. It takes less time and involves fewer people. Even if there is a cursory screening call with a human resources person, the first real interview is always with the hiring manager. That initial conversation or meeting, whether it is on the telephone or in person, is the first true test of whether or not there is potential for developing Personal Chemistry. Hiring managers make the decision to invite candidates to continue to interview and meet other team members based on three things: Qualifications, Experience and Personal Chemistry.

Peer Approval is the most resource intensive and therefore, usually the last phase of an interview. Candidates only get to the Peer Approval component if the Qualifications and Experience fit, there's Personal Chemistry with the hiring manager and, importantly, the candidate wants to continue. If the Qualifications and Experience don't match the immediate needs, there's no reason to explore Personal Chemistry with the hiring manager. If there's no Personal Chemistry between a hiring manager and a candidate, there's no need to seek Peer Approval.

Of course there are always exceptions. Even though Anthony's interview with Kyle is for a different job, it is still a second interview. What's different is that he's bringing a lot of Peer Approval from Jeff, Tonya, Diane and even Gerald. Kyle has high expectations and a green light from enough peers to be able to make a quick decision once he's interviewed Anthony. Obviously, Kyle will want to review Anthony's Qualifications and Experience to see how well he really fits, but he's got great feedback from Jeff already. The most important component of Anthony's interview with Kyle is Personal Chemistry. Kyle and Anthony need to figure out if they want to work together.

Typically this interview wouldn't take place since Anthony already interviewed for the job he was pursuing. However, not much of Anthony's progression has been typical. He was invited to an on-site interview without a telephone interview. He already had some Peer Approval from Diane and Gerald based on their referrals. His first on-site interview included a detailed exploration of all four decision making components with both Jeff and Tonya. Now he's bringing all of that to the meeting with Kyle. However, no matter how much momentum he has, Anthony can't ride the coattails of his previous interview. He still needs to be able to demonstrate that he can really help Kyle.

Why weren't the four decision making components broken down earlier? Because, even though Personal Chemistry and Peer Approval make a big difference in whether or not an offer is forthcoming, Qualifications and Experience are still more important. Just as important, if not more so, is being in the right place, talking to the right people and doing it often enough so that eventually it becomes the right time. These are the things that we can control: the quality of our message, who we contact, and the volume of activity. Personal Chemistry and Peer Approval are hard to control.

Karen's bad interview experience in Chapter 9 is a great example of why spending time worrying about Personal Chemistry and Peer Approval is not that productive. There's no way Karen could have prepared for the interviewers jet lag, apathy, bad weather or who knows what that made her interview go so poorly. As we discussed, she did a great job preparing for the interview itself. However, our conclusion about her experience was that even if she got the job, she probably wouldn't have liked working with that team anyways. In that way, for Karen, despite the fact that she didn't consider it consciously before her interview, being aware of, or making a positive effort in order to develop Personal Chemistry and Peer Approval during the interview worked for her. She got a result, even though it was negative, it was still a clear result. She exited the interview with feelings that came directly from a lack of Personal Chemistry with the interviewers. We figured it out in our post interview discussion and it completely changed Karen's perception of what happened. Perhaps if she had thought about Personal Chemistry and Peer Approval this way before her interview concluding that she wouldn't want to work with this hiring manager or his team probably would have been a lot easier and less stressful. Even so, she still couldn't prepare any more than she did.

Being invited to continue to interview beyond the first serious exploration of Qualifications and Experience is a huge step in the hiring process but it doesn't mean that things get easier or that an offer is guaranteed. Nothing is certain until you're working there. So don't slip up, don't relax, don't make any assumptions or become overconfident. The most important thing to do is to focus on them, their needs, goals and requirements and show a real desire and interest in helping.

Anthony and I have spent a lot of time preparing and I'm crossing my fingers for him. He knows about the interviews I'm managing too and since we've spent so much time talking about all of this, he's wishing me luck as well. This is the fun part. Things are in motion and there are real possibilities.

Chapter 12: Opportunities on the Inside

It has been a while since I heard from Karen, a couple of chapters in book-time and more than a month in real time, so it was nice to hear her voice when she called.

"You wouldn't believe how busy things have been! I've been meaning to call you for a few days to share some big news but every time I turn around something else is happening. Can you talk for a few minutes now? Is this a good time?"

"Sure, now is great. What's happening? And, before I forget, did you ever hear from that sports apparel company?"

"Oh, okay, yes, thanks for reminding me. I did finally hear from them, I guess about three weeks after the interview. They sent what looked like a form letter email from someone in their human resources department. It basically said that they appreciated me coming in to interview but had no further interest in continuing. That was it. To be honest, with everything else that's happening, it completely slipped my mind. Our conversation after the interview helped with that. Thanks again."

"You're welcome. Now tell me about what's happening that has you so excited."

"So…"

The way Karen sounded was a lot different from when we last spoke. She's in a really good mood and definitely excited about something. Her language has a purposeful tone and pace. She's moving along pretty quickly and I'm not at all surprised that she forgot about the sports apparel company. She tells me that since the interview, she's been on the road giving seminars, presentations and pre-selling business to business wireless networking services all over her region and more. She didn't have time to think about the interview. She had hoped there would be some useful feedback but she didn't really expect anything.

Things were changing for Karen other ways. One of her colleagues left the company a few weeks ago and Karen was asked to cover the region next to hers as well as her own. It has meant a lot of extra work but she's been doing a good job managing everything. The new region is significantly larger than her current territory and working both regions is a lot more responsibility. Her reporting structure changed too; now instead of just reporting to her current boss, the Director of Regional Sales, Karen is also reporting to a Vice President of Business Development. Needless to say, she hasn't been able to spend much time looking for a new job. However, she tells me she's enjoying the challenge of the additional responsibilities and that work is exciting again. Better still, and the main reason she called, her "big news," is that she has been invited to interview for a Director level position internally.

"So the real reason I called was to tell you that I've been invited to interview for a Director of Marketing Strategy job at corporate!"

"Nice! That is big news. Tell me about it. What do they want to do? Do you know the people involved? What do you think about it?"

The new job represents a significant step up in responsibility, a Director level title and increased compensation. It's still in marketing but instead of being out on the front lines, if she gets this job, Karen will move to corporate and get to create and implement the overall strategy and marketing message for a set of regions. It also means relocating to a new city.

"What about leaving wireless networking and getting into another industry? When you first started talking about making a change that was one of the things you mentioned."

"It's true, and ultimately I think I would like to get out of telecommunications. However, our talk about the interview with the sports apparel company really got me thinking. My current situation is pretty good and might get even better soon. Because of that, there will need to be a lot more than a little excitement to make me want to leave and start something new. I knew that before, but going on a real face-to-face outside interview really put things in perspective. No matter what happens with the Director opportunity here, I am going to keep my eyes open and continue to cultivate relationships with new people. I really liked some of the dialogues that came from my networking efforts and I made some great contacts. When it comes to actual jobs though, I'm going to be very selective."

When Karen and I first started talking about her career she told me that one of things she worried about was the fact that she hasn't had to look for a job in a long time. She explained that while she had survived a few cut backs and staff reductions and was good at her job, she worried that if something happened and she had to find a new position she wouldn't be able to. Of course she knows how to go online, find advertised jobs and apply to them, but that doesn't give her any sense of control. Without a sense of control, Karen said she feels vulnerable and uncomfortable. She knows that sending her resume out into space is passive, and not proactive, that it doesn't seem to really go anywhere and it's not a satisfying activity. What she wants is to feel confident and comfortable, safe and in control, whether in her current position or while looking for a job. To do that she needs to have a sense that she can direct, influence and manage what happens during a job search instead of just leaving it to chance.

That's why getting the interview at the sports apparel company was not only very important but also a huge success. That failed interview changed things for Karen. She knows that her invitation to interview was the product of a very specific, repeatable process. She did the research, identified the contacts, learned the language, created a value proposition, sought out people who would recognize her abilities, started dialogues with them and found opportunities. The interview was a direct result of her actions. It doesn't matter that the interview itself wasn't so great. What's important is that Karen created the opportunity by following a step-by-step strategy. Better still, because she used a defined process, she can do it again.

Knowing this is empowering. It builds confidence in the same way that familiarity, knowledge, and skill create increased self-assurance and allow for better performance in any endeavor. Before, Karen didn't know what she would do if she lost her job and had to find a new one. Now she does. She'll simply go to the first step of the job search process, defining value, after that she'll go to the next step and so on. Because she did it, she knows it will work. Because she studied it, she knows what she needs to do on a daily or tactical basis and can set short term targets for herself. Before, having to seek a new job seemed like a vague, luck based type of process with little or no feedback or control. Now, regardless of what happens with the internal Director position or her current job, Karen is confident that if she suddenly has to find something new she knows what to do.

I don't know if Karen's new confidence contributed to getting the interview for this Director opportunity but I'm super curious about it. Even though it is an internal interview and, everyone knows everyone, it is still an interview and she thinks it would be a great idea for us to meet for lunch and talk about it. I'm a sucker for a lunch invitation so of course I agree.

Internal interviews are serious job interviews, though there are some important differences. In an internal interview the participants on both sides already have a lot of information about each other, the position itself and the organizational structure. The decision makers, management and stakeholders for the Director position are familiar with Karen and like her work. Inviting her to interview shows that they already think she might be a good person for the job. Karen has more information than in a normal interview situation as well. She knows the business, understands the general objectives of the position and the organizational structure surrounding it. She may even have known the last person who had the job. She probably also has a good sense of some of the more specific challenges, needs and goals, and likely some of the internal politics too. Both sides know that, in terms of her career, this job represents a good logical progression and makes sense. There's no mystery about the level of the position, the increase in responsibility or higher compensation. Because all of this is already out in the open, the main area left to explore is whether or not Karen will fit in with the hiring manager and his or her immediate team.

An easy way for us to talk about this is to use the four interview decision making components to separate what's known from what's unknown going into her interview. Like in Anthony's second interview for the Talent Acquisition Specialist position, all four decision making components are there but they are not coming up in the usual order.

For example, Karen has been with this company for several years; if she's promoted it will be her third position with them. There are lots of people familiar with her Qualifications and Experience, and in fact, their knowledge is what created the desire to interview her in the first place. So, for the most part, excluding specific job related details to be explored during the interview, we would say that knowledge of Karen's Qualifications and Experience is well established.

In determining who to contact internally for this position, the hiring management team sought guidance from various other managers, some of them Karen's. So Karen's level of esteem with them and her other positive internal relationships, her level of Peer Approval, has also already been a contributing factor.

So what's left? Not to over simplify, but the only one of the four decision making components remaining is Personal Chemistry. Karen, the hiring manager, and his or her team all need to figure out if they can and want to work together. There will still be thorough discussion of the hiring manager's specific goals and needs and Karen will have to cite examples from her experience in order to demonstrate that she can really help. However, because so many of the normal unknowns are known, Karen's conversation with the hiring manager should be more focused on solutions rather than more general interview style questions and answers. If it works well, Karen's interviews will include plenty of good exchange conversations, sharing of ideas, concepts and goals as well a review of personal style and compatibility.

What does Karen have to do to make this happen? How should Karen approach it?

First, she has to really think about all of the known information and figure out what to use and what not to. She can use some of the known information to her advantage by not talking about it. As before, this means self-interested items. Karen knows what the job means for her, both professionally and personally. She doesn't need to ask about any of the compensation, benefits or relocation items at all. She doesn't have to worry about them either. Instead she can focus all of her attention on trying to figure out how she can help the hiring manager and his or her team the most. Her angle of approach or frame of reference should be exactly this: "I'm Karen and I'm here to help. Tell me what you want to do and we'll get it done!"

Next, Karen needs to use the known information to think about the origin of this position, where it fits into the organization, and from her perspective, to try to understand the priorities of the role and the core needs of the team. As a regional Head of Customer Marketing, Karen has been working from the corporate marketing strategy. She has front-line experience and knows what works and doesn't work in her region. She probably also has some ideas about how things might be better. Her experience and insights should allow her to ask the hiring team very specific questions about where they want to take the business and what areas need attention or repair. Karen already knows that the best way to demonstrate her knowledge, share her ideas and even point out criticisms is to use questions instead of statements. Questions engage people.

Karen also has to use her experience to understand that she is seeing things from her vantage point and not from theirs. Organizationally speaking, in any major move up, and going from a Manager level to Director level is a big move, being able to demonstrate the ability to think and act strategically is important. For Karen, this might mean not being too assumptive in the interview, not over selling her own ideas right away but rather listening, asking questions and learning about the bigger picture and overall goals first. Karen needs to demonstrate a level of organizational and strategic maturity beyond the fact that she has been a very good front line manager. This sounds much more abstract and challenging than it is. However, Karen already knows a lot of other Director level people at her company and can use her experience with them to consider what she needs to do. She also knows the organizational structure of her company, her peers, the other regional Heads of Customer Marketing, and how they interact with the various directors who manage them. If she thinks about it, Karen can probably already envision herself as a Director.

The unknowns are the specifics. What will this hiring manager want to accomplish? What challenges need addressing? Actually this is starting to feel pretty familiar. With all of the information that is known on both sides, Karen's internal interview is not much different than either Tom or Anthony's second interviews. Looking at it that way, our preparation conversation should be pretty easy. All Karen and I need to do is review some of the second interview preparation points and questions I discussed with Tom and apply them here. The first interview that is missing from Karen's interview process was never necessary because they know Karen and she knows them. Here are some of the most applicable points from my preparation with Tom in Chapter 10, skipping the first few that don't apply:

- Show that you understand where the position resides in the organization and the impact it has overall

- Demonstrate that you have considered the needs of every stakeholder, internal and external customers and the challenges they face or goals they would like to achieve and how those things relate back to the mission of the Director of Marketing Strategy

- Create opportunities for more specific exchange type conversations by keeping answers concise and following up with questions or eliciting feedback

- Be sensitive but assumptive and show that you want to take ownership and assume responsibility for accomplishing the mission

- Remember, this is still about them, focus on their needs, goals and desires. Don't sell yourself, instead, selflessly offer to help and be able to provide solutions

- Don't rush the process when it comes to your own needs and goals; be confident that if you do well on this part there will be time to discuss everything as things progress

Every job interview is different because every job is different. Each requires its own analysis in order to identify and understand the priorities of the hiring organization. The maturity detail in Karen's internal interview is a good example. Because it is a Director level job, the field of vision is broader and to have an impact, Karen needs to be a strategic thinker as well as someone who can still get down on the operations floor and get the job done. In Karen's company, Director's bridge the gap between Executives and Operators. This is part of their company culture and Karen knows this and can use it to her advantage in the interview.

When we talked everything through, it was pretty clear that Karen was already thinking along similar lines. However it was still invaluably helpful for us to actually break it all down and discuss things, to actually talk in person. No matter how well prepared you think you are, it is always good to speak with someone before going on an interview. Making yourself verbalize your ideas and thoughts and opening yourself up for criticism before it really counts is good preparation.

Karen did most of the talking and I tried to prompt her with questions. In typical Karen fashion, she's ready to rock the interview. She is excited about the opportunity. She knows what to do and is confident that no matter what happens, she'll be fine. If her interview goes well, the decision making and offer processes should go pretty quickly too. Karen could be packing up and moving on in a matter of just a few weeks. I have feeling she's going to get this job and even though I'll miss her when she moves, I also think it's a great opportunity for her.

At the start of our job search conversation, Karen thought she wanted to leave her company, find a new industry and generally change her life. She told me that she felt out of control in regard to her career and was unsure about her future. She didn't think she could make things happen if she needed to and that made her uncomfortable. Things are a bit different for Karen today. What changed?

It would be a few weeks before I heard from Karen again. I was right and they did move quickly. The email she sent this time travelled a lot further than the last one. Karen is the new Director of Marketing Strategy now and in the process of moving a few hundred miles away instead of being figuratively around the corner. In her note, she said she really appreciated the work we did, particularly the analysis after her interview with the sports apparel company, because it helped her think more strategically about her career and life choices as well as giving her a process to use to achieve her goals.

Even though she ended up staying in the telecommunications industry and at the same company, things are a lot different. The new Director job is a part of that. I suspect that Karen will still leave the telecommunications industry someday, just not right now. When she does though, I'm pretty sure it will be on her terms. For Karen, the thing that changed is control.

Chapter 13: Receiving an Offer

Tom was walking out of the main office complex on his way to pick up his rental car and drive to the airport when he called. His interviews just finished and he was in a hurry because things ran a little over time. Again, it's usually a good sign when interviews go long but I knew Tom wanted to make his flight home so I promised to keep our call short. I didn't have to promise anything though, Tom wanted to call and tell me how it went. He was pretty excited.

"So how did it go?"

"I think it went great. I'm kind of overloaded with information right now but my gut feeling is that it was really good. I know, for my part, I'm definitely more interested than I was before."

"Excellent. What did you think of the people you met? Did you get along with Carl in person?"

"I liked the team. Carl and I seemed to click. His style on the phone is much like he is in person, pretty direct and clear. I could see myself working with him."

"How did you guys leave it at the end of the interview?"

"Well, the schedule changed a little as the day went on, so I actually met with Carl twice. The first time was in the morning after Sheila from HR, and then again in what became an impromptu group interview at the end of the day. I was meeting with Laura, the Director of Supply Chain, and Carl came in with Paul, the Director of Sourcing and joined the conversation. It kind of threw me at first but I think it ended up being a good thing. As we wrapped up, Carl walked me out to the lobby. I told him I understood what they wanted to do and believed I could really help. He thanked me for coming in, said he thought it was a productive day and that he felt very good about our discussions. He smiled and told me that he would be in touch very soon. In what I took as a positive, he made it clear that he personally would contact me. We shook hands, I thanked him again, said I was definitely interested and would look forward to hearing from him, and that was it. I think it was literally five minutes ago!"

"That sounds like a pretty strong close to me. It's a good sign that Carl wants to follow up with you directly. We've got a lot more to talk about but I know you're in a rush to make your flight so we'll have a longer conversation later. Before we break, let me leave you with a couple of questions to think about while you're on the plane. The first question is about the job: Do you want it? And, if so, why? The second question is about you and it's a little more involved: What has to happen to make this work for you and your family? Think about both of those and we'll dig into them during our next couple of calls. I'll try to get some feedback from the company and we'll connect again in a day or two."

"Okay, that sounds good. I am pretty interested so hopefully they thought it went well too. I'll send you an email as soon as I figure out my schedule and we can setup a time to talk. Call me anytime if you get some information though. I'm really curious!"

"I will, definitely. Have a good trip."

Off he goes. Wait a minute, let's go back for a second. What did I say to Tom to preface the second question? I said: "The second question is about you." Notice, this is the first time in the entire process that I've suggested that there is a part of this that is about Tom. Obviously, just like Tom's, your job search really is about you, however working from that viewpoint will lead to failure. To get to where Tom and I are today we have had to stay focused on trying to determine how to help, contribute, improve, and generally add value to the companies we've been targeting. Going all the way back to the beginning, our very first step was defining our value proposition in an economic context, which by design forces us to consider how others view us, not how we view ourselves. Our next step was taking that value proposition and working to identify people who would recognize and validate it. We tailored our language and approach to meet their standards based on how they described themselves and how they defined the types of help they needed – the jobs that we're after. All of our communications and actions so far have been about discovering who, where and how we can help the most and then demonstrating the ability to do so. Throughout the process we have maintained faith in the idea that if we did the right research and connected with the right people, our ability to help would be recognized and valued appropriately. Now though, it's time for Tom to think about how this job and the move that comes with it will impact his family and what is essential to make it work. That means we need to get into the details about things like compensation, relocation and his and his family's specific requirements and desires. He's had his interviews and he feels good about them. Based on our understanding of the process, we expect that if the company is interested their next step will be to signal their intention to make Tom an offer. Instead of spending this time waiting around to see what they'll do, Tom and I need to get prepared.

How do we know the next step would be for the company to make an offer? Because I asked. I didn't ask about Tom specifically, nor did I ask about the timing. I asked about the process. Earlier, in one of my emails to Paul, I simply asked him to describe a typical interview process. It's a fair question. Anyone can ask it. He told me that they usually setup telephone interviews with the hiring manager, have selected candidates fly in for a day of one-on-one interviews with members of the hiring team, then, after that they make a decision and begin the offer process.

This doesn't mean that we know for sure that they are ready to make an offer, or even if Tom is the top candidate and likely the first to receive an offer. However we still need to get ready for the possibility of receiving an offer. This is not about getting excited. In fact it's more like a dispassionate analysis of the physical things that need to happen in order to make this job and location work for Tom and his family, like a project checklist. My job is to guide Tom into identifying all of things involved so that he can enable himself to ask the right questions if and when the time comes. This is another of the things that anyone can do for themselves if they know the right way to approach it. Tom and I know that he may not get an offer. Even so, we made it to this stage, we know that the company's next step is to make a hiring decision and it would be a mistake for us to be unprepared.

Do you want the job?

This is not a yes or no question. It's an essay question. I didn't tell Tom that when we spoke but he'll get the idea during our next call. Even though there won't be any further interviews, I still want to debrief Tom so I can understand what happened. We'll talk about all of the people he met over the course of the day, their roles on the team, their goals, concerns and challenges, and how Tom would work with each of them. I want to hear what Tom likes or doesn't like about the job, the people and the company. By now, Tom should also have a good sense of what his mission would be, if he can do it, and if he wants to. If he doesn't know enough about the job yet, we'll use this exercise to identify the areas where he needs more information and make a list of questions.

Our conversation will start with the interview for a couple of reasons. The first is to help Tom recall, breakdown and understand what happened and what he learned so that he can better evaluate whether or not this is a good job now and potentially a good career move for him over the longer term. We're going to literally list the positives and negatives. Then we're going compare this list to the notes I started and have continued taking since our initial conversations in the first chapter. What notes? Over the last few weeks, we've spent a lot of time talking about motivation, career goals, family and personal goals, why Tom wants to make a change, and why he wants to do it now. The notes I've captured will enable us to compare Tom's goals with the reality of this job. The answer to the question "Do you want the job?" comes from understanding if it satisfies enough of the items we identified in our first few talks. We know a lot of the basics match up already. If they didn't we would have stopped things much earlier. Going through all of this now is more about measuring how much this job corresponds with his hopes and expectations instead of simply asking if it does at all. If we're on the right track, we'll arrive at the end of this part of the call with the conclusion that, yes, Tom does want this job.

What has to happen to make this work for you and your family?

This is a big question, encompassing everything required to get Tom working at the new company and his family happily re-settled and living in Houston, TX. It's going to take some work. In order to organize the conversation, Tom and I will break it down into three parts: Career, Quality of Life and Compensation. The parts are all relative to each other. Think of it this way; the opportunity to live in a dream location or have more family time might be worth a lesser salary; a job that requires long hours and a lot of travel might justify seeking a higher salary; or, the chance to get into a rapidly growing industry might offset taking a lateral position instead of holding out for a clear move up.

The first part, Career, carries over from the question "Do you want the job?" and explores the possibilities beyond this job. For example, is Houston a good place to find other similar or higher level jobs in case Tom wants to make another move later? Will there be other jobs in the same industry there? Hopefully he won't need to consider leaving this company any time soon but it's smart to think about everything that can happen. If this job was in a much smaller city, or if this company was the largest employer in the area, then Tom might have to relocate again for another job if this one doesn't work out. How would that impact his family? Should a risk factor like that influence his desired compensation level?

The second part of the question, Quality of Life, includes everything from the length of the new workday and commute, how the move will affect other family members and children, the impact on a spouse's career, their social life, closeness to other family members, to the sale of their home and care for personal property. For example, Tom and his wife have kids in school, how will relocating impact them? Are there good schools near where the new job would be? They own a home that will have to be sold and have personal items and property that will have to be shipped. Will the company take care of this? If so, how? Because Tom has a family and owns a home, there are a lot of steps to take in getting them from Memphis to Houston. Having a good sense of what's involved will allow us to ask questions and fill in the blanks later.

The last part of the equation is Compensation. Everything leads to compensation. That's not cynicism, nor am I saying that money can solve all problems. This is a cumulative process. As we did when we moved from Career to Quality of Life, Tom and I really only need to talk about his potential compensation if everything else adds up. If he thinks the job represents a good opportunity, both short and long term, and his family feels positive about the idea of moving to Houston, then we'll continue. If things fall apart somewhere along the way in either the Career or Quality of Life discussions, then we won't bother to talk about money. Compensation is last because it is where the positives or negatives from both of the other parts of the answer can be reconciled. There is no level of compensation that can turn Houston, Texas into Paris, France but Tom's income will effect where he and his family might buy a home, which in turn influences several other things like schools, commute times and social opportunities. We'll spend a significant amount of time talking about compensation because it is a pivotal part of the equation.

For Tom to be able to properly evaluate an offer, he needs a structured way to compare where he is now to where this offer will take him and how both situations impact his career, family and personal life. Doing the work to answer the questions, "Do you want the job?" and "What has to happen to make this work for you and your family?" is our preparation. If the company makes an offer, we want to be ready. Right now though, Tom's on a plane and it will be a few days before we know anything further. It takes some effort to pull my mind away from all of the possibilities that he and I need to visualize but it's time to move on to something else for a while. I have other things to pursue and, like it is for anyone else, it is best for me to be productive instead of just waiting around.

"He didn't say anything about the personality test."

It's Anthony. His interview just finished up and he's calling me afterward just like Tom did. I wish I was getting paid for this... kidding. Really I just hope Anthony gets the job.

"What did he say?"

Anthony thinks the interview went well. He actually sounds kind of excited, which is unusual because he's been pretty unemotional about his job search work lately. I can't remember when exactly, but in a previous conversation Anthony mentioned that the satisfaction of doing the daily work has really helped him flatten out the emotional highs and lows that come from doing research, emailing, calling and interviewing. The ups and downs from activities that generate hope, result in failure, disappear without reply or lead to real potential all end up as numbers in a spreadsheet or notebook ultimately becoming a living body of work with its own momentum. Anthony's purpose, or mine for Tom, or yours as you're looking for a job, is to keep feeding the machine new material. In the end, it will be the weight of our effort and the force behind it, the previously mentioned critical mass that makes getting a job inevitable.

Anthony knows this now too. He sees that he's onto to something process-wise so he's not too worried about this job or that job because he's sure that one of them will come through eventually. He's much more focused on putting forth a quality daily effort towards completing a defined set of tactical tasks and meeting short term goals. Even so, he can't help but be a bit anxious now because it's really starting to feel like something might happen.

"The thing that sticks out the most, I guess, the best thing, was that Kyle said he thought I would do really well there. He said it right at the end of the interview. He was talking about some of his ideas and short term goals. It was kind of weird in a way, and reminded me of something you mentioned earlier, I heard him use the word 'we' several times and it seemed like he was talking about me and him, not him and the other team members. We were at his desk, he was behind it and I was sitting in front. I remember this very clearly because you told me to look for it: He leaned forward, put his elbows on the desk and used his hands to emphasize his ideas. Without even thinking about it when I did it, I leaned forward too so I could hear better and just, I don't know, feel closer to the action, if that makes any sense."

"That all sounds really good so far. Nice job recognizing and acting on Kyle's body language and his use of inclusive pronouns. Joining him like that cultivates the very type of exchange conversation that leads to both of you visualizing working together. It's very positive. Okay, tell me more. How did it wrap up?"

"Well that's when he said it. Right after the part where we were talking about some of the most immediate things he wants to do. He glanced at his watch, said something about having a meeting and began to get up. I matched his actions, seeing that the interview was ending, and then he said: 'I think you'll do really well here.' I almost felt like I didn't hear it. To top it off, as we shook hands he added: 'I really liked meeting you Anthony. I'm going to have someone else in HR give you a call as soon as possible.' I am not sure how I worded it exactly because I was still trying to take it all in, but I'm pretty sure I told him that I liked meeting him too and was really looking forward to hearing from HR. That was it. I left and then called you."

"Again, I have to say, it sounds like it was a good interview. I think you're doing great and I'm really curious about what will happen next."

"Do you think HR is going to call me about the personality test? Should I have asked Kyle about it during the interview? I know we already talked about it and I did do some research online so I guess I'm as ready as I can be but it still makes me nervous. Is there anything else I can do to keep this moving?"

"Try not to worry about the personality test too much. You've had some really positive interviews and met a lot of people. You've done some homework on personality tests and like I said before, the best way to approach it is to be honest, decisive and consistent. We know they have applicants take personality tests. However, we don't know how much the results impact decision making. Remember, it's only one part of their interview process and you've already done well on all the other parts."

"Okay, so what do I do next? I mean, after I send Kyle a note to thank him again for the interview and then get back to work on my other networking efforts."

"Remember that guy Tom I'm working with for the big company in Houston?"

"Sure, yes, how is that going?"

"I think it's going pretty well. Actually, excluding the personality test, you guys are at almost the same stage in your interview processes. If you have a little time I can share some of what I'm telling him now. We're pretty sure the next step for Tom, if there is one, will be an offer. We won't know anything for a few more days but he felt like his interviews went well so we are getting ready."

"What do you mean? How do you get ready for an offer?"

"Okay, so here is the thinking behind this. Let's imagine that you get through the personality test, based on everything you know, you should be at the end of their interview process, right?"

"Yes, as far as I understand, there shouldn't be any more interviews or anything after the personality test."

"Okay, so it is very likely that the next step, if they are interested, would be to make you an offer. Based on how positive Kyle sounded about the interview, his visualization of you working there, his inclusive language and his desire to get someone on board as soon as possible, for the sake of this exercise, let's assume there aren't any other candidates and that you're the guy he wants to hire. Are you ready?"

"Sure, yes, I'm ready. If anyone offers me a job, I'm taking it!"

"Well, wait a second. I know being unemployed has been really hard for you but it is important to keep things in perspective. Yes, if they make you an offer it will be your first and it will have taken a lot of work to get it. I don't mean just the work you did to get to this point with this organization, but also all of the work you've done during your entire job search. Any and all offers are a result of the total effort. So it is important to ask yourself a couple of questions and think things through before accepting. Remember the momentum you've built up and the fact that there is potential, as distant or abstract as it may now seem, to get other offers too. Taking this job means making a commitment. I'm not saying that you should turn off your ongoing networking because you accepted a job, however it may pull you away from your other current activity. It's the same for Tom. We don't know if there are other jobs out there that are better. Nor do we know if we'll ever find them or get access to the decision makers involved. A viable offer is the proverbial bird in the hand and the rest of our activity is the hidden potential of letting the bird in our hand go to see if there are two more in the bush. It's a risky decision. It always is."

"Okay, I see what you're saying. It's hard to think about other potential offers right now but you're right, I do have some other things going and, sure, yes, I guess if I took this job, I might be walking away from other opportunities. I suppose that's the case anytime you have to make a choice. How do you deal with it?"

"You need to figure out if this job is worth it. When I first started working with Tom we took some time to discuss his motivation, goals, and interests; considering both his career aspirations and his personal and family's needs and desires. We documented his thoughts and calibrated our search to find jobs that would satisfy his targets. With this job, we think we have. Knowing for sure will come from working through two key questions. When Tom called me after his interview and before he got on the plane to go home, I suggested that he think about these two questions: 'Do you want the job?' and 'What has to happen to make it work for you and your family?' While your situations are very different, you can think about it in the same way. It's starts out very simply. Do you want the job?"

Anthony tells me he's really liked all of the people he's met. They feel like the kind of people he'd like to work with. He's done so much research on what the organization does that he thinks he really knows them and he likes their mission. In addition, he had a rare chance to experience some of their internal culture by attending the Open House with Diane. Regarding the job itself, he thinks it will be fun, something he can do well, and a great opportunity to meet people and build up some good experience. By asking Jeff and Kyle about their own backgrounds and career trajectories, Anthony learned how he too might be able to move from Talent Acquisition Specialist to Talent Acquisition Manager or perhaps even another role in their Human Resources organization. He likes the possibilities. He's spoken to other companies about similar positions and had a few telephone interviews and this job seems comparable. Anthony has never been a Talent Acquisition Specialist so no matter where he goes, the experience itself will be new. His conclusion: Yes, he thinks that this would be a good job for him right now.

What has to happen to make this work for Anthony?

Tom and I are working on breaking this question down into three areas. Anthony's situation is a lot less complicated since he isn't married, doesn't have children, won't need to relocate and is currently unemployed. However, like anyone else, he should still go through the exercise and look at how this job will affect his Career, Quality of Life and Compensation.

As Tom did, Anthony can include the answer to the first question about if he wants the job into the answer to the first part of the second question, about how it impacts his career. As a career, is this the type of work that Anthony wants to do? On paper, his education and limited professional experience point in this direction. Anthony studied and received a degree in Human Resources Management. He tells me he likes recruiting, professional development and the problem solving opportunities and experiences that come with it. He says he appreciates the fact that human resources departments can make a significant contribution to an organization's effectiveness and shape its culture. He has a sense of the types of positions that he can strive for in the future and finds the potential very appealing. And, he likes people. Again, this seems like a good potential fit for him.

From a Quality of Life standpoint, Anthony has an established social life in the area and a variety of activities he enjoys outside of work, none of which would change if he took this job. Based on what he's observed from his exposure to the other employees there, the working hours seem pretty normal too. Actually, Anthony is hopeful that his quality of life will improve with the addition of new people in his circles and more resources available to use to pursue his interests.

In terms of Compensation, Anthony is starting at zero and fully expects some improvement! Actually, he's been able to do some research and has a sense of what the salary level should be for a position like this. Not only was he able to get general ideas using a variety of websites with salary information organized by job types and locations, but he also got a couple of specific examples from contacts on LinkedIn.com who have similar positions. He said it was pretty easy. After a few emails back and forth with each, he framed the question by telling them that he was interviewing for a similar position with another organization and was curious about what he should expect. Since he's not competing with them and was always genuine and professional in his emails, he got answers. He did the math on his own and concluded that if he gets an offer anywhere in the range that his contacts suggested it would make for a good entry level salary for that type of job in his location. And, significantly, it would work out just fine for him.

Overall, this was a pretty easy exercise for Anthony. He's young and his life is much simpler than Tom's. It is still very helpful though, not only for considering this job but also as a template for how he can measure the plusses and minuses of future opportunities. He still has a few steps to go, including completing the dreaded personality test, so I remind him not to become overconfident. Visualizing the next steps and potential results in a realistic way will enable Anthony to manage his expectations, avoid surprises and hopefully continue to move forward. It doesn't mean he can relax, lose his focus or give up his other activities though. Lastly,

I remind him that his hopes and expectations are to be kept to himself. The next move is theirs, not his.

As planned, Tom and I reconnect a few days after his interview. Neither of us has heard anything from the company yet but that's fine. It hasn't been very long and we still have plenty of work to do. Tom tells me that he's spoken with his wife and she thinks that this could be a good move. They haven't talked to the kids about it yet because they don't want to get them excited or nervous before there's an actual offer. The two of them are positive, curious and anxious though. Tom says he wants the job.

We talk about the level of responsibility, the team and organizational structure, and the size and health of the company. We also discuss their level of sophistication, the overall health of the business and of the industry. Tom thinks this could be a good learning opportunity. From what he's seen, they do things a bit differently and are a bit more advanced than his current company. There are challenges but those, if met, can become his accomplishments. He tells me again that he liked the people he met and spoke with. Partially echoing Anthony, Tom said he felt like they were like him, or that he was like them. Either way, he's pretty confident that he would fit in on the team and would be able to develop some good relationships.

Longer term, Tom thinks there will be chances for continued growth. While he made sure not to ask about it in a self-interested way during the interviews, Tom was able to get Paul and Laura to talk about how they liked the company and how long they had been in their respective positions. On a positive note, both Paul and Laura told him that they were originally recruited into more junior positions and promoted to their current, Director level jobs. Ideally, Tom should also become a candidate for a Director level job in the near future, so hearing that the company promotes from within addresses some of his curiosity about growth potential.

To cover our bases, Tom and I finish talking about the career aspects of this move. Getting to Houston with this company could be a good thing even if he does find himself seeking another job in a year or two. We have enough experience to know that all jobs are risky so we can speak pretty candidly about this. Everyone knows that corporate jobs can disappear at a moment's notice. One day you're working along just fine and the next day your number comes up in the next round of cutbacks. It could happen just as easily at Tom's current company. The key is to think beyond the job and the company and imagine where you will end up in the best and worst of circumstances. Again, we agree that for someone like Tom, in energy related manufacturing, Houston, Texas is a pretty good place to be.

The next step is to get him and his family there and make sure the move doesn't negatively impact either their finances or future quality of life. Fortunately, this won't be their first job related relocation. They have sold houses, packed up belongings and changed schools before and have a pretty good idea of everything involved. Tom and I talk about their house and what it will take to sell it, if the market is good in his area and if they will earn or lose money on the sale. Again, both of us have some experience here so we know that there will be realtors, movers, open houses, house hunting, and generally a lot to do. We also know that there will be expenses and that it will take some time. Talking through all of these steps helps us prepare to be able to compare Tom's needs to what the company provides for relocation assistance and ask questions. If there's something missing from a forthcoming offer, it is up to us to identify it and ask about it before Tom accepts the job.

Tom and his wife have family and friends in Houston. Even though they haven't lived there in a while, they are pretty familiar with the area. However, they are still doing additional research. Houston is a big city and it is important to consider commute times, neighborhoods, schools and more. The location of the position will have a big influence on where they end up buying a new house. And, the location of their new house will impact the schools their kids might attend, their immediate potential social circle and a lot of their daily activities. We suspect that the company will provide an opportunity for Tom and his wife to travel to Houston for a house-hunting trip either before or immediately after he accepts an offer but we don't know for sure. A house-hunting trip is a good example of the type of detail to ask about though. Both of us are familiar with the practice, however, if it isn't something the company normally does and we don't ask about it, chances are it won't happen.

Building a solid understanding of whether not this job represents a good move, visualizing how the change will affect their quality of life, and cataloguing all of the things that Tom and his family will need to do helps us transition into talking about the last piece of the puzzle: Compensation. Previously I said that everything leads to compensation. It's true. The right compensation level and relocation package can bring the whole thing together. Conversely, if the compensation package isn't right, the work we did in answering the first two parts of the question will contribute to exposing the gaps and help us address them if possible.

At the end of this process, if Tom gets an offer, there will be some time for discussions, but eventually, he's going to have to say yes or no. There is no middle ground. He can't say maybe and he shouldn't try to wait for other offers or a counter-offer, or start negotiations unprepared. Tom's been around a bit so he knows how salary and bonus structures work. He also has a pretty good sense of the value of his experience in the market. What we're doing now is developing scenarios so we'll know exactly how to respond if the company starts talking about numbers.

Tom and I are pretty confident that the position we're pursuing should come with a reasonable increase in responsibility and provide a strong chance for greater compensation and future growth. All of our research, networking and experience with comparable jobs tell us that a job like this with a company of this size and level of sophistication in the oil and gas industry ought to represent a move forward from Tom's current position. We are also fairly assured that the benefits packages will be comparable and that there won't be any glaring omissions. If there are significant differences in benefits we will bring that up later during negotiations, after the offer.

Both parties have been very transparent and have qualified and tested each other at every step, starting with my original presentation of Tom's resume, notes and compensation to Paul, all the way through this last set of interviews with Carl and his team. We've spent considerable time and shared a great deal of information so there should not be any surprises if they decide to make an offer. Nobody at the company has given any indication that Tom's current compensation represents an issue and I believe they understand that to be able to hire him, they must improve upon it.

Again, compensation is only one part of the equation. Depending on his goals and motivation, Tom may value the location, more family time, or the company itself over the immediate compensation package. For now, we're operating with the idea that the company knows they have to pay Tom more than he's paid now for him to change jobs. We're also assuming the company wouldn't have wasted all of our time if they knew that they couldn't improve upon Tom's existing pay.

Tom and I discussed his compensation level in our very first in depth conversation after I received his resume. We also talked about his expectations. Part of what I screen for in the candidates I market is realism. I can't afford to burn time marketing candidates who have unrealistic expectations about compensation. They turn down good jobs. The truth is that it is unbelievably rare for someone to double their salary when making a move. Large increases, larger than 20% of a person's current total compensation, are not common. In fact, depending on the health of the overall job market, type of position or industry, and level of competition, getting even an additional 10% can be tough. The job market is competitive and it is a mistake to think about your desired compensation in a vacuum. There are almost always others who are just as qualified and might work for less. That said, getting a good increase is possible, however it is important to consider the big picture, factor in the risks, and think long term.

Moving forward, Tom and I need to define three numbers. The first number is Tom's current compensation, which is comprised of a base salary and a bonus. The bonus is calculated as a percentage of the salary. There's an upper limit but no lower limit. In Tom's case, the upper limit is 15%. The amount of the bonus payment is based on a combination of company and personal performance measured against pre-set goals and paid out up to the maximum limit depending on the results. In practice, if Tom's salary is $100,000.00 per year and he receives the maximum bonus of 15%, his total compensation for the year would be $115,000.00. When we talk about the last few years, Tom says that the bonus has been pretty much on target, paid out at, or just below 15%. Tom is also eligible for an annual increase in salary. For the past three years, his annual increases have been around 4% per year which is pretty average. He just got his increase for this year so that's not a factor right now. In this example, the number we'll be working from is $115,000.00.

The second number is the "drop dead" number and it will always remain our secret. The drop dead number is the absolute minimum in total compensation that Tom would consider before telling the company, or in this case telling me to tell the company, to "drop dead." Without ever revealing this number, it will form a base to help me steer the company away from failure. For example, if they tell me they plan on offering something less than Tom's drop dead number, I will stop them before they do it and ask them to reconsider or face a turn-down. As I explain this to Tom, I make certain to stress the seriousness of this number. If the company comes back below the drop dead number and I tell them that he'll turn down the offer, there's always a chance they won't want to negotiate.

To put this in perspective, sometimes it is helpful to break down the total amounts into small increments. For example, if a candidate tells me that their drop dead number is $100,000.00 per year and the company offers $99,000.00 I need to know if they really want to walk away over what likely amounts to around $14.00 per week after taxes. This isn't about lowering candidate expectations but rather to encourage them to think about everything they stand to gain or lose.

To balance this out, I also explain that even though the companies are my clients and I have to do my best to help them succeed, the commissions I earn are based on a percentage of the salaries I negotiate. Higher salaries mean higher commissions. As a result, I have incentives to work hard for both clients and candidates. It's my job to help my client companies only make offers that have a chance for success. However, it's also my job to negotiate the highest possible salaries for my candidates. Explaining this to candidates and being as transparent as possible about all of the motivations involved, including my own, builds trust and helps us get to the bottom line.

As Tom and I talk about it, he tells me he wants to balance his desire to return to Houston to be closer to family and friends with his career ambitions, strong aspiration for continued growth and greater income opportunities. His current position is not under threat and he feels like he's doing pretty well at the company. If he stayed there, there's a chance he could get promoted. The Houston job, based on everything we know, really does represent a step forward. He's encouraged about what he's learned about growth opportunities at the company and the health of the industry. However, he doesn't see any reason to accept an offer that is lower than his current total compensation. He also believes that the cost of living in Houston is a bit higher than in Memphis and thinks it might be a factor.

Where does that leave us? Tom wants his family to be in Houston but he doesn't feel like he should have to make a lateral move to do it. After some back and forth, he says that he's pretty sure he would decline an offer that only matches his current compensation. That means Tom's drop dead number is the same as his current total compensation, $115,000.00 per year. If the offer isn't higher than that he will decline.

I've made placements where candidates have taken jobs for less than they currently earn to move to a desirable location or leave an overly expensive one, to change industries and follow their passion, to get into a more secure position, or to simply get a job after being out of work. Conversely, I've worked with candidates who were in situations where they could be more demanding and establish higher drop dead numbers. This has happened in cases where they have multiple offers, a rare and highly sought after skill set or education, or already had great jobs.

The drop dead number that Tom and I agreed upon is our secret. It only becomes necessary as a limitation if the company comes back with an offer that is below it. If they come back above it I'll explore higher possibilities.

The last number is Tom's "goal" number. This is the total compensation level he'd like to arrive at if we can do it. This is the number that answers the question, what will it take for Tom to say yes right now, without further discussion? Depending on how the company approaches the offer, I might reveal this number during the process. We'll discuss how to use the goal number a little later when we get into actual negotiations. For now though, it is good enough for us to define it so we understand our target and are on the same page. How do we determine a goal number?

To come up with a goal number, Tom and I do a little more research. We go online and do some specific cost of living comparisons, we get on some of the salary calculator websites to see if they offer any help and we review what we know from our own experiences, talking to peers, or in my case, working on similar jobs. The goal number we come up with reflects the value we place on the job in the market, potential cost of living differences, and a premium for a making the move; tempered by realism and the competitive nature of the industry. Specifically, Tom is hoping for an increase in total compensation that will allow him to earn around $135,000.00 per year, up from his current $115,000.00, which works out to around 15%. Tom tells me that he will accept the offer and start as soon as possible if the total compensation meets or exceeds his goal number.

What we know from this exercise is that Tom will definitely turn down anything at or below $115,000.00 and that he will definitely accept anything above $135,000.00. That leaves a $20,000.00 gap between the absolute bottom and the absolute top. Neither of us expects to have to utilize the drop dead number at all and the goal number is just that, a goal. Both of us acknowledge that those are the extremes so the gap isn't really as large as it seems. In practice, if there's an offer, we think it will probably end up somewhere in the middle, and if it does, and everything else lines up, Tom agrees that we should be able to make this work.

Tom's numbers are Tom's numbers. Yours will be different and depend on your individual circumstances and most important needs. If, like Anthony, you're unemployed, you may want to compromise more on the lower end of your range. However, if, like Tom, you're considering leaving a good job for one that has the potential to be better, then your range might skew upward more. Considering your limitations and desired compensation is about understanding priorities, risks and benefits. No matter what, coming up with a realistic range, including a drop dead number and a goal number, will help you figure out what to do in an objective and unemotional way once an offer is received.

The last thing Tom and I talk about is the pending call from Carl. During our first conversation after his interview, Tom told me Carl said he would call him directly. We both took this as a positive sign but neither of us said any more about it at the time. The only remaining question now is whether or not Tom is getting an offer. Remember, we did all of this preparation without knowing anything other than that Tom wants the job and that we think his interviews went well. Hopefully, we didn't waste our time.

"So what are you going to say when he calls?"

"I guess that depends."

"I think it was pretty bold of him to commit to calling you. It suggests that he's already made up his mind and simply needs confirmation from his team. I don't think he would be the one calling if the answer to the bigger question was 'no.' Do you see what I mean?"

"Right, exactly. So we think I'm going to get an offer?"

"We don't know anything for sure but as we've been doing, it's smart to prepare for every possibility."

"Okay, so what do I do in either case?"

"Well, if the answer to the question is 'no,' and you're not getting an offer, ask him why not? Don't worry, if the answer really is no, we'll talk more about getting constructive feedback later. For now, let's focus on how to handle the positive. If they do want to make you an offer, Carl might leave it at that, basically signaling their intent, or he may go as far as discussing a specific salary level. The key thing you need to understand is that no matter how much he says, a verbal offer is still only intent."

"So how do I respond?"

"Well, you've told me that you're really interested in the job, so with Carl, start there. Thank him for contacting you directly. It's nice for him to share the news with you like this instead of having Sheila contact me and then me calling you. Thank him for the offer itself and tell him that you can't wait to move forward with the process. Don't negotiate or respond positively or negatively to any numbers outside of saying that you're looking forward to seeing it all in writing. Be positive, genuine and appreciative. However remember that a verbal offer is not binding and really only signals their intent to make you a real offer. It would be a big step forward if it happens but it is only one step in the offer process and a pretty loose one at that."

It is always a bit of a challenge to keep our emotions in check while we visualize the remaining steps with the hope of getting an offer. Even though I know Tom wants the job and we've both put in some time and effort we are aware of the fact that not everything works out. I think it's harder for Anthony because he really needs a job but I also believe that he, like me, is confident that he's on target. He knows he will get this one, the next one or the one after that. We've reminded ourselves that even though we're closer, this is still not about us. The goal of our potential employers, or potential client in my case, is not to hire either Tom or Anthony specifically. Their purpose is to fill their open jobs with the best candidates possible. Remembering that helps us maintain objectivity and patience. The groundwork we've done is not about trying to preempt the process, help guide the company or provide them with additional information. It's about getting our side prepared. They'll get back to us when they're ready. It's our turn to wait and focus on other things. When we do hear back, the result will be binary: yes, or no, and because we did the work, we'll be ready in either case.

If you are here right now, along with me, Tom and Anthony, this is a good time to remind ourselves that this is where we belong. The opportunities we're pursuing aren't random. The companies didn't appear out of nowhere. We selected them. It was our research that put them on the list. The contacts we discovered and the dialogues that led to interview opportunities and potential offers came from our efforts. No matter the outcome, the process to this point has been clear and each completed step along the way reinforces its integrity. If we don't get offers this time, we'll get them next time. Getting interviews means getting offers and being at this stage right now means we can get interviews.

Chapter 14: The Written Offer – It's Finally About You!

Anthony was so excited I thought his head might literally pop out my phone. At least with me, he's pretty much lost his normal calm cool demeanor.

"I can't believe it! It's actually going to happen! I just spoke with someone from Human Resources in Kyle's office and I'm getting an offer."

"Awesome! Tell me everything."

"Well first, in kind of a double whammy of good news, they said that I won't have to take a personality test either!"

"That's probably a bit of a relief."

"Exactly. I was dreading it. I don't think I was worried for any good reason, it was just one more thing that might go wrong. Anyways, it's history now."

"How did you find out? Did you ask about it?"

"I asked but I didn't mean to. The guy who called began by saying that they wanted to start putting together an offer and that he'd send me an email with more information, links to some forms and an application. It was all pretty business-like. Somewhere in there I stopped him and blurted out something about the personality test. He said that they didn't do that for entry level positions anymore and went right back to talking about applications and forms. I regretted asking about it immediately but he really didn't react. I can't believe it. I'm getting an offer!"

"This is great news. You've still got a ways to go but hearing that they intend to make you an offer is a big step."

"Wait, slow down… What do you mean I've still got a ways to go? I'm getting an offer!"

"You are but there's a difference between getting an offer and having a written offer after all the background checks and other paperwork have been completed."

"Maybe, but I'm still getting an offer!"

"You should be excited but the most critical thing now is that you convert their intent to make you an offer into a cleared written offer."

"Damn your detachment! Joking – Okay, tell me what you mean by a 'cleared written offer.' Obviously I know what you mean by written but what about cleared?"

"Let's talk about the forms and application that you've got to complete and you'll see what I mean."

Anthony is so close. I am really happy for him. He's worked hard to get here and it looks like things are coming together. However, there's still a lot to do and he needs to complete every step to ensure that he does actually receive a written offer. There's a significant gap between learning of a company's intent to make an offer and receiving a written offer cleared of contingencies. In my undiplomatic way, this is what I tell Anthony (and everyone else I work with):

"Until you have a written offer in your possession, you do not have an offer. Until you have cleared all of the necessary background checks, education verification, drug tests and reference checking, even your written offer is worth less than the energy required to brighten the pixels on your computer screen as you read it. Be cool and don't do anything stupid."

All of the employers I work with perform some sort of background checking, drug testing or at a minimum, will contact references as part of their offer process. The first written offers my candidates usually receive come bracketed by contingencies. Somewhere in the small print it is typically stated that the offer is "contingent upon satisfactory completion of…" whatever list of tests, forms or applications are required. This is probably not true of every employer. Perhaps there are still real offers given with handshakes and smiles but that's not the norm. Contingencies are normal.

Right now, Anthony has intent, meaning that he has been informed that he will receive an offer. If that sounds about as firm as ether, it is because it is. I didn't tell Anthony that I've seen intent turn into nothing based on as little as a calendar deadline or a temporary hiring freeze. There's no indication that it could happen that way for him and he doesn't need the stress. Instead, we talked about the rest of his call from HR, the instructions he received and the forms he needs to finish to get things moving.

Anthony was told that he will have to complete an employment application in order for them to generate the offer. He's done plenty of applications so we don't spend any more time than is required to mention being accurate, thorough and honest. He will also have to sign authorization forms allowing the company or one of its contractors to complete both a background check and a credit check. The email he'll receive will include instructions and contact information so that he can find the closest drug testing clinic and report in for a standard test. Lastly, he will need to provide three to five references who can speak to his conduct at previous positions or as a student.

The HR contact goes on to explain that once Anthony's completed the application and entered it into the system, the Human Resources Manager will produce an offer letter that will need to be approved by the immediate hiring manager, Kyle, and Kyle's Program Director. Once both of them have signed off on the letter, it will be delivered to Anthony via email along with a benefits handbook. It will take a few days. They will start the background checks as soon as Anthony signs off on the authorization forms and he should get the drug test done and submit the names and contact information for his references as soon as possible.

All of these things could take up to a couple of weeks to sort out. Background checks are often outsourced to third party providers, drug test results take a few days to come back and sometimes references are not easy to reach the first time around. Anthony will probably receive his written offer before all of the tests and checks are done and it will be contingent upon favorable results.

There's not much I can say to Anthony about the drug test or background checks. I don't know what he does with his spare time but hopefully there won't be any surprises. We can talk about references though.

There's a difference between a reference and a good reference. I don't think this is much of a secret. In fact, many of my large corporate clients don't even do references anymore. Between potential liability issues and candidates only providing vetted reference contacts, frequently the available information is not worth the effort required to get it. However, there are employers who insist on receiving references so it is important to be prepared.

Doing the work to provide good references is part of an overall job search effort and something Anthony needs to control. He may be getting an offer and feel like his work is almost done but he could just as easily lose everything by not having good references. He may not remember but back in Chapter 3 we spent a moment talking about whether or not references should be included on his resume. My advice then was short and simple. I said: "Wait until someone asks." Now someone has.

Fortunately, Anthony already has a short list of people in mind who can speak to his work ethic, interests and basic character. He's stayed in touch, networked with them during his search and has previously asked if they would consider being references if the time came. For them to be good references for this job, Anthony needs to let them know what's happening. He should contact each of them again, tell them about the position, verify that each is willing to receive a call and will provide a good reference before submitting their names and contact information. It's a bit of work but not taking control of this situation is irresponsible. As a headhunter, I'd consider anything less than ensuring good references a mistake. Anthony gets it too. He's worked too hard to get here to take chances now. He assures me that his references will be informed and ready.

Before we finish up, I let Anthony know that he should call or stop by once he's received the written offer. I don't know how complex it will be but if he has questions about the offer itself or any of the benefits it is a good idea to talk them out with someone before going back to the hiring manager or the human resources team.

The time to ask questions and negotiate an offer varies depending on the parties involved, how the offer is delivered and the timing. In Anthony's case, he won't be receiving a verbal offer. His written offer will be delivered via email by the human resources team and will come after he completes the application but before the background check and drug test results. We expect it in a couple of days or so. Because this is a fairly entry level type of position and there's no relocation involved, the highlights of the offer will be the job title, compensation and structure, benefits, and proposed start date. It is likely that there will be an expiration date on the offer as well. When he gets it, we'll review it together and look for anything that appears out of place, note any questions and determine if the offer falls within the range that Anthony and I discussed previously. If everything lines up, accepting the position should be pretty automatic. However, if he has questions about the offer or the benefits, he needs to ask before he signs. One of the advantages of discussing an offer with someone is getting the chance to practice asking questions. Once any questions are resolved and everything is clear, Anthony can sign the offer and accept the position. Of course, that doesn't mean that he's got the job, only that's he's agreed to the terms. He still has to wait out the contingencies.

For now though, Anthony can take a moment to bask in the glory of his pending offer. He's got some paperwork to do, a cup that needs filling and hopefully not too long to wait. It's going to be tough for him to keep networking and pushing his other leads but he knows he should. Nothing is certain yet and it can't hurt to try to increase the odds, especially now with one offer already on the way. In fact, having a pending offer may help him network with a little extra energy and confidence.

Now it's my turn. Or Tom's rather. I don't know if life is like this for everyone but in my little world it always seems like everything happens at the same time and everyone calls at once. It takes me a couple of rings to get to the phone and Tom is already talking fast when I pick up.

"Guess who just called!"

"I'm not much of a guesser but I'm hoping it was Carl."

"It sure was and it sounds like things are moving. He said that he's had opportunities to speak with everyone on the interview panel and that the feedback was all very positive."

"Fantastic. What else did he say?"

"Basically, he said that he felt very comfortable with the idea of having me join the team and he wanted to know if it was something I really wanted to do. I told him the same thing I told you, that the more I learned, the more I felt like this job was a great opportunity and that I would be excited to work with him and his team."

"Good answer. What happens next?"

"Well, it's a good thing we did all that preparation work. Carl couldn't get into any details but he said he's going to speak with Sheila in HR and that they will start putting together an offer. He just wanted to call to tell me himself and get my reaction. The official offer, all the paperwork and stuff will go through you."

"I like that he called you directly. The rest sounds pretty typical. And yes, it is a good thing we talked everything through ahead of time, isn't it? How did the call finish?"

"I did what we discussed. I told him that I was really glad that he called, that I was excited about the opportunity, and that I would look forward to hearing from you with the details. After that he gave me his email address and direct phone number and said if I had any questions or just wanted to talk about some of what's happening at the company I could call or email anytime. Then he repeated that they were really looking forward to having me on board. That was it."

"Okay, I'll wait to hear from Sheila and get with you as soon as I have some details. I'm sure you will have to complete an application, probably online, sign an authorization for a background check and perform a drug test. This is all pretty standard and I'll make sure you get everything and help you get through it. It will probably take a few days or more for them to produce the offer so we just need to hang in there for a little while. So far, things sound great though. What do you think? Are you excited?"

"Yes, I'm definitely excited and really curious. I can't believe I called you before I called my wife though!"

"Well, get off the phone with me and give her a call!"

Just like Anthony, Tom now knows that the company intends to make him an offer. It's exciting, not only for Tom but for me too. I did a lot of work to get us to this point. It may not seem like it but remember we're not talking about all of the things that failed. Still though, I have to keep us both grounded and make sure we get through everything.

Learning about a company's intent to make an offer doesn't always happen like this but its common enough. As we said previously, intent is great but it can be very dangerous. Sure, Carl is a VP and it's doubtful that anyone will block him from hiring for a critical position like this but it does happen. Companies announce hiring freezes all the time with little concern for unfilled positions or ongoing interviews. Carl's intent to make an offer doesn't guarantee that it will really happen. Our job, mine and Tom's, is to stay cool, make sure we're prepared and wait. Hopefully HR will call and start talking specifics soon but until they do, it is absolutely critical not to reveal anything that might disrupt the process.

Another reason that Tom's situation is different than Anthony's is because of his current position and the risks involved in leaving one job to take another. We need to be really sure that everything is okay with his offer and that all of the contingencies have been cleared before he even thinks about telling anyone or talking to his current employer. For him, this is not a time to celebrate. This is a time to be quiet, objective, patient and thorough.

For me on the other hand, just like I said to Anthony, this little waiting period is a good time to concentrate my effort and see if I can come up with any other options. It will take the company a couple of weeks to get everything together. The offer letter won't go out for a few days and we have to wait for the background check and drug test results. I doubt they'll bother with references but if they do, that too may add some time to the process. In the meantime, Tom's pending offer is a great reason to check back with a few of the more promising contacts from our original networking campaign. Recall, there were a handful of people who replied and said they might have something in a few months, or in the next quarter, or that they were thinking of creating a new position. The simple and direct email I'll send them effectively says:

> "Remember that guy I told you about? The one you said you might be interested in? I'm afraid he's getting an offer soon and may become unavailable. However, there's still enough time to make things happen and there's no harm in talking. Would you like me to setup a quick phone conversation?"

I'll add a little more detail to make sure they remember who I'm talking about but that's pretty much it. Action, action, action! No matter how it is phrased, this is what I want to make sure the recipients take from my message: The person they were interested in is also valued by other people, which is validating. Time is limited, however I can still put something together. A phone call to explore possibilities is harmless and easy to setup. This is a potentially high impact, immediate result message. The number of replies will be low but any hiring manager who does reply knows that he or she will need to act immediately and decisively.

As surprising as it is, I've been able to use small email campaigns like this to setup new telephone conversations and interviews. Once I was able to improve an existing offer by increasing competitive interest and another time I made an entirely new placement. In the second situation, the candidate's first offer was through another headhunter and I was able to get my client to act quickly enough to make a better offer before the first company completed the background check. The candidate was thrilled, I earned a commission after being sure I'd lost both candidate and commission, and my new client, with just a little prodding, got to hire a great candidate they would have otherwise lost. And, yes, we beat the other headhunter. What can I say? It's a competitive world. The important thing is recognizing that sometimes all it takes is a deadline to get someone to act. Obviously, only two incidences in almost 15 years is not a trend but those two placements represented over $50,000.00 in commissions for me. It's not something I'm going to forget. Nor should you.

How is the message I'm sending different than what you or Anthony could send in a similar situation?

As it has been with many of the tactics I've used, it's just not that different. My message is more direct and aggressive than what I would suggest a candidate send but the points to cover are the same. You want the recipient to know that you remain interested in them. You want them to know that you're valued by others too, possibly even their competitors or peers. There's a deadline now, since you're getting an offer. However, there's still time and a conversation is easy. A good way to put all of that might be something like this:

> "Hi (First Name),
>
> I wanted to check in with you regarding a potential opportunity you mentioned previously. I'm still very interested, however I am going to be receiving an offer from another company soon and may become unavailable. There's still time for us to talk though and, if you're interested, I'd welcome the opportunity.
>
> Sincerely, (Your Name)"

Remember, this is meant to be very action oriented and while there will be few if any replies that result in conversations, those that do have the potential to develop very quickly.

It took a while for Sheila to call so I had time to send a few emails about Tom's offer to some of the people from our original list. I don't know if anything will come of the effort but I'm a big believer in tangential results or unintended positives. For example, another of the messages I want to convey in the email about Tom's offer is that, as a recruiter, I work with high demand candidates who are good enough to get offers fast.

The instructions Sheila gave me are very similar to what the HR contact that Anthony spoke with told him. Tom will have to fill out an application and sign authorizations for background and credit checks. He'll get instructions about how to find a drug testing clinic in the Memphis area and complete the drug test. In a few days, Sheila will email me an offer letter that will include the job title, salary and bonus structure, and a potential start date. She says that she is meeting with Carl and the Sr. VP in the next day or two to talk about the numbers and that we'll see everything in the letter. Along with the letter will be a New Hire Relocation Guide that describes all of the services the company provides and their Benefits Handbook. They don't check references so we don't have to worry about that.

As I suggested to Tom and Anthony, during the call with Sheila I kept my responses short, acknowledged that I understood the process, ensured that I'll convey everything to Tom and that we will follow her directions. While it is important that I get all of the instructions right, it is also important to understand that Sheila's call to me is little more than another demonstration of intent. Until we see everything in writing, I need to be just as careful and patient as Tom or Anthony. During our call, I purposely neglected to ask Sheila for more details about the salary numbers or anything else that will be included in the actual offer letter.

Not only did she already tell me how things will happen, but more importantly, I know she's not a decision maker in this process. She may have input regarding the salary level and other compensation items but Carl makes the final decisions. It's not useful to press Sheila for more information than she has or do anything that might prove unhelpful later. Sheila and I need to work together to get this done. If I want her to work with me and treat me as a professional, then I need to make sure I am prepared before I start asking questions; which means waiting for the information, then reading everything and discussing it with Tom before doing anything.

It's more subtle, but I'm also trying to be empathetic and aware of the relationships between all of the people involved. That means thinking about Sheila's job as well. The fact is Sheila and I have a common goal. Her job exists in order to help hiring managers identify high quality candidates and fill critical positions. My job is also to identify high quality candidates and fill critical positions. We even have the same customer, Carl. Thinking of Sheila as an ally and acknowledging that we share a common goal will help keep our dialogue positive. By respecting her time and recognizing that Carl's job is probably not the only one she's working on I am demonstrating that I know how this process works. Hopefully, my efforts now will encourage her to respond quickly and clearly when I do have questions later. This may seem like the kind of thing that doesn't apply to individual job seekers but it does. Sheila's role is no different than that of the HR guy who called Anthony. He also is responsible for making sure jobs get filled. Anthony needs to help him get Kyle's job filled just as much as I need to help Sheila fill Carl's job. Anthony's HR contact and Sheila aren't decision makers in their respective processes. They didn't select the candidates that Carl and Kyle want to hire. Their job is making sure that the selected candidates get through the hiring process and are able to start as soon as possible. Without meaning to be repetitive, I think both Tom and Anthony are also pretty interested in getting through the hiring process and starting as soon as possible – me too!

How can Anthony help his HR contact? Empathy and understanding are good starting points. Anthony also needs to continue to have faith in the process.

"According to the letter, I'm going to be a 'Talent Acquisition Specialist Level 1.' They want me to start on Monday of the week after next, pending the results of the background check and drug test. Do you think the results will be in by then?"

"Probably, though if they aren't it's not a big deal. They'll just change the start date."

"So this is it, isn't it? I'm really almost there!"

"What do you think of the offer? Have you read the Benefits Handbook?"

"I read everything this morning and it seems clear enough. I'm fairly pleased with the salary level and the vacation and health insurance seem fine. Really, it's all pretty simple since I don't have dependents and I'm not moving."

"What were the numbers, if you don't mind me asking?"

"Oh, sure, of course, first, remember when I told you that my research suggested a range of somewhere between $33k and $40k per year, depending on the location and industry? Well, they came in almost in the middle at $36k. There's no bonus or anything so that's it. I think it is fine. Should I ask about annual increases? Is there anything else that I should look for in the offer letter or Benefits Handbook? What do I do next?"

"I'll read it to be sure, but if you're comfortable with everything, I think you're ready to sign it and send it back to them."

"Great! Wait, I do have one question. I don't think it is important for me right now but I'm curious anyways. Why does the offer letter have an expiration date? What would happen if I did have questions and ongoing discussions took us past the expiration date? Would I lose the offer?"

"That's a good question and a good reminder of something I've said throughout your entire job search. Remember, from an employer's standpoint, this job search is not about you. For them it's not even a job search, it's a candidate search. This is the last time I'll get to say it because now that you have a written offer, it is your decision. However until you're working there, they still have a job to fill. If for some reason you turned down the offer, they would have to go to the next candidate or start over. The reason there's an expiration date is so that they will know, one way or another, by a certain time. To answer your other question, I've never had a situation where a client let an offer expire or withdrew it while we were still talking. Like the proposed start date, if we couldn't get everything done on time, we just changed the expiration date."

"Okay, that makes sense and you're right, it does add one last bit of perspective. I have to say, all the time we've spent talking about how employers think about their jobs has really helped me. I never thought of the relationships and process like that before. Anyways, I guess I'm ready to sign the letter."

"Excellent. You've done a great job with everything and I'm really happy for you. I'll save my formal congratulations until after you've received the background check and drug test results and the references are all cleared. It looks like you're pretty much there though."

Despite how it may seem, the end is not anti-climactic for Anthony, however each step takes time and pin-pointing when it's over is tough. For my money, it's not over until I get paid. For Anthony, it's over when he receives written notification that the background check, drug test and reference checks are all completed. That's the moment his offer and acceptance become official. While it may seem like a detail, insisting on being notified in writing is important, even more so if you're leaving one job to take another. Having both an accepted offer and an email or letter that states that all the contingencies are cleared is the only way to move forward to the resignation process.

Getting the offer was exciting; it signaled the end-game but not the end. However it brought the finish line into view. Getting notice that the contingencies are out of the way, while not exactly an event, does mean that Anthony's got the job.

It was a few days before I heard from Anthony again. He didn't come flying through the phone to announce it this time either. Instead, I got a text message. The background check, drug test and references were all completed satisfactorily. Anthony has a job. As planned, he invited me to lunch to celebrate, and this time he paid!

Anthony's new job isn't just any job, it's the one that he wanted and pursued. He'll start working in a week and in a few more weeks he'll receive a paycheck for the first time in a good while. His whole life just changed. How cool is that?

Tom's offer isn't so simple. Despite the fact that the company knows his current compensation level and is probably aware that they have to improve upon it, there's always the possibility of a surprise. We've done our part though. Both Tom and I are comfortable with the numbers we've discussed and are prepared for anything.

The email I received from Sheila included everything that she said it would. The offer letter was in the body of the message and attached as a PDF file for printing and signing; the Benefits Handbook and New Hire Relocation Guide were there as well. The email was sent directly to me to forward to Tom. Before calling Tom with the news, I took a few minutes to read the offer letter, relocation guide and benefits summary in order to get familiar with the key elements.

The title is Senior Procurement and Materials Manager. The salary is $110k per year plus a bonus of 10%. The vacation allowance is for two weeks. The proposed start date is about three weeks from today and the offer expires in 72 hours.

The relocation policy is competitive and includes many of the same benefits I've seen in other large corporate relocation policies. They are offering to help him sell his current house and buy a new one in Houston. This includes payment for real estate closing costs on both the sale of his existing home and purchase of a new one, movement and 30 days of storage for their household goods, 30 days of temporary living in Houston for him and his family, and shipment of one personal vehicle. They outsource fulfillment of these services to a third-party provider and will set Tom up with an account manager if he accepts the offer.

The benefits also look competitive compared to other similar sized company benefits guides I've reviewed. Tom will need to go through it in detail and compare it to his current benefits package to see how they line up though.

Overall there is nothing shocking, which is good. There might even be some room to maneuver. Once he's read it, Tom and I will discuss everything and I suspect, respond to the company with some questions and requests. There's a lot of work to do here and the clock is ticking.

"I was kind of hoping for a little bit more."

"I understand. I think the best first step is for you to go ahead and read everything to get a feel for the whole package, including the relocation and benefits. Call me when you're done and we'll start to talk about the areas that you want to address. Don't worry, this is normal. We have time and can get more if necessary."

"Okay, that sounds good. Do you think they will be receptive to making changes if we want to go back to them about things like the salary level or some of the relocation items?"

"We'll do the work to get specific in our next call. The most important thing will be to make it easy for them. Think about it this way, their offer is the first real, tangible thing in this process. Up until now, we've been playing poker. You don't know if they have other candidates and they don't know if you will really take the job. However, by making an offer, the company has shown their cards. They have revealed that you're the candidate they would like to hire. Without getting carried away, their offer signifies a transfer of power."

"How do you mean?"

"For the first time in this process you are a decision maker. Obviously you could have withdrawn at any point, and that too would have been a decision. However, assuming you want the job, you don't really have any decisions to make until you get an offer. Without an offer, all of the decision making power is theirs. They could have stopped the interviews at any time. Keep in mind however, your offer doesn't mean you're the only decision maker. For example, they have decided that your offer should expire in 72 hours. They can also decide not to make any changes or offer the position to someone else."

"Right, I understand. So, how do we approach this?"

"We need to keep their goal in mind when we go back to them. Remember, their goal is hiring a Senior Procurement and Materials

Manager. By making you an offer, they are telling us that hiring you is the easiest way for them to satisfy their goal. That doesn't mean that you're the only person they could hire but the offer is a commitment. Now that they've made it, it's up to us to show them that adjusting it, if necessary, is still the easiest path to achieving their goal."

"That makes sense. How do we keep this easy and still get them to make changes?"

"When we talk again later one of things we'll do is list all of the different moving parts included in the offer. This means the salary, bonus, vacation, items in the relocation package and potentially specific benefits. We'll talk about what's good and what's lacking and rank them based on importance. Then we'll develop a strategy for how to frame your requests and how to respond to their actions. As you can imagine, some of the moving parts are easier to adjust than others. The key to keeping this easy is having a sense of where they have the most latitude to make changes and where they don't."

"Do you think it will work?"

"It seems like the interviews went really well and that Carl is pretty interested. In the end, he'll make his decision based on several things, including what you're asking about specifically, how well you guys have connected so far and the prospect of having to start over if this fails. It will also depend on how we present everything. Don't worry, I have some ideas on how to handle it."

"Okay, let me read it all and I'll get back to you in a little bit."

I tell every candidate I work with that their goal should be to get into a position where they will get a chance to make a decision. The only way to do that is to get an offer. Anything other than receiving an offer means that the company has decided for you. Tom and I have reached that point. He's got an offer. He doesn't have to accept it but had we not done the work to get here, he wouldn't even have the choice. Now that we're here we have the opportunity to see if we can make it work.

Tom's offer has three main components: Compensation, Relocation and Benefits. Each main component is made up of smaller separate items, some of which are the moving parts I mentioned earlier. Compensation, for example, includes the salary, bonus percentage and vacation allowance. Relocation consists of home sales assistance, realtor fee reimbursements, movement of personal property and temporary living. Health insurance, sick or personal day allowances, pension or 401k plans are all benefits. Specifically, Tom's offer looks like this:

Compensation:

- Salary: $110k per year

- Bonus: (up to) 10% per year

- Vacation: 2 weeks per year

Relocation Package:

- Miscellaneous Expenses: $1000.00

- Real Estate Closing Fees (Buying and Selling): Paid

- Temporary Living: 30 Days

- Storage of Personal Goods: 30 Days

- Vehicle Shipping: 1x Paid

Benefits:

- Eligibility for medical, dental and vision, accidental death and dismemberment, long term disability, and employee, spouse and child life insurance

- Eligibility to participate in the company's retirement and savings plan 401k with up to 4% matching contributions from the company

- Five personal or sick days

Not all of the items listed above are moving parts. Some of them are universal for all employees, like the number of sick days. Other parts of the offer are based on the level of the job like the bonus percentage, some of the health and wellness benefits, and the percentage of matching contributions to the 401k or retirement plan. These items typically can't be changed for individual employees and companies rarely negotiate them. If there are gaps it is typically easier for an employer to find a way to compensate using one of the other more flexible items.

In Tom's offer, we believe the parts with the most elasticity, the moving parts that we'll focus on, include the salary level – to a point, the amount of vacation, the miscellaneous expense allowance and the time limits for both personal goods storage and temporary living.

The salary level is only really negotiable to a point because in larger companies the specific job levels come with defined salary ranges. Ideally, employers like to hire people in the lower-middle or middle of a defined range, anticipating that the person will be there for a few years and receive annual salary increases. Hiring someone at the high end of the range can result in lower percentage annual increases which might cause them to become dissatisfied and leave the company.

Because I marketed Tom into the company without having an assigned job, I was never made aware of the salary range for the position. We don't know if his offer is in the lower, middle or higher parts of the range. Moving forward, we'll operate as if it's is in the middle though. As I said, companies are reluctant to hire people at the top of the range and both Tom and I believe his experience level and current compensation put him above the lower end.

Salary level is important to Tom. When we talk about it, he says it's his highest priority item since the starting salary forms the base from which all of his future increases will be determined. He wants to join the company with the highest salary he can get. He also feels strongly about getting another week of vacation. He has three weeks' vacation now and really wants to avoid taking a step back. Tom and his wife agreed that they would really like the company to provide an opportunity for them to travel to Houston on a house-hunting trip too. The location of Tom's potential new office is important on a lot of levels and they want a chance to take a look before making a final commitment. Some of the other things Tom mentioned were that the miscellaneous expense amount, at $1000.00, seemed low and that when he joined his current company they provided up to 60 days of temporary living and personal goods storage. He'd like to ask about both of those things too.

When we're all done going through the offer letter, the New Hire Relocation Guide and the Benefits Handbook, we have a pretty good list of items we'd like to explore. We are also pretty sure that we've picked the items with the most potential flexibility.

Now we need to do two more things: Get specific and prioritize. We don't want to go to the company with an open list of items and make them figure out what Tom wants. Instead, our chances will be greatly increased if we do the work to show them exactly what they have to do to get what they want. Tom and I also need to agree about which items are the most important, the ones that will kill the whole deal unless they are addressed and which items might have potential for compromise if his exact requests can't be met. When we talk about it, Tom reiterates that his highest priority is the salary level. After that he wants more vacation, the house-hunting trip and adjustments on the miscellaneous expense, temporary living and storage allowances, in that order.

For us to cover all of the potential variables, we need to also consider what happens if the company can only partially accommodate Tom's desires. Will he turn down the job if they can't provide a house-hunting trip but can meet his salary request? What if they can't increase the salary but can add a week of vacation, provide additional funds for the miscellaneous expense allowance, and extend the temporary living and personal goods storage times? What if he can get everything but the additional week of vacation? It's hard to predict every possible combination of potential responses however we can discuss the options and define some limitations. To make this simple, I typically suggest categorizing items into four areas: "Deal Closers," meaning changes that will result in automatic acceptance; "Compromises," for adjustments that get close enough to say yes; "Giveaways," for things that are not that important and won't impact the final decision; and "Showstoppers," for items that, left unchanged, will result in turning down the offer.

For example, Tom feels very strongly about the salary. His current salary is $100k and his current bonus is payable up to 15%, making his total compensation potential around $115k per year. The new offer comes with a base salary of $110k and a bonus of up to 10% for a total compensation potential of approximately $121k. While this only represents an increase in total compensation of around 5%, the amount of guaranteed income, the salary, is 10% higher. Still, even though the total falls in between his drop dead number and his goal number, Tom says it is just not enough to justify relocating and changing everything. He would like to see the salary level at $120k. He says that if they can increase the salary to $120k per year it's a "Deal Closer" even without adjustments on any of the other items. However, if they can't do anything about the salary level, it's a "Showstopper" no matter what other changes they make.

300

Vacation is a little bit different. I explain to Tom that some companies have the ability to recognize years of experience with previous employers and give seniority to new hires making them eligible for additional vacation. Hopefully, that will be the case here. However, sometimes there is no official way to grant additional vacation time so we have to find alternative ways to address the issue. The most common is to simply discuss it with the hiring manager and informally agree to allow for additional days out on request. If this sounds loose, it is because it is. That said, I've been involved in negotiations where a handshake agreement regarding extra days off is the only way we can move forward. It won't show up in a revised offer letter or in a personnel file but it can work. Tom says that he could be receptive to either solution regarding vacation time, particularly if there are positive adjustments in other areas. Vacation is not a "Giveaway" but he is willing to compromise.

Despite their strong desire to have it, Tom views the house-hunting trip as optional. Depending on how the company handles the other items, the trip might be something they could do on their own. For him, it's a potential "Giveaway" depending on everything else.

On the relocation items, Tom would like the company to match what his current employer provided when they relocated to Memphis. Their relocation benefit included a miscellaneous expense allowance of $2500.00 and up to 60 days for both temporary living and storage of personal goods. It's not a "Showstopper" but it is important.

That's our list, from highest priority to lowest, including "Deal Closers, Compromises, Giveaways and Showstoppers."

Number one is the salary. Tom is committed to accepting the position if we can get the offer increased to $120k from $110k. Next is vacation, he's earned three weeks' worth over the years and wants to keep it. The house-hunting trip is important but they could live without it or do it on their own if it became a sticking point. They do think they'll need help on the relocation expenses and worry that 30 days is not enough time to get into a new house. Getting improvements would be a real positive, but again, depending on the other items, they might compromise.

With some flexibility, Tom's ideal offer looks like this:

Compensation:

- Salary: $120k per year (an increase of $10k over the original offer)

- Bonus: (up to) 10% per year (no change)

- Vacation: 3 weeks per year (an increase of one week over the original offer)

- House-Hunting Trip: 3 days, 2 nights including flights, hotel and rental car (new addition)

Relocation Package:

- Miscellaneous Expenses: $2500.00 (an increase of $1500.00 over the original offer)

- Real Estate Closing Fees (Buying and Selling): Paid (no change)

- Temporary Living: 60 Days (an increase of 30 days over the original offer)

- Storage of Personal Goods: 60 Days (an increase of 30 days over the original offer)

- Vehicle Shipping: 1x Paid (no change)

Benefits: (no changes on any item)

- Eligibility for medical, dental and vision, accidental death and dismemberment, long term disability, and employee, spouse and child life insurance

- Eligibility to participate in the company's retirement and savings plan 401k with up to 4% matching contributions from the company

- Five personal or sick days

Notice there are only changes in the items that we felt had some level of flexibility. Tom understood what I meant when we talked about it and is familiar enough with corporate compensation structures to know that things like the bonus percentage and the benefits items have less potential for individual adjustment.

Now that we know exactly what it will take to make this work we need to see if the company is receptive to making the necessary changes. We've come a long way and Tom doesn't want to jeopardize the offer so we need to be careful. At the same time, as it is, it is just not enough. Going back to what I said previously, our best chance for success will be to keep this easy. They've told us what they want and we're going to show them how to get it. To do this well we need to consider not only how we present Tom's requests but also to whom.

One aspect of this project that is different for me, but actually makes it more relevant to individual job seekers, is the fact that I'm not dealing with the hiring manager directly. Usually I act as a buffer between the two and negotiate with the hiring manager myself. However this time, my contacts are Paul, the Director of Sourcing, and Sheila in Human Resources. Neither of them are the decision makers for this job and I've promised not to contact the hiring manager, Carl, who is the ultimate decision maker. Because the most direct communications are the easiest and often most effective, it would be best to approach Carl instead of going through either Sheila or Paul. Speaking with either Sheila or Paul first means that we would be relying on them to make our case to Carl as convincingly as either Tom or I might. That would be a mistake. At the same time, if I contact Carl directly, not only would I be breaking my promise to Paul but I'd also be going around Sheila. Neither of those things will help our chances. Instead, Tom and I decide that since he and Carl seem to have established a good rapport, it would be best for him to call Carl directly and present his requests. Tom says he can do it as long as we prepare.

There is one method of negotiating in situations like this that has been more effective for me than anything else. It goes back to what we've been saying all along, showing the customer, in this case Carl specifically, and the company overall, the fastest and easiest way to get what they want. Tom will be most successful in his negotiation if the first thing he says makes Carl happy.

Think of it like taking the classic If / Then statement and turning it around. An If / Then statement defines an event or a set of circumstances that will bring about a certain outcome. For example: If I win the lottery, then I will buy a new car. The event is winning the lottery. The outcome is buying a new car. Turning it into a Then / If statement results in a sentence like this: I will buy a new car if I win the lottery. By turning it around, the outcome is first and the circumstance that creates it is second.

How does this apply to negotiating with a potential employer? Again, what will be the first thing Tom says when he calls Carl? Tom is going to tell Carl that he will be able to accept the offer and then he'll define the circumstances. What Carl will hear first is that he's going to get what he wants; Tom is going to join the team. Carl's candidate search will be over and everyone will be able to go back to focusing on the greater mission.

By immediately telling Carl that he will be able to accept the position, Tom is starting the conversation with a strong positive statement. Specifically, when we talk about his opening statement, I tell Tom he needs to be definitive and clear about what he intends to do. He needs to say something like:

> "Thank you for the offer. I'm really excited about the opportunity and am looking forward to joining the team. I will be able to accept the position and start as soon as possible if…"

Starting with a strong positive statement is engaging instead of being confrontational or adversarial. It reinforces the idea that everyone wants the same thing. This is subtle. The difference between starting out with a positive statement and a negative statement can hinge on a single word. For example, the word "if" that sets up the second part of the statement is a lot different than the word "but."

"If" is a word filled with possibilities. Using "if" to transition into the second part of the statement promises solutions and puts both parties on the same side of the equation.

> "I can accept the job and start in two weeks if…"

"But" highlights separation and differences. Using "but" to transition into the second part of the statement divides the candidate from the company by stressing what's wrong with the offer without promising solutions.

> "This is a good offer but…"

> "I really want to do this but…"

> "I appreciate the offer but…"

Even if it is spelled out later, the negotiation still will have started from the negative and the company will not feel as good about it had they heard a positive, solution oriented opening at the beginning.

The "if" transition sets up the next part of the equation where Tom will define the circumstances that will make the offer successful.

"...if we can make the following small changes..."

Again, subtlety, using the word "small" to describe the changes Tom wants helps minimize them. Tom and I did a lot of work to try to ensure that his requests are actually small and, hopefully, easy for Carl to fulfill. The fact is, if the gaps in the offer weren't small, we wouldn't even be talking. Tom would turn the offer down and we would all move on. We never expected that to happen though because – why? Going all the way back to the first chapter, everything we did to get here was done to mitigate the risk of failure and help make sure that we ended up in the right place, with the right company and hopefully the right job. The differences between the offer Tom received and the offer he wants are indeed small.

When he gets to his if transition with Carl, Tom will need to be exact. His statement started with a definitive action, that he will accept the position and join the team under certain circumstances. To maintain the clarity and strength of the statement, Tom now needs to define the circumstances just as specifically. Part of making this easy for Carl includes showing him that we've made the effort to figure it out already. We don't want Carl to exit the call wondering what he has to do to make the offer work. We're going to tell him.

This is what Tom and I agree he should say:

> "Thank you for the offer. I'm really excited about the
> opportunity and am looking forward to joining the
> team. I will be able to accept the position and start as

soon as possible if we can make the following small changes: I would like the salary level to be $120k, three weeks of vacation to match my current allotment, up to 60 days of temporary living and personal goods storage, and a relocation expense allowance of $2500.00. We would also really like an opportunity to come out and look at housing and schools in the area. If we can do this I'm ready to sign on and start as soon as possible."

He may not get the wording exactly like this; every conversation is different, however this is the message he needs to convey in the most concise and efficient way possible. And, importantly, once he's said it he needs to stop talking. This is critical. If Tom continues to talk after he's made his Then / If statement he will weaken his position. Almost anything he might continue to say could be heard as a justification. As it is, we've only justified his request for additional vacation by referring to his current level of vacation. Trying to justify his other requests only opens them up for further conversation. To be most effective, Tom needs to let his requests stand on their own and wait to hear how Carl responds before adding anything more.

Knowing when to stop talking during negotiations is one of the most difficult things I've had to learn. It's really hard to let a pause happen in a conversation like this, especially on the phone. Tom and I have worked so hard and are so close that the temptation to keep talking after the initial statement is almost irresistible. If Tom does continue talking, or if it's me, or you doing the talking and we don't stop, almost inevitably we will set ourselves up for a premature compromise and negotiate away some portion of our requests. In Tom's case he might slip up and fill the silence by saying something like maybe the house-hunting trip isn't that important, or that they could probably find a new home in 30 days or less and perhaps won't need extra time for temporary living and personal goods storage. Compromising now, before Carl has a chance to reply, means that there will be fewer items to give away later and that future compromises might be more painful.

Once Tom has made his Then / If statement and explained to Carl how to get what he wants, Tom needs to wait and let Carl respond. We don't know if Carl will want to go through each item on the phone with Tom immediately, if he'll want to consider everything before getting back to Tom, or if he'll propose a counter offer right away. Tom is prepared in any event though. We defined his fallback positions when we discussed the moving parts of the offer. Tom is ready with his "Deal Closers, Compromises, Giveaways and Showstoppers." He knows how he will respond to almost any combination of proposed changes or lack thereof. Officially, no matter how the call concludes, Tom will still say that he is looking forward to seeing any revisions in writing.

Why do we do it this way?

There is no question that calling first is better than just sending an email. Tom will follow up with an email to Carl after the call, but he'll start with the call. Calling is more personal, cordial and dynamic and has the potential for faster and better results.

Presenting his requests in a Then / If statement is designed to do two things, first, to make it easy for the customer, in this case, Carl, to see the solution, and second, to avoid a prolonged, vague or unproductive set of conversations. We want to get this done quickly and I'm sure the company does too. If we enter into this discussion without specifics or rely on the company to try to figure out how to make the offer work, things may drag on and make it more difficult to start the job amicably once the negotiations are finished. We want the company to recognize that we've made the effort to show them what needs to be done and that we've demonstrated a commitment to accepting the position. They may come back a little lower than what Tom wants or perhaps can't make all of the changes he requested but he knows his limitations and how he'll respond, from compromising to turning the job down completely.

Starting with a strong positive statement does not guarantee that you will get everything you want. The definitive way of saying it I described sounds like an ultimatum but you still retain the final decision even if they come back with less. If they say, "We can't do that" after you've said, "I can accept the position and start as soon as possible if..." then what do you do? Just like Tom, you go to your pre-defined set of "Deal Closer, Compromise, Giveaway and Showstopper" scenarios to see what combination of things works or doesn't work and then act.

Negotiating means offering something in exchange for what you want. Using the Then / If approach does that. The final and most important thing a candidate has to offer is their acceptance. No company wants to start the interview process all over again. If you can offer an acceptance and a guaranteed start date in exchange for a realistic and reasonable increase in compensation or one of the other items included in an offer, more often than not, it is in the company's best interest to accept your proposal. However, negotiating can be risky. In conservative markets, where jobs are scarce, companies might have backup candidates identified and would rather move on than negotiate at all. Any negotiating has to be done carefully and expectations or requirements must be reasonable. Otherwise, the company will simply continue to the next candidate.

Forget about the concept of Win / Win. Expect to compromise and focus on the larger, long term target. In fact, expect everyone to compromise to get what they want. I've never been in a successful negotiation where all of the parties felt like they won. We might have achieved the goal, and if we did, we did it by compromising. Identifying one party as the winner suggests that the other party lost. The goal however was filling the job and if we reached an agreement, we satisfied the goal. Maybe the candidate got a little less than they wanted or the company had to pay a little more but in achieving our goal, we didn't create any winners and losers, we worked together to get the job done. Nobody won but everyone got what they wanted.

That semi unsatisfied feeling you may have, that feeling that maybe you left a little something on the table but you still got the job, that feeling you noticed in the last handshake, call or email, where you pushed it and they pushed it and now everyone is glad it's done but not super-duper jumping up and down excited, that's success.

Accepting or declining a job is a very personal thing. You have to decide if you can live with an offer or if it is better to walk away.

Chapter 15: Final Offer and Resignation

"Well, I did what we talked about and now I guess we'll wait and see what happens."

"Did Carl give any indication of what they might be able to do?"

"Not specifically. He said he understood my requests, wanted me to email him so he'd have everything in writing and then he said he'd get back to me."

"How was his tone? Did he say anything to make you believe that he could or couldn't make adjustments?"

"I think we both played it pretty tight. Like you suggested, I stopped talking after I made my opening statement. There was a little bit of silence. I could tell that he was waiting to see if I would say anything else or give any indication of compromising. When I didn't, he repeated that he'd like me to send him my list. He didn't sound too stressed or anything, almost like he expected us to come back with some requests."

"Good. How did the call end?"

"He finished up by saying that they definitely wanted me on board and was hopeful this would be sorted out as soon as possible. He said he'd talk to Sheila and that one of them would contact us in a day or two. I said that sounded great and that I'll look forward to hearing from them. That was it."

"Okay, so he didn't say no to everything out of hand and sounded somewhat receptive. I'll be curious see what they do. Call me if you hear something and I'll do the same."

It didn't take long for Sheila to get in touch with me. She wanted to go over some of Tom's requests and see if there were any flexibilities, as well as discuss some of their limitations before re-typing the offer letter. She would have called Tom directly and had the same conversation with him if there wasn't a recruiter involved. Essentially, this is another negotiation. However, this time, I have even less to say. The same would be true for Tom if he was on the call. The requests have been made and it's time for us to listen to their response.

Sheila was pretty much all business and dove right into the numbers. They expected us to request an increase in salary but can only add another $5k taking the total to $115k. I didn't really respond when she said it, honestly thinking she would keep talking and address the other items, but she didn't initially. Instead she asked if I thought $115k would work. Sensing a small opportunity, I very politely replied, that Tom was hoping for $120k and immediately stopped talking. There was a pause and then she spoke first and said that they could offset the difference with a $5k sign-on bonus if I thought it would help. I don't think she would have volunteered that were it not for the pause. The sign-on bonus is not exactly what Tom wanted but I told her I thought it would work depending on the rest of the items on the list. Everything else was pretty easy. They recognized Tom's work history and experience level and increased his vacation to three weeks. Doubling the temporary living and personal goods storage to 60 days was something they did regularly and again, was not a problem. We got a little stuck on the miscellaneous expense allowance but we still got it up to $2k from $1k. Regarding the house-hunting trip, Sheila said that they can provide it but only after Tom has signed the offer letter accepting the position and has cleared the drug test and background check. I told her I thought that sounded fair considering the improvements they were able to make to the original offer. Sheila said she would have the revised offer letter out to me before the end of the day would like to hear back from Tom in 24 hours or less.

With the changes that we discussed, Tom's new offer looks like this:

Compensation:

- Salary: $115k per year (an increase of $5k over the original offer)

- Bonus: (up to) 10% per year (no change)

- Vacation: 3 weeks per year (an increase of one week over the original offer)

- House-Hunting Trip: 3 days, 2 nights including flights, hotel and rental car (new addition)

- $5k Sign-On Bonus (new addition)

Relocation Package:

- Miscellaneous Expenses: $2000.00 (an increase of $1000.00 over the original offer)

- Real Estate Closing Fees (Buying and Selling): Paid (no change)

- Temporary Living: 60 Days (an increase of 30 days over the original offer)

- Storage of Personal Goods: 60 Days (an increase of 30 days over the original offer)

- Vehicle Shipping: 1x Paid (no change)

Benefits: (no changes on any item)

- Eligibility for medical, dental and vision, accidental death and dismemberment, long term disability, and employee, spouse and child life insurance

- Eligibility to participate in the company's retirement and savings plan 401k with up to 4% matching contributions from the company

- Five personal or sick days

I received the revised offer letter in an email from Sheila about an hour after our call ended. It contained everything we talked about, with the addition of the sign-on bonus, post acceptance house-hunting trip and the new 24 hour deadline. I called Tom immediately, told him the good news and alerted him to the check his email and call me back after he'd read everything. It didn't take long.

"We're going to do it. We just talked it over and we're both pretty excited."

"Great! I'm glad to hear it!"

"Obviously, I was hoping for a higher salary but it looks like they made a good effort with the $5k increase and the sign-on bonus."

"We knew there could be resistance on the salary so the sign-on bonus was a nice touch. Sometimes that's an easy way for a company to work around salary limitations."

"I think with that, getting to keep three weeks of vacation, as well as having extra time on the relocation stuff, it all comes together. So what do I do now?"

"Let's do two things. First, print, sign and scan the revised offer letter so you have a signed version as a PDF file that you can email to Carl, Sheila and me. Then I think you should call Carl and tell him that you're accepting the revised offer and can't wait to get to work. That will make him happy. I'll call Sheila to let her know to look out for the signed offer letter from you. I'll also check on the status of the background check and drug test results to see where we stand. You completed everything, right? Getting the contingencies cleared is our next step."

"Yes, I did my part for the application, drug test and background check when I got the original offer paperwork. We're just waiting on them. How long do you think it will take?"

"I would hope less than a week since it's already been a few days. In the meantime, we need to keep this quiet. You can't tell anyone at your current company and I would go further and advise not sharing this with anyone outside of your immediate family. Please remember your offer only becomes official when we have written verification that the background check and drug test results are cleared. I can't imagine anything happening to jeopardize things but it is smart to play it cool and wait."

"Got it. I'll follow your lead on this."

"Great. Sheila will send me an email as soon as she has the results. That's all we need. I'll forward it to you and then we can confirm the start date and start talking about the resignation process."

"I guess we still have a little ways to go, don't we?"

"We're almost there. It's a little too early to celebrate but we're past the hard part!"

Confidentiality has been important throughout the process with Tom. He's currently employed so we've worked hard to keep his entire job search as discreet as possible. The fact that he's accepted an offer doesn't change anything because we are not done. I know he wants to tell people, maybe some colleagues or friends in Houston, but as I said when we spoke, it's much smarter not to.

I've never had a situation where a candidate didn't clear the background check or drug test but there could always be a first time. The possibility alone merits attention. Imagine, you've just signed an offer letter and accepted a new position. Not thinking, you mention it to someone in passing and word gets out at your current company. Your boss doesn't appreciate the fact that you've been looking for another job and decides to take the opportunity to terminate your position. Then you find out that for some reason there's a flag on your background check, something about your credit history, more than likely an error, but even so, all of a sudden, your accepted offer is in danger. Sure, the chances are slim but if this happened, it would be a lousy way to become unemployed.

The job search process wouldn't require a whole book if there weren't a lot of important details. That holds true all the way through to the very end. This little part, the quiet time between agreeing to terms and accepting an offer and waiting for clearance on any contingencies, is a step just like all the others. Getting a new job is a big deal and there's a time for telling everyone. It's just not yet.

The time stamp on Sheila's latest email told me she was up late but I was glad her message was the first thing I saw in the morning. It was good news and she wanted to share it right away. Tom's background check and drug test results came back and everything is fine. His offer is cleared and they want him to start as soon as possible. In my reply I told her that I really appreciated her sending me this in an email instead of just calling and that I would relay the news to Tom immediately.

Why is it so important to have this in writing? Remember, earlier, I said anything can happen. I don't know what the possibilities are, but I want this in writing for protection, for both Tom and myself, because the next thing I'm going to do is help Tom quit his job.

No candidate should ever leave his or her current job without being 100% in-writing sure that their offer is official and that all of the contingencies are cleared. Having it spelled out in an email from a responsible company representative is just as good as having a letter. No matter what the format, before anyone resigns from anything, we have to be absolutely sure.

Before we get into that though, it's time for me to give Tom a call, in fact, my favorite call:

"Congratulations! You're now officially the new Sr. Procurement and Materials Manager at (undisclosed company)! I got an email from Sheila last night confirming that the background check and drug test results are in and everything is fine. The offer is cleared. I'm forwarding her email to you now."

"Awesome! Awesome! Awesome!"

"This is it. We've got a few more things to do but you've made it. I need to get back to Sheila with a specific start date so we'll talk about that and we'll also want to discuss your resignation to make sure things go smoothly."

"No problem. Let me call my wife to tell her the good news and I'll call you right back. This is great! I'm really excited and we both can't wait to get there."

The company wants Tom to start on a Monday. They have an on-boarding process that all new hires go through that includes completing the paperwork for setting up payroll and benefits and a tour of the local facilities. He'll also need to give two weeks' notice to his current employer and take a few days to get things together at home ahead of the trip to Houston. That puts his start date about three weeks out. After confirming the date with the company, the next step for Tom is resigning from his current position.

Resigning from a job represents a big change and as much as it might be goal for some, it's not always an easy thing to do. No matter how much you may dislike your current job, if you've been there a while you've established relationships. We spend a lot of time at work and it is a core part of our daily lives. Leaving colleagues, a manager or mentor, and familiar routines is stressful. Confronting your boss and telling them that you're moving on can be uncomfortable, no matter how much you want to do it.

When Tom and I talked about his resignation he told me that it's really important for him to help his team and manager transition his work to other people. They've all been good to him and he wants to make sure he doesn't leave them with a mess. His boss specifically has been like a mentor over the last few years and they've become friends. He's not looking forward to telling him but he's determined to move on.

Like everything else, resigning is also part of Tom's overall job search. His impetus from the very beginning was to leave this job to go to another one. From my own perspective, I don't consider the process complete until Tom is started at the new company and working, and later again, after I've been paid. That means resigning from his current position is one more thing we need to manage. Our desired outcome is for Tom's resignation to be as painless as possible, that he's able to depart on a positive note with his relationships intact, and that he doesn't leave things worse than when he started. How do we achieve this?

As he mentioned previously, Tom has had a good run with his current company and gets along well with the other team members and managers. He wants to do the right thing and offer them two weeks' notice so he can help with the changeover. Most of the time, two weeks are really all that is necessary. I've worked with plenty of candidates who thought they needed more than two weeks only to later realize that they are no longer as critical by the end of the first week. People move on, companies transition. I've also had candidates who were escorted out of their offices immediately after resigning despite offering two weeks' notice. This happens in situations when someone goes to a competing company or sometimes in a secretive industry. I still suggest that every candidate plan for and offer two weeks.

Beyond providing an adequate notice and transition period, Tom wants the process to go cleanly without an ongoing discussion during his last couple of weeks. He tells me that he's worried that his boss will keep bugging him about staying on and that will make him uncomfortable. He and his family want to go to Houston and he's made a commitment. He's hopeful that his boss will respect that but not sure how to communicate it.

From a process standpoint, there are a few key steps we can take to influence how things go. The first is his resignation letter. A resignation letter needs to be clear, concise and leave no room for misinterpretation. In his, Tom needs to state that he is resigning his position, that this letter serves as notification and that his last day will be two weeks from the day he presents the letter. He should also stress the finality of his decision. Lastly, he wants to express how much he appreciated the opportunity to work with everyone and that he wants to spend the two week notice period helping with the transition. For reference, I sent Tom the following sample letter containing all of the important elements:

(Greeting and Name),

This letter serves as my formal notice of resignation of my position at ABC Corporation. With two weeks' notice, my last day of employment will be Friday, Month / Date / Year. During the next two weeks, I will do my best to help ensure a smooth transition.

Please understand, my decision to leave was not made lightly. I believe that this move will be good for my family and beneficial in helping me reach my career goals.

Thank you for all of the support that you have shown me during my employment here. I've enjoyed working with you and value our relationship.

Sincerely, (Your Name)

Everything is included and the letter itself is short, clear and to the point. Tom should use his own language to make the letter more personal but he doesn't have to add anything else.

The next step is figuring out the timing. The company already said that they would like Tom to start on a Monday, and in addition to the two weeks' notice, Tom needs to get himself from Memphis to Houston. We have a little over three weeks until the proposed start date. Ideally, Tom will be able to setup a time to meet with his boss in person on the next Friday or Monday. Fridays and Mondays are best for resigning for several reasons. Recall, Tom has some concern about his boss trying to convince him to stay during the notice period. Picking the right day and time to resign can help mitigate some of that and help everyone concentrate on what needs to be done. If Tom can meet with his boss to resign and present his letter on a Friday afternoon, his boss will have the whole weekend to let it sink in, hopefully returning on Monday having accepted the fact that Tom's leaving. As a second option, if Tom can meet with his boss on Monday morning, he can immediately start talking about how his departure impacts their plans for the week to try to get things focused. Either of these are better options than doing it in the middle of the week. As well, resigning on a Friday afternoon or Monday morning makes his last day a Friday adding the following weekend to his preparation time. As always, in person is better than over the phone and over the phone is better than via email.

What will he say? Tom tells me this is the hardest part. It makes sense, Tom likes his manager and for him, this is not good news. It can be an uncomfortable situation. The key to diffusing this stress is empathy. Tom wasn't sure what I meant when I first said it but when I asked him how long he's known his current boss the light bulb went off. Tom met him when he joined the company as his new Director, which means he made a move to get there, resigning from a previous job to take a new job. He did what Tom's doing. In fact, everyone has. When Tom puts it to him that way, he'll understand. When he emphasizes that he's thought about it and is sure that it's what he wants to do, it will sink in. When he promises to help avoid a mess, it will be appreciated.

Specifically, Tom can start the conversation with a statement as simple as this:

> "I've just accepted a position at another company and
> my last day will be two weeks from today."

No matter how he says it, just like in the letter, Tom needs to be clear and direct. The other elements he needs to employ in the conversation are also the same as what he used in the letter. State the facts, reiterate the thought that went into it, emphasize the finality of the decision, express gratitude for the experience and focus on the transition.

It's important to stress the finality of the decision in order to help stave off counter offers and ongoing pressure. Nobody wants to spend their two week notice period having their decision questioned by his or her manager. As a recruiter, I've seen the articles describing the perils of counter offers and have experienced it first hand through candidates who have received them. I can't say definitively that every counter offer is bad, however I will say that unless it specifically addresses a person's original motivation for looking, it probably won't work out over long term. Most of the counter offers I've seen haven't done that, despite often including more money, a change in title, or even position. I've never worked with someone for whom money, or short term compensation, was the only motivating factor and many of the other things can come off as reactionary and not genuine. If the main reasons for seeking a new job are things like growth opportunities, increased stability, a different location or industry type, and money; then most of the time a counter offer won't make a difference.

I've only had one candidate accept a counter offer. It was late in my first year as a headhunter, I was still working at the firm and I really needed a commission. I remember being so excited when all the background checks were finished and we fixed the start date, imagining out loud how I would spend every penny of my pending paycheck. I really believed we solved every problem and that the deal was done.

He had already resigned and was in the second week of his notice period when it happened. The VP from corporate personally offered to increase his salary by fifty percent and add the word "Senior" to the beginning of his title if he would just stay on. This was in the nineties in the PC industry and companies were growing like weeds. My client was a big Houston based name brand company that was expanding their supply chain team to support ongoing growth. The position was for a Global Commodity Manager for Hard Disk Drives with an annual spend responsibility into the hundreds of millions. My candidate was in southern California at a much smaller PC maker. He had exactly the right experience and was admittedly underpaid. It was a great match. The interviews went really well and the company made a compelling offer. He accepted it without negotiating and we set about completing the process as normal. He assured me that there was nothing that could keep him from the new job.

Nobody expected him to get a counter offer with increase that big. On one hand it was a significant amount of money. On the other hand, had I had more experience, I would have seen it for what it really was – a warning – and given better advice. In the end, I lost the commission. It hurt. My candidate took the counter offer and stayed in the old job. The client understood that it was out of my control and the amount of the counter offer was more than they were willing to match, so they let it go. It was easy for them. I didn't get the paycheck I needed so badly and worse, because of the amount of money and drama involved, and my excitement about getting paid, the whole thing became one of those bull pen stories that the other recruiters never forgot. It was so bad that the candidate's name became a euphemism for worst case scenario counter offer situations. Topping it all off, I heard from the candidate six months later. His job at the original company was eliminated soon after the supply chain issues with Hard Disk Drives were resolved. His salary simply didn't match up with his peers and they didn't have another position for him. He was out of work and looking for a new job.

I told Tom this story too. We've been working together for quite a few weeks now so he's used to my stories. To reassure me, he said counter offers like that never happen in his industry so he's not too concerned. I told him I knew that and wasn't worried but then, in retribution for making him listen to another story, he half-jokingly added "but you never know."

"I wonder what he's going to say when I tell him I've just accepted another offer."

"I'd guess the first thing he'll do is ask if you're sure, or if there's anything they can do to keep you. It's a natural reaction and you should expect it and be prepared to respond. This is a good time to emphasize that you are sure and that your decision is final. After that, the next thing to do is to start talking about helping with the transition."

"What should I tell him when he asks where I'm going?"

"It's up to you, but if it were me, I'd default to the idea that your job search and our process is not done until you're working at the new company, so caution is the rule. You're not going to a direct competitor so you don't have to disclose anything. As you said though, you and your boss are close so you want respect that as well. To be safe, I'd tell him that you'll share the name of the company with him as soon as you actually start. Can you do that?"

It's not that all headhunters are totally paranoid about everything, though it's helpful to be, let's say, thorough. Obviously earning a commission is a big part of this for me and that means looking out for all of the stupid little things that can come along and ruin a good deal. Tom wants to take this job and the company wants to hire him. Part of my job at this stage is ensuring that everyone gets what they said they wanted. Mostly that means guiding people through the end of the process and being wary of potential distractions. It includes details like practicing resignation conversations with candidates, or on the company side, getting Sheila to come up with the idea that Carl and Tom might meet socially with their spouses during Tom's house-hunting trip. We still have a ways to go before Tom is started and there are things to do, or more importantly, things we shouldn't do until it's finished. Tom and I end our conversation about resigning with a few more points about stemming counter offers and avoiding awkward situations, and some general guidelines for what he wants to happen during his resignation.

One of the things I suggest to Tom is that as soon as he tells his boss and presents his resignation letter he should ask about exit interviews, meeting with Human Resources and beginning to talk to colleagues about the impending changes. Making the news more public after he's resigned to his direct manager is a very effective way of both forwarding the effort to transition his responsibilities and reducing the potential of continued counter offer discussions. Telling his colleagues that he's leaving puts a lot of pressure on the company not to make a counter offer. If everyone knows that Tom accepted another job but ended up staying at the company, then they will all want raises too.

Beyond that, we talked about the fact that he'll be leaving friends at the company and wants to maintain relationships. I tell him that I think it will work out okay if he focuses on four main things: Planning ahead, which we've done, communicating clearly and decisively, respecting relationships and demonstrating empathy, and being fair and professional. The world, and certainly the specific industries we work in, is getting smaller every day. We're all connected in a lot of different ways now and it's easy to stay in touch. People end up working together again at other companies or in other projects and it's important to maintain a network. As an example, I reiterated that he and I should definitely stay in touch and in addition, that I am always interested in making new connections and developing my network. In fact, right now, I'm getting ready to see if I can find someone to talk to about a lead for a new purchasing and materials management job that will become available in Memphis in a about three weeks.

Our project is coming to an end. After I get Tom through his resignation, there's not much more for me to do. I'll connect him with Sheila and any of the other staff members at the new company he'll need to reach and make myself available to both sides for questions. Tom and I will stay in touch up until the start date, mostly so I can hear about how his resignation went, what's happening during the notice period, how he's getting on with relocation services, and about the move in general. If he needs something, I'll be there to help. Generally though, now that everything is official, he's a company employee and it's time for my role to diminish.

In contrast, Tom has a lot to do. He'll start working with someone from the relocation services team and they'll begin the task of getting his family moved to Houston. Initially, Tom will go to Houston on his own to start working and stay in the temporary living accommodations provided in the relocation policy. They'll setup the house-hunting trip so he and his wife can become familiar with the area and start searching for a new home. When they sell their house in Memphis their belongings will either go into storage or will be moved out to their new house in Houston. In less time that we imagine, Tom and his family will be settled into their new home and new routines.

I typically send my invoice to the company on the start date as soon as I verify that my candidate actually started. Then it takes anywhere from thirty to ninety days to receive my commission check. For me, a project is done when the commission check clears the bank. I don't celebrate. By then I'm already working on the next set of projects trying to do it all over again.

Chapter 16: Conclusion and End Notes

Tom called to tell me thanks a couple weeks after he started. We'd been in touch a few times via email during his first week just so he could tell me he got there okay and is getting used to where things are but hadn't had a chance to talk. He told me that he thought things were going fine so far. They had the house-hunting trip a week ago, found three places that they liked and are hoping to pick one and make an offer in the next week or so. He's making progress at work too. It's challenging but he's happy about the decision. He thinks they will like living in Houston again and is hopeful about the long term prospects.

I wrote a lot about Tom in the last couple of chapters but the recurring theme, the message I wanted to get out was that there was nothing that I did for him that you couldn't do for yourself. Nothing. It is simply a matter of having a plan and knowing what to do. The process I went through with Tom, Anthony and even Karen may not be perfect but it works and has done so consistently over a long period.

Every situation is unique and there are no one-size-fits-all solutions. However, every job starts with someone somewhere trying to figure out how to do something or solve a problem and discovering they need help.

What if Tom didn't get an offer? Or, what do I usually do when I take a candidate all the way through a set of interviews and we don't get an offer? Well, for me it happens constantly. It happened on two other projects during the time I was working with Tom. Those situations were not included in the book because they were not important. Failure is part of my job and something I deal with by being satisfied with my daily work, running multiple projects to increase my chances for success, and being persistent. I was going to add more about what to do when an offer doesn't come but, when I thought about it, all that needs to be said is this: If you didn't get an offer this time, try to figure out why, go to the sources and ask, improve if you can and repeat the process until you do get an offer, and not just any offer, the one you want.

Maybe you've gotten all the way to this point and you're thinking I made it sound easy, that I'm a professional headhunter who deals with this every day, makes a ton of money, drives a fancy car and wears million dollar suits to work. You still don't have a job and you feel like a loser. You think you did everything in the book and did your best but it didn't work for you. I've been there too.

I wasn't born knowing how to get access to jobs and how to get offers. I had to learn and it took a long time. There's probably space for another story in here about how my father was in the Army and how we moved around, how I attended multiple high schools and colleges, how I spent most of my teen years overseas, and how I popped out of college and into an economy knowing nothing. Honestly, I have a degree in literature! Nothing I studied or was exposed to prepared me to look for a real job. To say that joining an executive search firm as a headhunter on commission was a baptism by fire overlooks the fact that I couldn't afford fire.

Perhaps you remember when I told Karen the story about how I had to go digging through big giant manufacturing directories to get leads and that I had to cold-call hundreds of people to try to break in and get projects or candidates or anything. It was hard and it took a long time, literally years, for me to figure it out. Without going into everything about my early challenges, one thing that you might take from this is that if someone starting with as little experience and knowledge I had could make it as a headhunter, then maybe what I'm saying works. Maybe it's worked well enough for me to have made a decent living for all of these years. Maybe it's worked well enough for me to have found time to write it all down in a book!

I'm not promising you that this book will make your job search easy. In fact, I'm pretty sure that if you're reading this and using these techniques to try to get a really good job, your job search will be hard because the best things are never easy. I will promise that the accumulated knowledge in this book will give you the kind of head-start I never had as a candidate when I was looking for a job or as a headhunter when I first started out.

If you've reached this point in the book and you have a new job, or if you're revisiting this section after getting a job, then you know there's still a few things left to do. Like Tom or Anthony, you probably didn't get your job in a vacuum. There were other people involved. Anthony for example networked and met quite a few people at the non-profit that hired him before he got a job there. Most of them are not directly involved with the job he has now but all of them were integral to the process. Now that he has a job, he should let them know and more importantly, thank them for their help. Who are we talking about? Remember Diane? She was the very first person Anthony ever contacted there. They shared a common degree and Anthony sought her advice about how she got her first job after graduating. She replied, a conversation developed, they met once and she invited Anthony to the open house where he met Gerald, the Project Manager who helped him get his first interview. No doubt Diane would appreciate an update. Anthony should send a note to Gerald too since he introduced him to Jeff and Tonya who interviewed him for the first Talent Acquisition Specialist job and later referred him to Kyle, who hired him. Obviously, he should reach out to Jeff and Tonya as well. These are all little things but they make a difference.

More important than staying in touch and thanking the people who helped him find a job, Anthony should also take stock of where he is now and remain open to helping others when, later on, he's receiving advice requests from other people trying to find jobs. As I mentioned to Tom when we were preparing for his resignation, it's a small world, particularly within specific industries, and it pays to maintain good relationships with your peers, colleagues, and mentors.

I know Anthony is going to continue to do well because even though I never told him to do it, he did send little thank you notes to all the people who helped him along the way. How do I know? I got one. In mine he reminded me of something else we talked about. He told me he's keeping all the notes from our work together because one of the messages that really sunk in for him was that there's a good chance he'll be looking for a job again sometime in the future.

Now, finally, the fun part. Everything in this book is true. The people I wrote about are real. The situations and as much of the dialogue as I could capture and recreate all happened. The companies, how they operate, the salaries and fees involved are all accurate.

Two of the characters in the book are friends, Anthony and Karen are in real life, Antonio and Kira. Tom is a real candidate I marketed and placed. His name is Todd.

Antonio really was a recruiter in his first job out of college. Now he works for non-profit consulting firms that help new EU countries secure grant funds for infrastructure projects. His last couple of jobs have been contract jobs lasting 18 months to two years. He recently got new contract using the exact methods described in this book – doing research to find relevant hiring manager contacts on LinkedIn.com and seeking their advice. We talk all the time. He told me that he really focused during his most recent job search and only contacted hiring managers at competing consulting firms. He couldn't believe the results. He was invited to interview at every firm he contacted. He ended up only getting one offer but it was enough.

Kira is a Head of Customer Marketing at Nokia Siemens Networks. I won't say where because she's still there. She did go through a rough patch and wanted to find something else for a while. There were interviews with other companies and Kira did call me one night after a bad interview destroyed her confidence and left her in tears. That interview was with Nike. She still likes them but doesn't want to work there anymore. She told me that talking about it helped her regain her confidence and not look at interviews in such a one-sided way anymore. Things are better for her at Nokia Siemens Networks too.

As I was going through the replies I got from marketing Tom (Todd) in Chapter 6, there were three that showed some promise. The first was the director who replied that he may have a need for someone like Todd in 6 months. I sent a resume and my notes, followed up a week or so later, and then again when Todd got his offer. Nothing ever happened. I can't remember the name of the company. It's only worth mentioning because it was one of the three instances out of a hundred emails that merited sending out a resume and following up.

The second situation was with the director at the super-major energy production company. She said that they didn't have a position right now but that they liked to hire people like Tom. She sent me to their human resources department where I ended up going through their vendor qualification and sign-up process to get access to work on supply chain jobs. It worked and my firm was able to become a vendor. I was assigned a good internal recruiter as a contact and developed the company as a client. Of course Todd was long gone by then but I did end up placing four people with them. Those four people were the four I referred to when describing the "Skills Testing" in Chapter 11. The company is BP.

The last of the three marketing replies I received for Todd was the one from Paul. His real name is Ron. At the time Ron was the Corporate Director of Raw Materials Sourcing at Halliburton in Houston. The VP of Manufacturing who hired Todd was named Chris, not Carl. The candidate who Todd referred to me when I told him that Ron (Paul) needed a Metals Commodity Manager was Robert. Todd still works for Halliburton and continues to do very well there. Ron hired Robert from me too so I actually ended up making two placements. Halliburton became one of my better clients hiring almost ten people from me over a several year period. Nothing is constant though and after a long productive period in which Ron rose to become the Corporate Sr. Vice President of Procurement, his job was eliminated. Robert's position was eliminated too. I tried to help Robert find a new job but was not fast enough. He ended up getting an offer from another energy related manufacturer in Houston through another recruiter and took it. Ron is taking his time to explore new opportunities. I'm sure he will find something interesting soon. I still maintain a vendor relationship with Halliburton and will help them if I can.

Clark from the first chapter really is Clark. He and his wife Carol, gave me my first shot at being an executive recruiter and taught me a lot. I will never forget the opportunity they provided. They are retired now. The other person hired right out of college, or in his case, the U.S. Marines and college, for Clark's grand experiment was my good friend Kevin. He started about nine months before me and did well enough to encourage Clark to hire and train someone else without prior experience. Kevin lives in Houston now. He and I talk frequently and continue to work together on headhunting projects from time to time.

The rest, well, I'm still just a headhunter based in Georgia, marketing and recruiting candidates for supply chain and sourcing jobs in manufacturing and energy. If you know someone with that background who's looking or needs help, tell them to contact me. I'm always interested.

Before closing I need to thank my girlfriend Zrinka and my parents, Carol and Ron, for their ongoing support and encouragement. I don't think I could have finished without them. Thank you!

Made in the USA
Middletown, DE
27 August 2022

72469676R00186